SERVICE AREA APPROACH

A New Concept in Rural Lending

SERVICE AREA APPROACH
A New Concept in Rural Lending

MANJULA TYAGI

RBSA PUBLISHERS
340, Chaura Rasta, JAIPUR (INDIA)

Published by :

Deepak Parnami

RBSA Publishers
340, Chaura Rasta
Jaipur - 302 003
Phone : (0141) 2575826

First Published : 2006

ISBN : 81-7611-363-8

Laser Typesetting by :
Sanchit Computers, Jaipur
Phone : 0141-2552417

Printed at :
Sheetal Printers, Jaipur
Phone : 0141-310543

PREFACE

Indian banking has witnessed many revolutionary changes since independence of the country. The first banking revolution was started with the nationalization of 14 major commercial banks in July, 1969 when the concept of Lead Bank Scheme was launched and later on under the Lead Bank Scheme district credit plans were formulated and implemented in each district of the country. This brought about the changes in the objective function of banks. The emphasis of lending was shifted from 'credit worthiness' to 'purpose worthiness' and nature of banking shifted from 'commercial banking' to 'social banking' and from 'class banking' to 'mass banking'. Area development approach was adopted for quantitative expansion of credit in rural areas, but this approach suffered from many deficiencies. For effecting vibrant rural credit delivery system, a new and innovative concept of Service Area Approach was launched on April 1, 1989 with the purpose of linking credit with production, productivity and generation of income. The main purpose of this new approach was to improve the quality of lending besides that of its quantitative expansion. The service area approach is basically a command area approach where in 15 to 25 villages, on an average, are covered for their intensive development which is known as 'Service Area' of the branch. These villages are placed under the particular bank branch for formulating and implementing the credit plans at village and branch level. Thus, the service area approach could really be termed as 'micro-level credit planning' taking down to the village level and meant for intensive development of a particular service area under a particular bank branch.

The 'second banking revolution', which was an offshoot of financial sector reforms launched since 1991-92, has altogether changed the present Indian banking scenario of the country. In the changed scenario the functioning of service area approach has become a matter of concern for one and all. This book examines critically the various aspects of service area approach in length and depth with a view to find out the real situation at grass root level. This book also throws light on to what extent the service area approach has succeeded in achieving its objectives in Hadoti region. The present work is microscopic in nature as it confines only to Hadoti region of the state of Rajasthan, but its findings are applicable/relevant for the whole nation as the philosophy and methodology of formulating, implementing and evaluating the credit plans are the same in all districts of the country. The book is empirical in nature as analysis done and inferences drawn in it are based on field survey and authentic published data/information. I not only presume, but also believe firmly that this book will be useful not only to academic community, but also to the policy planners and executors who are engaged in the gigantic task of formulation, implementation and evaluation of credit plans prepared under service area approach in the country.

Although I have tried my level best that no mistake should remain in the book, eventhen some mistakes may remain inadvertantly. Prudent readers will excuse me for this. It is my proud privilege to express my deep sense of gratefulness and indetedness to Dr. Gopal Singh, Head, Post Graduate Department of Economic Administration and Financial Management, Govt. Commerce College, Kota, whose scholastic and generous guidance, unfailing encouragement, inspiration, constructive suggestions and keen interest have been instrumental throughout in completing the present book.

I shall be failing in my duty if I do not acknowledge the profound debt to my father late Major V.N.S. Tyagi and mother Vimla Tyagi for their obvious blessings to my present book. I also express my affectionate thanks to my all brothers Pankaj, Ajay and Vijay for their all out support and encouragement in completing and giving final shape to it. I cannot forget to express my heartly thanks to my husband Sh. N.K. Tyagi, daughters Sonal and Tanushree and son Mohit who have sacrificed a lot due to my business in this present book.

I also extend my heartfelt thanks to all those bank officials of Hadoti region who have helped me not only by providing necessary data/information for the present work, but also for making valuable comments and giving practical suggestions for improving my work. At the end, I also extend my sincere thanks to Shri Surendra Paranami of RBSA, for publishing this book in a nice and elegant form.

–Manjula Tyagi

CONTENTS

ABBREVIATIONS

AAP	–	Annual Action Plan
ACT	–	Annual Credit Plan
BCKGB	–	Bundi Chittorgarh Kshetriya Gramin Bank
BCP	–	Branch Credit Plan
BLCP	–	Block Level Credit Plan
BDO	–	Block Development Officer
BLBC	–	Block Level Bankers Committee
BLCC	–	Block Level Consultative Committee
BM	–	Branch Manager
BOB	–	Bank of Baroda
BOI	–	Bank of India
BOM	–	Bank of Maharastra
BOR	–	Bank of Rajasthan
CAGR	–	Compound Average Annual Growth Rate
CBI	–	Central Bank of India
CCBs	–	Central Co-operative Bank
CDR	–	Credit Deposit Ratio
DCCB	–	District Central Co-operative Bank
DCP	–	District Credit Plan
DDM	–	District Development Manager
DDP	–	District Development PLan
DIC	–	District Industry Center
DLCC	–	District Level Consultative Committee
DLRC	–	Disctrict Level Review Committee
DLRM	–	District Level Review Meeting
DRDA	–	District Rural Development Agency
DRI	–	Differential Rate of Interest
GOI	–	Government of India
HKGB	–	Hadoti Kshetriya Gramin Bank
HPC	–	High Power Committee on the Working of Lead Bank Scheme
IB	–	Indian Bank
IOB	–	Indian Overseas Bank

KVIB	–	Khadi and Village Industry Board
KVIC	–	Khadi and Village Industry Commission
LBO	–	Lead Bank Officer
LBR	–	Lead Bank Return
LBS	–	Lead Bank Scheme
LDO	–	Lead District Officer
NIBM	–	National Institute of Bank Management
NPA	–	Non-Performing Asset
NGOs	–	Non-Government Organisations
NPS	–	Non-Priority Sector
OBC	–	Oriental Bank of Commerce
PLDB	–	Primary Land and Development Bank
PLP	–	Potential Linked Plan/Potential Linked Credit Plan
PMRY	–	Prime Minister's Rozgar Yojana
PNB	–	Punjab National Bank
PSB	–	Punjan and Sindh Bank
RACO	–	Rajasthan Agriculture Credit Operations
RBI	–	Reserve Bank of India
RCC	–	Regional Consultative Committee
RFC	–	Rajasthan Finance Corporation
RODA	–	Removal of Difficulties Act, 1974
RPCD	–	Rural Planning and Credit Department (RBI)
RRB	–	Regional Rural Bank
SAA	–	Service Area Approach
SAP	–	Service Area Credit Plan
SAR	–	Service Area Recovery and Outstanding Statement
SBBJ	–	State Bank of Bikaner and Jaipur
SBI	–	State Bank of India
SGSY	–	Swarnjayanti Gram Swarozgar Yojana
SJSRY	–	Swarn Jayanti Shahari Rozgar Yojana
SLBC	–	State Level Bankers Committee
SLCC	–	State Level Consultative Committee
UBI	–	United Bank of India
UCCB	–	Urban Central Co-operative Bank
UCO	–	United Commercial Bank of India
VCP	–	Village Credit Plan
VVV	–	Vikas Vahini Volunters.

Chapter 1

A Brief History of Banking Development in India

The history of banks in India ·finds its way back to Bank of Hindustan, which was the earliest Indian Bank setup in 1870. Banking on modern lines started with the establishment of three presidency banks under Presidency Bank's Act, 1876. Bank of Calcutta, Bank of Bombay and Bank of Madras, were amalgamated to form the Imperial Bank of India in 1921.

Prior to establishment of RBI in 1935, Imperial Bank used to carry out limited central banking functions also. It engaged in all types of commercial banking business except dealing in foreign exchange. Reserve Bank of India Act, 1934 made RBI as an Apex bank without major government ownership. Banking Regulations Act passed in 1949 brought RBI under government control. Under the act, RBI got wide ranging powers for supervision and control of banks. The Act also vested licensing power and the authority to conduct inspections in RBI. On the basis of the recommendations of the Gorewala Committee the Imperial Bank of India was renamed as State Bank of India by merging eight private banks floated in the erstwhile princely states, which is known as 'SBI Group'. RBI was empowered in 1960 to force compulsory merger of weak banks with the strong ones. Due to this the total number of banks was thus reduced from 566 in 1951 to 85 in 1969.

14 major commercial banks (CBs) were nationalised in July, 1969 and other 6 banks in April, 1980 with the intention to convert the Class banking to Mass banking, Urban banking to Rural banking, Commercial banking to Social banking and credit worthiness banking to purpose

worthiness banking. This resulted in the spread of the banking network specially in the rural and semi-urban areas of the country.

Nationalisation of banks was to make them play the role of catalytic agents for economic growth. To further accelerate this spree of rural growth, the country witnessed emergence of Regional Rural Banks (2 October, 1975) having local base and concentrated approach for poverty alleviation programmes through employees possessing with local accent and knowledge. To support functioning of RRBs and financing agencies in rural sector, NABARD (1982) was constituted, which is an apex institution accredited with all matters concerning policy, planning and operations in the field of credit for agriculture and other economic activities in rural areas. It is an apex refinancing agency for the institutions providing investment and production credit for promoting the various developmental activities in rural areas. It takes measures towards institution building for improving absorptive capacity of the credit delivery system, including monitoring, formulation of rehabilitation schemes, restructuring of credit institutions, training of personnel etc. It co-ordinates the rural financing activities of all the institutions engaged in developmental work at the field level and maintains liaison with GOI, State Governments, RBI and other national institutions concerned with policy formulation. It prepares on annual basis rural credit plans for all districts in the country, these plans form the base for ACPs of all rural financial institutions. It undertakes monitoring and evaluation of projects refinanced by it and promotes research in the fields of rural banking, agriculture and rural development.

The RBI is the Central Bank of the country and as an apex bank, it regulates and controls the whole banking structure of the country. The whole banking sector can broadly be classified into CBs, Co-operative banks, Development banks and Non-Bank Finance Companies (NBFCs), which all operate under the umbrella of RBI.

Commercial Banks

CBs can further be divided into scheduled and non-scheduled CBs. At present there are 27 Public Sector Banks which account for more than 80% banking business of all CBs in India. These include 19 nationalised banks, SBI and its 7 associate banks. Besides these, there are 31 Private Sector Banks which accounted for about 12% banking business. Side by side, 44 Foreign Banks are also operating in India, which accounted for about 8% of banking business.

Co-operative Banks

These can be classified into two main categories :

1) Short-term lending oriented co-operative banks which include Primary Credit Agricultural Societies, District Central Co-operative Banks and State Co-operative Banks.

2) Long-term lending oriented co-operative banks, which include Primary Land Development Banks (PLDBs) at the State, District and Village level.

Development Banks

These banks were established to provide medium and long-term financial assistance to various industries for setting up projects for expanding and modernising. These among others include mainly ICICI, IDBI, SLDBI, EXIM Bank and NABARD. These institutions, provide project finance, risk capital assistance and advisory services have played a vital role in India's industrial growth and used to have access to concessional funding. However, in recent years, they have had to access other avenues of funding, including public deposits. With permission to provide short-term lending, many of these institutions are moving towards 'Universal Banking' and transforming themselves by diversifying into a wide array of financial services.

Non-Bank Finance Companies

NBFCs, which are generally known as non-bank financial institutions in other parts of the world, provide various financial services outside normal banking services. Their activities include equipment leasing, hire purchase, bill discounting, loans and investments, venture capital, housing finance, factoring, short-term loans, inter-corporate loans, equity participation, corporate financing and bridge finance.

Other activities include issue management, portfolio management, corporate counselling, project counselling, advice on mergers and acquisitions, capital structuring and foreign collaboration, corporate advice, corporate structuring and market research.

The structure of scheduled banks and the overview of rural credit structure in India have been exhibited by the following schematic charts :

Structure of Scheduled Banks in India at a Glance

(as on March 31, 2001)

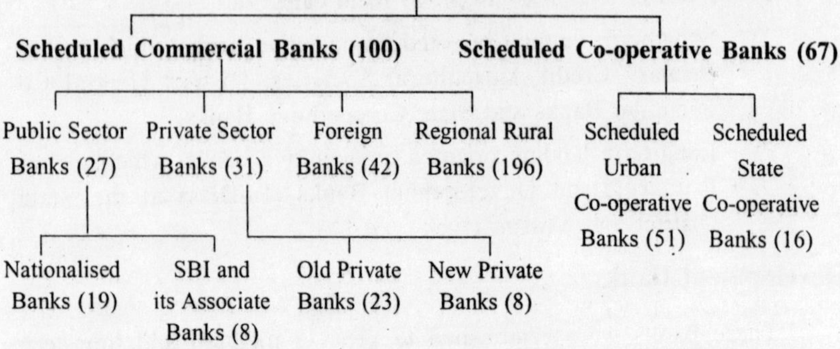

Note : *Figures in brackets indicate number of banks in each group.*

Source: RBI report on Trend and Progress of Banking in India 2000- 2001

Overview of Rural Credit Structure

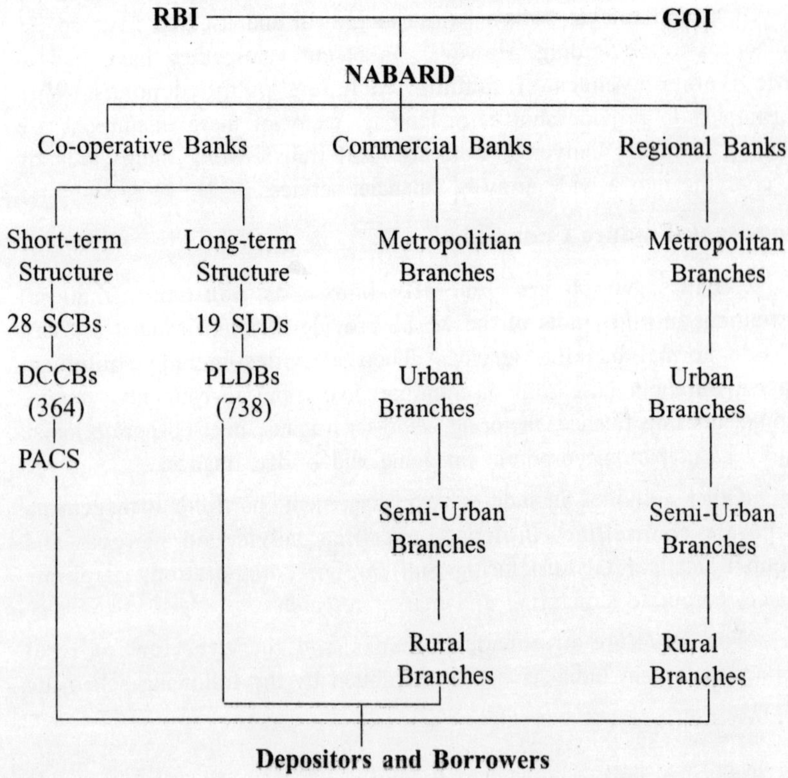

Recent Developments

During the era of 1985-1990 the world saw failure of banks with lower capital base on a large scale. Consequently, after Basle meet of 1988, all over the world the need was felt to strengthen the capital base. Other global events, like 'Urguay Meet' for talks on Trade and Services, further reiterated the importance of sound banking with strong risk management techniques. In India, the **Narsimhan committee** suggested wide ranging reforms for the banking sector in 1992 to introduce internationally accepted banking practices. The committee recommended prudential norms and practices for Indian banks, which mainly include prudential accounting methods (transparency and disclosure norms), Exposure Norms and Income Recognition and Asset Classification (IRAC) norms. With globalisation newer techniques and process have come into being and banking, at present, it not merely a vehicle for economic growth, but has become an activity to bring about changes in life style of the society through various deposit and lending schemes. The RBI has also prescribed the Capital Adequacy Ratio of 9% for banks to strengthen their financial position.

Post liberalisation years have seen significant pressure on banks in India with a few banks repeatedly showing signs of distress, primarily for want of effective risk management systems. The government has, however, categorically the intention to bring about the required financial discipline, introduce and strengthen appropriate systems in banks, even at the cost of privatisation in the sector.

Consolidation and Convergence in Banking Services

The Indian banking system had few mergers until recently, which were mainly triggered by events such as insolvency (Bank of Karad with Bank of India) or closure (Bank of Credit and Commerce International with State Bank of India) or losses (New Bank of India with Punjab National Bank). However, in the past two to three years, the world wide trend of consolidation and convergence has begun to manifest itself in the Indian banking industry as well. Times bank, a new private sector bank, has been merged with HDFC bank. In keeping with the concept of Universal banking, the Industrial credit and Investment Corporation of India (ICICI) has now moved from a traditional term lending institution to a one stop shop for financial services. It has entered retail financial services aggressively and acquired two NBFCs engaged in retail finance to provide itself with a retail asset portfolio, experience and a distribution network.

The RBI intends that the principle of universal banking is a desirable goal. It also says some progress has been made by permitting banks to diversify into investments and long-term financing and allowing development finance institutions to transform into banks provided they satisfy the prudential norms of banks. ICICI and IDBI have already expressed their intention to transform and become universal banks providing a wide array of financial services. Recently ICICI has transformed into an universal bank.

Present Position of Indian Banking

The progress of India banking based on certain parameters has been depicted in **Table no. 1.1** The analysis of the table throws light on the progress of Indian banking during 1950-2000. The total number of banks operating in the country was 297 at the end of March, 2000. The total number of bank branches in India, was 65,521 at the end of March, 2000. The total deposits and advances of bank branches were Rs. 9,00,307 crore and Rs. 4,43,469 crore respectively at the end of March, 2000. The total investments of all banks was Rs. 4,13,187 crore; while the net profit of these institutions was Rs. 7306.36 crore at the end of March, 2000.

HISTORY OF CREDIT PLANNING

The concept of credit planning originated with the idea of linking bank's credit input with financial/physical targets incorporated in the plan. Efficient & Optimum allocation of resources is fundamental to the process of credit planning. The credit planning denotes the rational allocation of resources available with banks. The essence of credit planning is to utilise the scarce resources for the "greatest good of the greatest number." In this context, credit planning has greater significance and more positive role to play in the process of economic development. In a planned and agro-based economy like India, bank credit constitutes an important component of resources. Thus, development of credit has to be properly planned so as to match with national planning objectives and targets as the credit planning and physical planning are supplement to each other.

Keeping in view the importance of concept of credit planning, the plan makers realised the importance of credit planning for achieving the national plan objectives. The economic planning commenced in India in early fifties, but credit planning which must have been an integral part of the growth process did not receive due attention at the that time.

Table No. 1.1

Progress of Indian Banking at a glance (1950-2000)

(Rs. in Crores)

Parameters of Progress	***1950***	***1960***	***CAGR (1950-1960)***	***1970***	***CAGR (1960-1970)***	***1980***	***CAGR (1970-1980)***	***1990***	***CAGR (1980-1990)***	***2000***	***CAGR (1990-2000)***
No. of Banks	605	345	-33.26	83	-27.26	157	6.6	274	5.7	297	0.8
No. of Branches	4163	4870	1.6	11146	8.6	34594	12.0	58914	5.4	65521	1.1
Deposits	1002	1953	6.9	6194	12.2	43987	21.7	202720	15.8	900307	16.1
Advances	553	1217	8.2	4653	14.4	27267	19.3	111274	15.1	443469	14.8
Investments	389	724	6.4	1825	9.7	13455	22.1	66832	17.4	413871	20.0
Net Profit	-	14.09	-	13.80	54.23	-	14.7	555.33	-	7306.36	29.4

** The figure of 1990 and 2000 are as on March end and others on December end.*

CAGR - Compound Average Annual Growth Rate

Source: Statistical Table relating to the Banks in India, Various issues of RBI.

The systematic credit planning in India was started with the launching of 'Lead Bank Scheme' in 1969 with the nationalisation of 14 major commercial banks on July 19, 1969. Before nationalisation of 14 major banks the RBI used to hold discussions from time to time with major users of credit in the private and public sectors and also with commercial banks in order to get an idea of the demand for credit.

To make credit planning more meaningful the RBI set-up a National Credit Council (NCC) in 1968 and a Credit Planning Cell in April, 1970 to undertake the exercises for macro-credit planning and to provide guidance to banks for credit planning at the micro-level.

Since 1973, due to the growing emphasis on balanced regional development and control of inflationary pressures, the need for deployment resources rationally among the various regions/sectors as well as strong monetary measures together with fiscal and administrative restraints on spending was seriously recognised. This required credit planning at the micro level as well as the macro level starting from the level of banks credit plan upto monetary management at the macro level.

Credit Planning as an instrument of overall monetary management was in operation since 1975 and banks began to workout their plans on a half yearly basis in that year. Later on, in 1976, credit planning was adopted on a quarterly basis.

In other words, for the system as a whole, the RBI undertakes formulation of a broad credit plan taking in to account the national priorities, the anticipated pace of deposit acceleration, general economic situation and likely developments in different sectors alongwith their credit absorption capacity.

Thus, by and large the broad guidelines issued and sincere efforts done by the RBI for smooth and rational deployment of resources, RBI has continued this exercise and perfected the modalities time to time. While these techniques of credit planning may be regarded as more directly relevant for short-term credit planning. From the long term point of view credit planning also aims at bringing about certain 'structural changes' in commercial bank credit planning. National targets for banks lending to priority sectors and in rural sectors, Credit Authorisation Scheme 1965, Lead Bank Scheme 1969 and the latest remarkable approach in this field is modified Lead Bank Scheme i.e. Service Area Approach 1989 have been introduced for the desired changes in the structure of commercial bank credit planning.

Meaning of Credit Planning

Credit planning means the rational allocation of resources available with financial institutions according to national priorities. Infact, credit planning is an effective instrument of planned economic development for achieving the ultimate objective of 'economic growth with social justice' in an economy. Thus, it is an exercise of estimating the credit demand for both existing and emerging bankable schemes, which are technically feasible and economically viable, of a specific region for the attainment of development goals in a given time horizon.

Indeed, Credit Planning is a conscious effort on the part of the banks and other financial institutions to allocate their loanable funds among various sectors of the economy according to the national plan priorities. It's basic tenet is to utilise the scarce productive resources judiciously, productively and efficiently. The credit planning can be for the whole economy as well as for a specific segment/sector of an economy. Thus, it can be done at macro level as well as, at micro level.

The macro credit planning has to take into account the total volume of credit expansion to meet the demand of different segments of economy; while the micro level credit planning is concerned with a detailed exercise of allocating credit to various sectors, *i.e.* agriculture, industry, trade etc. and also to maintain balance with various parts/sectors of the economy. Each component is given due weightage. This exercise has to be done by all financial institutions.

Credit planning not only stresses on quantitative extension of credit, but also emphasises on the qualitative aspect of credit by linking credit input with production, productivity and generation of income. In other words, credit plan is a plan of rational allocation of financial resources to various sectors/segments of the economy for meeting out their developments needs. It also implies the areas/activities to which credit will be extended in a specified period of time. In the words of D.J. Kanvinde - "Basically credit plan is an exercise in indicating the lines on which credit can be extended in a given area in a given period of time, on the basis of the anticipated demand for credit from existing or development induced economic activities."

Thus, in nutshell, "Credit Planning is a tool of the planned economic development. It consists of such economic schemes which are technically feasible and economically viable and can be taken up for financing by financial institutions.

Objectives of Credit Planning

Credit planning is undertaken with several objectives. Among them few important objectives are as under:

- To provide banking facilities to hither to unbanked areas of the economy, thereby enabling people to have easy accessibility to institutional credit. The rationale behind this objective is to actively foster the growth of new and progressive entrepreneurs and to create fresh opportunities in neglected and backward areas. This is intended to correct sectoral and regional imbalances in the distribution of credit and bring about a wider diffusion of economic power.
- To serve the farmers in a better way so that agricultural production and productivity may improve substantially. The easy and timely accessibility of institutional credit to farmers will make them free from the clutches of money lenders and thus stop their exploitation.
- To curb the use of bank credit for speculative and other unproductive purposes.
- To meet the legitimate credit needs of industry and trade and to eliminate undesirable features of lending such as over financing and double/multiple financing.
- To achieve the goal of 'target financing' i.e., to provide minimum amount of credit to priority sectors, new entrepreneurs, backward areas and down-trodden people of society. Here the logistic behind is proper deployment of credit rather than 'mere distribution of credit.'

Thus,in brief, the basic objective of credit planning is to channelise the investment and output deliberately along the lines postulated in the national plans and to reduce the regional and sectoral imbalances in the economy, so that the twin objectives of 'growth with stability' and 'growth with social justice' could be attained.

Significance of Credit Planning

The principal objective of reducing regional and sectoral imbalances in the disbursal and deployment of credit signifies the need for credit planning. Indeed, credit input is an important ingredient of economic development or in other words, credit is just like a lubricant for the engine of economic growth. In this context, it has been very aptly remarked that the flow of credit is very much like the circulation of blood. Just as the circulation of blood has to be smooth and uniform in all organs of the human body, in the same manner credit should also flow steadily and according to the needs of various sectors of the economy. If credit flow is not proper and timely, it would do irreparable harm to the economy just as clotting of blood vessels leads to fatal result to human body.

As we know that one of the important objective of credit planning is to ensure that the expansion of credit should be non-inflationary, i.e. it should be just enough to meet the genuine needs of production. This can be achieved if the credit expansion is strictly production oriented. In practice, it can be ensured only through proper credit planning.

Thus, it is quite obvious that in any economy especially in a developing economy like India, credit planning has a vital role in bringing about structural transformation and in allocating the resources optimally in to productive channels. For an efficient and judicious allocation and use of physical resources, it is quite necessary that there should not be mis-match between physical planning and credit planning.

Adequate and timely availability of credit is supposed to be the kingpin of the process of rapid industrialisation. The modern business is entirely dependent on credit, therefore the modern age is termed as 'Credit Era'. Credit planning helps in mobilising and channelising the resources in comparatively more productive and needy sectors of the economy and thus helps in industrialisation of the economy.

To achieve the objective of balanced regional development, credit planning plays a catalytic role by allocating credit to the backward hither to neglected areas and also to priority sectors for their development. Credit planning contributes to the development and better use of local resources,development of entrepreneurship and local talents, thus raising the level of overall development of the backward regions. Hence, it is clear that credit planning is potentially a very powerful tool for shaping the destiny of the economy and that with the help of proper credit planning policy it is possible to encourage specific activities/industries selectively and discourage others according to the priorities established for the purpose.

Besides these, Credit planning has a great significant role to play as an instrument of monetary control. Credit planning , which seeks to achieve need-based credit extension to various sectors and borrowers, is in many respect superior to overall quantitative control of credit. The significance of such planning is enhanced when banks have to operate principally with the deposits they are able to mobilise and when resources to borrowings from the central bank is restricted and itself turned to overall plan and monetary requirements.

In nutshell, credit planning has a greater significance and a more important role to play in the overall development of economy. Credit planning becomes essential from the point of view of mobilisation and better utilisation of scarce economic resources on desired lines.

Stages of Credit Plan

Credit planning passes through the following three stages–

1) In the first stage, impressionist surveys are conducted to get a bird's eye view of the existing growth potential, current and proposed development schemes and the felt-needs of the people in the planned region. It helps in identifying the centre for branch opening which would make optimum contribution to the development of the area. In India, a massive branch expansion programme during 1969-75 was undertaken on the basis of impressionist surveys. During there surveys an in-depth study of the area is conducted to select economic activities, which are technically feasible and economically viable, for the purpose of financing by banks.

2) In the second stage, resources requirements for the further development of the region are estimated. The credit gaps are identified and the credit supply estimates are made with the purpose to make the best possible use of credit available.

3) In the third and final stage, fixation and sharing of the responsibilities among the various financial institutions operating in the area are planned.

Monetary Planning v/s Credit Planning

The term 'monetary planning' refers to the monetary system along with the measures to manage the money and credit supply in the economy including steps taken from time to time to regulate and control the interest rates. It may also include non-monetary measures taken by the government which have the effects of influencing the monetary situation in the economy. Such non-monetary measures may be wages and price controls,budgetory operations etc,which indirectly influence the monetary situation in the economy. Therefore, the role of monetary planning in this context is very significant. It is an important tool for the growth with stability of the economy–

- Whereas, credit planning means the rational allocation of the resources available with banks. Infact, credit planning deals with the problem of allocation of bank credit among different segments/sectors of the economy.
- the Government and Commercial sector or the rest of the economy.
- sectoral allocation of credit; allocation of credit within the commercial sector by main area individual borrowers classified by economic status or in some other manner which is justifiable.

In nutshell, monetary planning relates to controlling the stock of the bank credit and change in this total; whereas credit planning is one step forward than monetary planning as it not only aims at controlling the stock of the bank credit and change in this total, but also equally important in directing its allocation and cost to its various users.

In this context, it is important that some economists like Milton Friedman are of the opinion that monetary planning and credit planning are entirely different, but we do not agree with this view. For the developmental point of view of the economy, monetary and credit planning are equally important and both act as a supplement to each other. Changes in the volume of credit have exactly the same effect on the internal price-level as changes in the supply of money. In simple words, the monetary planning regulate the flow of money maintaining the economic balance; whereas credit planning refers the distribution of available bank resources for economic growth with social justice. So, both are interdependent and equally important for achieving the goals of national plans.

In brief, credit planning can be used as an effective tool of monetary planning/ management. Productive credit creation, as part of active monetary policy, has an important role to play in facilitating to achieve the goal of the rapid development with economic stability in a developing economy.

While considering this fact, there is an urgent need for a healthy and pragmatic co-ordination between monetary and credit planning.

Relation between Development Plan and Credit Plan

The main purpose of development planning is to attain the self-sustained growth in the economy. In this context, the development plan attempts to promote economic development in three main ways :

- by increasing the overall rate of investment;
- by carrying out special types of investment designed to break bottlenecks in production in important sectors of the economy; and
- by trying to improve the co-ordination between different segments/sectors of the economy.

Thus, a development plan may include any or all the following ingredients:

- A survey of current economic conditions;
- A list of proposed public expenditures;
- A discussion on likely developments in the private sector;
- A macro economic projection of the economy; and
- A review of Government policies.

A credit plan, in its spirit is a development plan for financing the various sectors by the financial institutions. Only such schemes which are technically feasible and economically viable should be included in the credit plan from the point of view of the lending bank, credit allocation should be on the basis of schemes which have the capacity of generating surplus for repayment of the loans. Credit plan should be drawn up on the basis of a strategy of development suitable for the area taking into account its natural endowment, principal economic activities and their potential for development. In simple words, credit plan is a plan which is prepared by a bank for advancing credit to the various sectors. It is also comprehensive and integrated in the sense that it includes various projects and schemes covering all the major agriculture and allied activities, industry and service sectors, depending upon their natural linkages. In other words, a credit plan is a exercise in estimation of credit demand for an area and a blue print for action by banks and other financial institutions.

In this context, a credit plan may, therefore, be regarded as the financial framework of a District Development Plan (DDP). The formulation of a credit plan thus involves simultaneously the formulation of development plan as well as their proper integration with each other. Inspite of that, there are some basic differences between these two.

The first and foremost distinction between DDP and DCP is that the DDP is prepared on the basis of social cost and benefit analysis; while the credit plan is prepared on the grounds of economic viability of the activities/schemes to be financed by it. Another important difference between these two is that in case of DDP the location of infra-structural facilities are decided on the grounds of population threshold, centre place theory, growth centre concept, felt-needs of the people etc; whereas the DCP covers those technically feasible and economically viable schemes which can easily be financed by various financial institutions operating in the concern district keeping in view the infrastructure and other extension facilities provided by the DDP.

Though it is quite clear that, of course, there are some distinctions between DDP and DCP, but it is also quite obvious that DDP and DCP both exist together and they are not only inter-related, but interdependent on each other.

In practice, credit plan is formulated within the overall framework of DDP with the main purpose of achieving pre-determined targets of the DDP. Thus, It can be said that despite the influence of credit plan on the DDP, the important thing is that the nature and size of the DDP determines the size of the credit plan.

In brief, for improving the quality of lending and effectively fulfilling the objectives of national plans, credit planning should be synthesised with development planning and infact, the later should precede the former. Keeping this fact in view, the guidelines issued by RBI for the preparation of the second round of DCPs suggested that the DCP should be dovetailed into the DDP, so that the DCP will aim at the same plan priorities as the DDP. In other words, the objective of 'growth with stability' can be achieved only when realistic target oriented credit cum development plans are formulated and implemented. Therefore, credit plan should supplement and integrate with the development plan in achieving its overall objectives of development without enhancing inflationary pressures.

Pre-requisites of a successful credit planning

For the proper development of agriculture, allied activities and other sectors of rural economy, there must be a good credit planning. In this context, there are several conditions which are essential for a sound credit planning. If a credit planning is to succeed as an instrument of credit allocation in line with the overall national policy, the following conditions appear necessary :

- **Low cost of credit**

  Cost of credit must include interest and a number of expenses incurred during the period of securing credit.The first and foremost condition for a successful credit planning is that the rate of interest should be reasonable. The expenses of various types should also, as far as possible, be low. Availability of credit at a reasonable rate of interest and with minimum other costs should be ensured.

- **Minimal Risk**

  One of the important pre-requisites of a successful credit planning is that there should be minimum amount of risk involved in extending the credit to the borrowers so that easy recovery of loan is ensured. The financial institutional are really the revolving institutions. Therefore, the loanable funds must rotate in the interest of the health of the economy.

- **Absence of Monopoly**

  The another important condition for a successful credit planning is that there should not be a complete monopoly of any one financial institutions in a particular area of operation otherwise the borrowers will be exploited. They will have to pay exorbitant rate of interest. Therefore, some element of competition should be there between the lending institutions.

- **Adequate and Timely supply of Credit**

  A successful credit planning should have the virtue of making available not only the adequate amount of credit for needy sectors of the economy, but also should have the timely availability of credit without any delay. Besides this, a successful credit plan should also be able to cater to meet the short-term, medium-term and long-term credit needs of the borrowers.

  If adequate amount of credit is not provided by single agency the borrowers may be constrained to approach other agencies and thus it may create the problem of multiple financing making the recovery of loan difficult.

- **Credit to needy person**

  Credit should be provided to those who really need it for development purposes. There must be proper assessment of credit requirements. The small and marginal farmers must be given priority in giving credit. Credit must be made available as near to his door step as far as possible and whenever needed. Through this step, it is possible to eliminate the role of money lenders. Unless money lenders are eliminated, the credit system cannot function effectively.

- **Sufficient Income generation and Asset building**

  Credit should facilitate asset building and help to generate additional income so that repayment of loan become easier.

- **Proper Supervision of Credit**

  The system of supervising the credit after its disbursement for ensuring the proper end-use of credit which is known as 'Supervised Credit System' or 'Post Disbursement, Supervision of Credit', Under this system, it is ensured that credit is used only for that purpose for which it has been sanctioned.

Besides the essential conditions mentioned above, there are some other conditions for a successful credit planning,which are briefly mentioned below :

- Full awareness of and commitment to the national priorities;
- Allocation of credit according to the national priorities; and
- Realistic estimation of credit needs of and extension of credit to each borrower strictly according to his requirement.

Thus, a sound credit planning must be multi-dimensional in its nature and context. Its operational efficiency depends on various factors as mentioned above alongwith the active involvement of the people, it is ment for.

REFERENCES

1. Dang, Ashok K. : Bank Credit in India (Classical Publishing Company, N. Delhi)
2. Narula, R.K. and Gopala Krishna, V. : Agricultural and Rural advances by Commercial Banks (UDH Publishers, Delhi)
3. Sharma, J.K. : Bank Credit and Economic Development in India (Classical Publishing Company, New Delhi)
4. Singh, Ajit : Rural Development and Banking in India (Deep and Deep Publication, New Delhi)
5. Subrahmanya, K.N. (Editor) : Modern Banking in India (Deep and Deep Publication, New Delhi)
6. Chawla, A. S.: Nationalisation and Growth of Indian Banking (Deep and Deep Publication, New Delhi)

7. Ghosh, D.N. : Banking Policy in India, An Evaluation (Allied Publishers Pvt. Ltd., New Delhi, Calcutta)
8. Garhwal, S. : Commercial Banking and Economic Development (Pointer Publishers, Jaipur)
9. Hussain, Farhat : Public Sector Commercial Banking in India (Deep and Deep Publication, New Delhi)
10. Rayudu, C.S. : Rural Credit in India (Mittal Publications, New Delhi)
11. Desai, S.S.M. : Rural Banking in India (Himalaya Publishing House, Bombay, Nagpur, Delhi)
12. Simbha, S.L.N. and Raman, A. Edited : Credit Planning and Policy (Vora and Co. Publishers Ltd., Delhi)
13. Desai, Vasant : Money and Central Banking (Himalaya Publishing House, Delhi)
14. Desai, Vasant : Development Banking Issues and Options, (Himalaya Publishing House, Delhi)
15. Deb., K. : Indian Banking since Independence (Ashish Publishing House, New Delhi)
16. Desai, Vasant : Indian Banking (Himalaya Publishing House)
17. Singh, Gopal : Rural Credit Planning (2000) (RBSA Publishers, Jaipur)

□■□

Chapter 2

Lead Bank Scheme

Famous economist Ragnar Nurkse advocated the idea of balanced growth as against the concept of unbalanced growth achieved through the all round development of all sectors of the economy simultaneously. For attaining the balanced growth as advocated by Ragnar Nurkse, it can be said that the institutional credit available should not be only adequate, but it should reach all regions, sectors and sections in due proportions that means the services of the banking sector should be in reach of all and to achieve this important aspect the Lead Bank Scheme was introduced on Dec.12, 1969, but here it is important to mention that Lead Banks did not spring up all of a sudden. They came to be established as an array of efforts by the Government putforth in the direction of making available financial resources to the rural and agricultural masses.

As per the report of the RBI, 1951 private creditors - the professional money lender, the agriculturist money lender and the trader still reign supreme in the field of rural credit, supplying 70 percent or more of the total requirements. The Government supplied as little as 3.3 percent. Out of this very little, the larger part went to the bigger agriculturist and only a minor fraction percolated to the small cultivators. The remaining 27 percent was from the commercial banks and co-operative banks. Nationalisation of banks was supposed to change the whole perspective.

Table No. 2.1

Loans & Advances of Scheduled Commercial Banks to Various Sectors (in %)

S.No.	Sector	1951	1968
1.	Agriculture	2.1	2.2
2.	Industry	34.0	67.5
3.	Trade	36.0	19.2
4.	Personal	6.8	3.7
5.	Others	21.1	7.4

Source : RBI report of the trend and progress of banking in India 1968-69

Table No. 2.1 depicts the loans and advances given by scheduled commercial banks to various sectors of the economy in 1951 and in 1968.

The figures given in table no. 2.1 clearly indicate that during the period 1951 to 1968 the percentage share of agriculture credit in total bank credit was very small (2.1%) in 1951 and remained almost stagnant (2.2%) in 1968. But contrary to it, the percentage share of industrial credit to total bank credit was not only large, but also increased substantially from 34% to 67.5% during the same period . Thus. it can be concluded that commercial banks did not pay much attention in providing credit to agriculture and rural sectors of the economy before the nationalisation of 14 major commercial banks.

The main reason of this state of affair was that commercial banks concentrated their operations mainly in urban and metropolitan centres of the country. It is evident from this fact that up to the end of December, 1968 the number of rural branches was 1507 (20% only) out of the total 7463 branches of commercial banks in the whole country. Thus, around 80% bank branches were in urban and metropolitan cities of the country. Besides this, there was glaring disparities between different states/ regions in the number of bank branches functioning.

The uneven spread of bank branches created the problem of uneven distribution of credit amongst various states and regions. For instance, major share of total credit given by commercial banks went only to two states viz. Maharastra and West Bangal. They accounted for 32.3% and 22.5% share of total bank credit respectively at the end of 1967.

Priority sector advances accounted for 13.9 percent of the total bank finance, the share of agriculture, excluding plantation advances was less than 1 percent and retail traders got less then 2 percent of the total bank credit. The share of the large scale industry, wholesale trade and commerce in the total bank finance was as high as 80 percent. Besides uneven distribution of credit, the direction of flow of credit was also not proper and desirable as it was from small to large population centres and from rural to urban centres. It is clear from this fact that credit deposit ratio was as high as 89% in centres with a population above 10 lacs; while this was only 41% in centres having population less than 10 thousands.

Before nationalisation of 14 major commercial banks in 1969, the banking network was very small in relation to its size and requirement. Only 617 town out of total 2,700 and 5,000 villages out of total 5,60,000 villages were served by commercial banks. The per capita credit was less than Re. 1/- in as many as 63 districts. There was no credit advancement in 13 districts. Average population served by a bank brand was about 2 lacs in 88 districts as against the national average of about 70,000.

On the basis of above facts & figures, it can be said that banking development was uneven and the benefits of growth were not equitably shared by the people. This kind of uneven and unbalanced development were mainly responsible for the imbalances in income generation and distribution. Although, in every plan period some efforts had been made to help the poor, specially in the fourth plan period, the emphasis was laid on district planning, area approach and micro planning in order to enable the poor to participate in the growth process in an organised manner. Hence, the area approach gained significance towards the end of sixties and there was a feeling that this may be introduced in the banking sector too. It was also felt that a purposeful and equitable distribution of credit should be ensured with the help of periodical assessment of the demand for bank credit, determination of priorities for lending and investment in various sectors of the economy and adequate follow-up of these by the banking system also.

The National Credit Council was set-up in February, 1968 with a view to provide a forum for discussing and assessing credit priorities on all India basis. The main tasks entrusted to it were as under :

- To assess the demand for bank credit form the various sectors of the economy;
- To determine priorities for the grant of loans and advances or for investments, having regard to the availability of resources and requirements of the priority sector, in particular to agriculture, small scale industries and exports; and

- To co-ordinate lending and investment policies as between commercial and co-operative banks and specialised agencies to ensure optimum utilisation of resources.

In pursuance of a decision of the National Credit Council, The Government of India constituted a study group under the chairmanship of Prof. D.R. Gadgil, the then Deputy Chairman of Planning Commission to go into the question of the building up of an appropriate organisational framework for the implementation of social objectives. The study group vividly analysed the most vexatious problem of maladjustment between the demand for and the supply of credit by the commercial banks with a particular reference to the gross negligence of priority sectors like agriculture, small industry, self-employment, trade, professionals etc. The study group, in its voluminous report, examined the existing structure of the banking system and the nature of credit gaps and recommended several steps to overcome the pitfalls of the system. The main findings of the study group were as under :

- There is uneven spread of bank offices and bank business between different states and population groups;
- There is a flow of resources from the smaller to the larger population centres and from the rural to urban centres;
- In contrast to the commercial banking system, co-operative banking has penetrated into rural areas and has provided credit at numerous and wide-spread centres.
- The effective coverage of co-operative credit is uneven as between different states.
- The areas where banking, both commercial and co-operative has recorded progress are common except in West Bengal.
- Apart from original disparities, there is an uneven distribution of credit between different economic sectors and virtual non-availability of credit to small borrowers and weaker sections of the community.
- There is a large potential demand for credit from several borrowers, artisans, fisherman, small farmers, adivasies, retail trader and for consumption and emergency needs;
- Commercial banks have a few difficulties in meeting these credit gaps.

Recommendations of Gadgil Study Group

Following were the main recommendation of Gadgil study group :

- Banks should adopt an area approach and evolve plans and programmes for the development of the banking and credit structure. Commercial banks should be assigned particular districts where they should play the lead role and set the pace;
- District plans should be prepared for banking and credit;
- Each district plan should have three following aspects:
  - ▶ The establishment of branches or new units in particular unserved banking areas;
  - ▶ The formulation of relationships within a structure; and
  - ▶ The formulation of proper policies and procedures.
- *Organisational arrangements should be made immediately for the establishment of:*
  - ▶ District or Zonal committees.
  - ▶ National committee for credit assistance.
  - ▶ Department of credit planning in the Reserve Bank of India.
- A close examination of the credit guarantee schemes should be undertaken to determine how it may be modified in favour of new areas, spheres and the weaker sections.

The Gadgil group submitted its report in October, 1969 highlighted the problems of credit gaps and strongly recommended the adoption of an 'Area Approach'. The group suggested that the 'District' should be the 'unit of planning' under area approach or 'District' be taken as 'nucleus' for this approach.

The recommendations of Gadgil study group were further examined and endorsed by a 'Committee of Bankers' (August, 1969) headed by Shri F.K.F. Nariman, the then chairman of the Union Bank of India. The committee of Bankers accepted the area approach and gave the practical shape to it under the name of 'Lead Bank Scheme'.

On the basis of these valuable recommendations, the RBI on December 12, 1969 accepted the Lead Bank Scheme, which has now become the main plank of the banking development.

The LBS was launched by the RBI with a view to mobilise deposits on a massive scale throughout the country and also for stepping up lending to the weak sectors of the economy. The scheme symbolises area approach to identify and study local problems and evolve an integrated credit plan for the district.

When the scheme was initially introduced by the RBI, all the district of the country (baring metropolitan cities and the union territories) were allotted to 22 public sector banks (SBI and its associates 7 banks and 14 nationalised banks) and 3 private sector banks (Andhra Bank Ltd.; Bank of Rajasthan Ltd. and Punjab and Sindh Bank Ltd.).

The lead bank designated would be responsible for taking lead role in surveying the credit needs of people's, development of banking and extension of credit facilities in the district allotted to it.

While allotting districts to the banks or distribution of districts among various banks, following points were taken into consideration :

- Resources base of the bank concerned;
- Regional orientation of banks;
- Districts were allotted in clusters to facilitate control; and
- In each state two or more than two banks were allotted lead districts responsibility and each bank was allotted districts in more than one state.

As on March 31, 2000 the LBS has covered 575 districts out of 597 districts.

In nutshell, a particular bank was assigned a lead role which was having comparatively large resources base and good foot-hold in terms of number of branches.

Concept of Lead Bank

The concept of lead bank scheme envisages a consortium philosophy. This concept is based on the principle of one among all and acting as a consortium leader. It shoulders the responsibility of the development of the district and solicits the co-operation of other credit as well as non-credit agencies operating in that district. It opens more and more branches in the unbanked areas of the district, particularly in the villages, so as to geographically extend banking operations for making available its services and benefits to the rural people.

Technically, the concept of Lead Bank encompasses three dimensional role :

- A commercial credit institution for mobilising resources and advancing loans;
- A planning agency for finding out the credit needs and problems and for solving them by setting up targets; and
- A development bank for working as catalytic agent for initiating and accelerating the development of the backward and the underdeveloped areas of the district.

Thus, the lead bank identifies and implements bankable schemes in the district. On the basis of surveys, the lead bank is expected to estimate the deposit potentials and the credit gaps that could be taken up to tap the deposit potentials and fill the credit gaps.

The lead bank is expected to act not as a monopolist in the district, but as a consortium leader for involving co-operation from other financial institutions functioning in the area and sharing responsibilities with them. The LBS was supposed to bring all the financial and government development agencies on a common platform with a sense of joint participation for the economic upliftment of the rural poor. In this sense, lead bank acts more or less as the 'Central Bank' of the district.

Scope of Lead Bank

The main job of lead bank is to formulate the DCP in consultation with other financial institutions and the development departments of the government in the district. It also monitors the progress in the implementation of annual action plans. It also acts as an exemplary body for other financial institutions operating in the district particularly in regard to financing priority sector and downtrodden people along with providing adequate support to government sponsored poverty alleviation programmes. Lead bank is also supposed to be a catalyst in mobilising and seeking co-operation from other financial institutions and government development agencies in formulating and implementing the DCP successfully.

The lead bank acts as the convenor of the DLCC and its standing committee at the district level. Thus, it provides an organisational framework for participating by financial institutions and government development agencies in an integrated and co-ordinated manner. On the whole, the lead bank is a commercial institution, a planning and co-ordinating agency and a development bank (all three rolled in one) of the district.

Objectives of Lead Bank

The paramount object of the LBS is to fill up the credit gaps in a designated district by allocating the responsibility to various financial institutions. Besides this, the LBS evolves plans and programmes for the overall development of the rural areas by adopting area approach.

The *main objectives* of the Lead Bank Scheme are as follows :

- To formulate a phased programme for expanding the bank branch with the object of providing banking facilities to the entire area covered;
- To earmark the potential area for promoting agriculture and small scale industrial schemes including entrepreneurs;
- To assess the major constraints on the development of the district and to induce the appropriate agency for taking up and follow-up the remedial action;
- To experient with financial schemes which can help in mobilising deposits and promoting investment among the local people;
- To identify the un-banked and under-banked centres in the district to grasp their profile - physiographic, agro-climatic and socio-economic conditions through quick and impressionistic surveys;
- To remove regional imbalances by extending banking facilities to unbanked areas;
- To estimate the credit gaps in the various sectors of the economy and to prepare the credit plan for each district;
- To develop rapport with all the financial and non-financial institutions including administrative authorities for the improvement of infra-structural facilities of the district economy; and
- To effect structural and procedural changes in banking.

In context of the above mentioned objectives, it is clear that the LBS has been introduced to give a proper shape to the "Area approach" for the overall development in the lead district.

Functions/Tasks of Lead Bank

It will not be out of place to mention that the commercial banks were allotted districts to act as lead bank far away from their main areas of operation. The lead bank undertakes economic survey with a purpose to identify bankable schemes which may be taken up for financing by the financial institutions operating in the district. The lead bank designated for the particular district also serves as the clearing house for discussing problems in formulating realistic credit plans and implementing them successfully particularly ment for priority sectors.

Thus, a lead bank has to performe various tasks assigned to it and also assumed task related to the main task. The RBI has also categorically issued the guidelines regarding the functions of lead bank. The main functions of a lead bank to be performed by as consortium leader of the district are mentioned as under :

- To conduct impressionistic surveys to estimate credit gaps and studying the availability of resources and finding out potential for banking development in the assigned districts;
- To survey the quantum of industrial, commercial units and other establishments and firms which do not have bank accounts and depend on moneylenders for their needs;
- To examine the facilities for marketing of agricultural produce, industrial production storage and warehousing space and linking the credit with marketing;
- To explore the facilities for stocking the fertilizers and other agricultural inputs and the repairing and servicing equipments;
- To recruit and train staff for offering advice to small borrowers and farmers in the priority sectors which may be covered by the credit insurance schemes;
- To assist other primary lending agencies;
- To maintain proper contacts and liaison with government and quasi government agencies;
- To follow-up and inspection of the end use of loans;
- To undertake in-depth studies in relation to resource mobilisation and credit extension and formulate bankable schemes in due consultation with respective functional specialists;
- To locate growth centres to geographically extend banking facilities;
- To prepare DCP to cater to the credit needs of the district in a planned and phased manner in collaboration with other financial institutions at the district level;
- To circulate background notes/minutes of the meetings of the standing committee/DLCC and communicate information regarding latest developments relating to the growth of the district's economy;
- To monitor the progress in implementation of credit plan and special programmes like the IRDP, SEEUY, SEPUP, TRYSEM etc.; (with the coming in to force of PMRY-Oct.1993, SGSRY-Dec.1997 and SGSY-April 1999, these programmes are no longer in operation);

- To inculcate the saving habits among the people and promoting investments and mobilise deposits in the local areas;
- To make a programme in a phased manner for expansion of banking facilities for designated district/area; and
- To undertake programmes of educating and informing the masses (particularly the rural masses) about the benefits that will flow from the implementation of the LBS.

Keeping in view the above, it can be said that the lead banks have been assigned an important task for development of banking and credit deployment in the lead districts. Infact, a lead bank is required to function as a consortium leader, whose prime responsibility is to identify the under-banked areas and also the areas suffering from credit gaps.

Thus, the lead bank is a financial house for credit and deposit mobilisation, a planning agency for finding out the needs and problems and solving them by setting up targets, a development bank for working as a catalytic agent for initiating and accelerating the development of the district and a co-ordinator of planning and implementing forum-all rolled in one.

In-depth studies

In-depth studies were conducted by lead banks in their lead districts. These studies aimed at identifying the economic activities in a given area, which can be developed with the help of credit facilities. The focus of these studies was preparation of loaning programmes for banks on the basis of bankable schemes evolved to finance viable economic activities. The various tasks in in-depth studies were :

- Survey of the economy of an area with a view to identifying economic activities with potential for development;
- Study of identified activities to verify whether these are technically feasible and economically viable and capable of generating enough surplus, in a reasonable time period, to repay the bank loan;
- Assessment of the infra-structural and institutional support necessary to ensure their viability;
- Ascertaining and soliciting support from the development departments of the govt. and financial institutions for their lending programmes;

- Estimation of the number of units under each scheme, which can be financed in the given time period, taking into account the linkages of various economic activities and the infra-structural support available;
- Preparation of 'credit-plan' for the area based on the bankable schemes and the number of the units which can be financed thereunder; and
- Allocation of the 'Credit-Plan' among various credit institutions for implementation in a time bound manner.

These in-depth studies were more purposive than the initial impressionistic surveys; their objective was more specific *viz.* to identify bankable schemes/activities. The emphasis was, therefore, on studying the techno.-economic features of the economic activities and collection of information about their cost and benefit. These studies increased the insights of the banks into the growth process at the grass-roots level. They also equipped the bank's staff with skills to interpret the economic environmental data in terms of demand for credit and deposit potential.

Phases/Stages of Lead Bank Scheme

The executing of the lead bank scheme has been divided into two phases as per the guidelines of the RBI as mentioned below :

- ***Conducting surveys and identification of credit gaps***

  In the first phase various districts of the country were allocated among all public sector banks as the lead bank of the district. This was based on the concept of 'area approach'. Under this first stage, lead banks conducted impressionistic surveys to identify the centres for growth existing and potential both. The lead banks have put in strenuous efforts in their respective districts in regard to collection of socio-economic data, identifying credit gaps, formulating developmental programmes and establishment of a network of branches. This resulted in massive branch expansion in under-banked/un-banked areas.

- ***Formulation and Implementation of area development programmes***

  The second and most important stage of the scheme comprises of filling in the credit gaps by formulating DCPs and their implementation. The lead banks have to identify bankable schemes in their districts and cover all economically viable and technically feasible activities. They should seek/invoke co-operation from other financing agencies in this task.

Advantages from Lead Bank Scheme

The close involvement of the lead bank with a particular area will not only result in deposit mobilisation, but also in the expansion of credit to agriculture and small industries. Individual lead banks used to make a detailed survey of the area of their operation and the potentials in that area for economic growth and evolve schemes to accelerate their involvement in their respective areas.

Important benefits observed from the Lead Bank Scheme are as under :

- The whole country is served by a well knit system of commercial and co-operative banking;
- Branch expansion, supervision and guidance has become effective;
- A dynamic relationship between commercial banks, co-operative credit institutions and government authorities at the district level has evolved;
- There is a close integration of credit and banking business with other activities;
- Major bottlenecks in the development of the district are identified and the lead bank has induced the appropriate agencies to take remedial actions.

The advantages of LBS can be better understood in the light of sufferings of millions of farmers and other rural people before the independence of India. Undoubtedly, some efforts were made to help them in rudimentary forms, but all in vain. In the words of Late Prime Minister Smt. Indira Gandhi (1969) "The banker must become the friend, philosopher and guide of the farmer, by providing technical assistance, inputs, supervision of credit and input use and by simultaneously financing the development of storage and marketing facilities."

Service Area Approach - Modified Version of Lead Bank Scheme

After nationalisation of 14 major commercial banks in 1969, commercial banks decided to go in for an 'Area Approach' for the development of banking in rural areas, but unfortunately, the primary objective of the area approach appeared to be not so much effective in the development of chosen areas. Owing to the avoidance of the pit falls of scattered and unsupervised lending, with a view to avoid scattered lending and to ensure better supervision of credit, another variant of area approach the 'Village Adoption Scheme' was adopted in 1977 by SBI, which was subsequently followed by many banks. Under this scheme with mutual understanding among banks each branch was allowed to adopt one or more villages for intensive financing to meet the entire credit needs of the village and to avoid multiple financing, but majority of the banks adopted those villages which were well connected with roads and comparatively more developed. The banks, however, discriminated against the small farmers and backward villages, with little or no consideration for viable schemes, loans were granted far and wide. The problems of bankable schemes like recovery, acute shortage of manpower and even of untrained hands started coming in. Then, it was realised that the scattered geographical locations of the adopted villages by a bank again leading to the system of 'scattered lending'.

Though the 'multiple financing system' and 'accelerated financing' through agricultural development branches, village adoption scheme and implementation of area specific schemes enabled these agencies to achieve their overall targets set out from time to time, but it had many weaknesses like overlapping of efforts due to lending in scattered and distant areas, poor quality of lending, poor recovery of advances, under utilisation of available natural resources and skills and generation of imbalances etc. To overcome these problems and to make rural lending more productive and extensive in nature, one of the most important structural change in the 'area approach' (LBS) was made in the form of the 'village allotted' in place of 'village adoption' to commercial banks and RRBs for the overall development of villages.

In view of the many operational problems of sporadic and scattered lending, it was thought necessary that some specific operational area should be fixed for efficiency and targetted results for a particular bank branch. Hence, the new approach came into being from April 1,1989, which is popularly known as 'Service Area Approach' (SAA) or 'Branch Command Area Approach'. The SAA is, infact, a modified version of LBS. It is altogether not a new approach, but an extension of the 'Village Adoption Scheme'. The only difference between these two is that the former was voluntary in nature whereas the later one was obligatory. The SAA is superior comparatively to the village adoption scheme as it helped in overcoming many pitfalls and flaws of the institutional credit which were prevalent under the old lending system.

Under the original LBS, the **'district'** was the unit for planning, but under the new scheme the **'village'** is the unit of planning. Thus, the focus of planning shifted from the 'district' to the 'village,' which ultimately mean the planning from below or grass root level planning so that the benefits of planning could percolate down to the masses and credit could be linked to the production, productivity and generation of income. In nutshell, the SAA could be able to improve the quality of lending drastically. The whole concept of SAA has been discussed in length and depth in the next chapter of this book.

District Credit Plan

The main objective of the lead bank scheme is to ensure adequate supply of credit for the rapid economic development of the district. In this regard, the lead bank is expected to estimate credit demands from the existing patterns of economic activities and also those emerging while growth-oriented programmes are being implemented and to evolve schemes for meeting these demands in co-operation with other banks and financial institutions. The role of the lead bank has, therefore, to be viewed in the perspective of credit planning. The concept of credit planning at the district level for credit and banking development can be traced to the Gadgil study group's report which advocated an area approach to the development of banking and credit structure. Prof. Gadgil, the champion of district planning, also recommended the adoption of district which constituted the main administrative unit as the base unit for the purpose.

Need of District Credit Plan

The essence behind the adoption of district for credit planning was the inability of the central plans to estimate credit needs of the various sectors in the district. The need for micro planning is recognised by the planning commission as well as by the GOI. There is no doubt that centralised planning based on macro level indicators has helped to increase agricultural and industrial production and Gross National Product (GNP), but such an economic growth has not brought distributive economic justice. The rate of unemployment and percentage of people living below the poverty line have increased during the period of agricultural and industrial growth prior to micro level planning.

One of the reasons for such problems was the centralised planning exercise in a country of sub-continental proportions and physical economic diversity, vast dispersed sectors like agriculture, traditional and small industries etc. Centralised planning in such situations creates astronomical requirements of information collection, processing, interpretation and their conversion into operational decisions with such a speed and frequency that, even irrespective of its cost, it may turn out to be an impossible task.

Another reason for focusing on micro planning is that macro planning has so far remained purely an arithmetical exercise at the national level with emphasis on heavy industries, major and medium irrigation projects and heavy machinery mostly feeding urban industrial complexes. In the rural areas, the only beneficiaries of this type of development have been the more affluent farmers, who have the resources to buy modern agricultural inputs. The poorer sections of the people have always been by passed by this type of development.

Owing to many weaknesses of macro level planning, the fourth Five year plan for the first time in the history of planning in India suggested the introduction of micro level plans at the district level to correct the imbalances of the centralised planning.

Infact, the fourth plan marked a significant departure from the past practice in that the states were not given even broad indication about their sectoral outlays and were asked to frame plan proposals with their own priorities and resources in view. The Planning Commission then, also defined the nature and scope of district planning and issued operational guidelines to the state and district agencies before the exercise on the formulation of the fourth plan was taken up. This was later accepted by the Government of India. The concept of DDP thus evolved and the district level plans were prepared and implemented during the fourth five year plan period. In district plan the district became the basic unit for planning.

Meaning of District Credit Plan

A district credit plan is a development plan for an area, consisting of technically feasible and economically viable schemes, which can be taken up for financing by financial institutions after slight modification of the existing framework. It is drawn on the basis of a strategy of development suitable for the area taking in to account its natural endowments, principal economic activities and their potential for development, current and proposed development projects and the felt needs of the people. A DCP can be defined as a comprehensive and integrated plan, which includes schemes covering all the major sectors of the economy of the district and depending upon their natural linkages.

Infact, a DCP is a development plan consisting of bankable schemes. The schemes should be such that they can be immediately taken up for implementation by the various credit agencies within the existing or marginally strengthened framework of infra-structure and other facilities.

In other words, the DCP is a financial plan of banks operating in the district for allocation and disbursal of available resources among various sectors/ activities/ borrowers in conformity with the plan priority. A district credit plan may, therefore, be regarded as the financial framework of a district development plan. Thus, a DCP is not a mere exercise in estimates of credit needs of an area on the basis of available data, but it is a blue print for action by banks and other financial institutions. In nutshell, the DCP is intended to be a 'Blue print of the lending programmes' of all credit institutions operating in the district.

Nature and Scope of District Credit Plan

District credit plan has three facets, namely-rural banking development, rural credit disbursal and deployment and ultimately the rural development. These three dimensions of DCP are interwoven with each other as they cannot be separated from each for the sake of success of any DCP. In other words, for making rural lending more effective, efficient and smooth with the purpose of filling up the credit gaps and improve the quality of lending, the concept of DCP was evolved. Though the exercise of formulating DCP began in 1973, but its actual formulation took place in 1975. DCPs are prepared by the respective lead banks of the district and then discussed at District Level Consultative Committee (DLCC), which are in existence in almost every district since 1974. Since 1980, the DCPs have been prepared on the uniform pattern as per the RBI's guidelines and split up in to an Annual Action Plan (AAPs) and block/branch-wise plans for its implementation. DCP spell-out targets scheme-wise, sector-wise and block-wise and also determine bank-wise participation for the grass root level programmes/ schemes.

In simple words, a DCP is comprehensive and integrated plan of action of bankable schemes in the district which can be taken up by the financial institutions for financing. The DCP is operationally successful to the extent of its soundness in terms of technically feasible and economically viable schemes with reference to location specific realities or 'Bankable schemes." Here, it is important to make clear that technically feasibility means that inputs, facilities and services required for implementing the scheme are available and market exists to the resulting incremental outputs, whereas economically viable means that the incremental income is sufficient enough to repay the loan and interest and then also to leave a surplus.

From the scope point of view, DCP indicates the scope of development in the specified district on the lines on which credit could be deployed by the concerned agencies in a given time. Although DCP has a specific time period, it is an on going exercise, through the annual action plans. Through the AAPs, the DCP is translated in to an action plan for realising its objectives. The AAPs are flexible in approach so that they can easily be implemented.

It is in consonance with the plan programme of the State Government and development agencies viz., DRDA, DIC etc. the DCP indicates the level of credit to be extended to the priority sectors covering agriculture and allied activities, rural and cottage industries, the SSI and other activities such as road transport, retail trade, self-employed professionals in the specified area. The DCP also takes into account the credit needs of the educational and housing schemes of Government. It also considers the need for consumption credit in its area of operation.

A DCP covers a wide range of activities under its umbrella including those meant for priority sector lending. While finalising the quantum of resources for DCP, the estimation exercise takes into consideration not only the credit requirement of the district, but also the amount of resources that can easily be raised within the district as well as those which could be available from outside the district.

Therefore, it is quite obvious that a DCP combines two distinct kinds of integrative functions : Firstly, it should bridge the gap between macro decision at the national level and the local project plans, blending them together by relying on the knowledge of other plans and familiarity with the minor decisions of the district. Secondly, at the same time it provides a convenient frame work co-ordinating a wide range of activities in terms of physical plans suitable to the specific condition of a region.

In nutshell, DCP provides a blue print of action for an all round economic development of the district and the plan is thus ideally suited to bring about a balanced regional development in general and of rural and backward area and weaker sections of society in particular.

Subject matter of the District Credit Plan

The document of DCP contains the following details :

- District profile and block profiles;

- Review of the performance (bank-wise and block-wise) of earlier credit plan;
- Details of developmental programmes of the government development agencies;
- Details of the SGSY and other specified programmes;
- Infra-structure and the supporting services required from the Government to carry out the targetted credit programmes;
- Credit demand estimation of various sectors/activities of the economy covered under the plan;
- Bank-wise, block-wise and scheme-wise details of credit deployment expected in the plan;
- Bank-wise and block-wise resources availability to implement the programmes;
- Specific responsibilities of individual financial institutions participating in the credit plan programmes;
- The details of Annual Action Plan (AAP)

Objectives of District Credit Plan

The first and the foremost objective of DCP is to accelerate the growth of the district's economy through the all round development of rural and backward areas. Besides this, a DCP has also more or less the same objectives as those of national plan or of DDP. Among them the main objectives of the DCP are listed below :

- To remove the unemployment and under employment;
- To reduce the 'spatial' and 'sectoral gaps' or inequalities;
- To attain social objectives through raising the standard of living and by fulfilling the basic needs of the people belonging to poorer sections of society;
- To improve the 'Credit Absorptive Capacity' of rural sector, specially of capital deficient areas and weaker sections;
- To promote balanced development of the blocks in the district;
- To establish meaningful linkages between credit for priority sector activities on the one hand and government subsidy programmes for such activities on the other hand;
- To facilitate expansion of credit in non-inflationary manner through the production oriented bankable schemes. This objective may also be achieved through better inter-sectoral and inter borrower allocation of credit as envisaged in DCP.

- To increase production and productivity through maximising the output from the existing and marginally strengthened production capacity of the available resources of the area.

In brief, the principal objective of DCP is to ensure optimum utilisation of available resources for economic development as per the plan priorities of the district. The main thrust of DCP is towards higher production, increased productivity and better standard of living for the masses. In other words, we can say that the object of DCP is to provide a contributory means of credit for fulfilling the developmental needs at the grass-root level.

Advantages of District Credit Plan

The concept of DCP was implemented due to certain inherent merits in it. The chief distinctive advantages of DCP are as under :

- DCP helps in optimum utilisation of local resources as it is based on potential local resources on the one hand and the felt needs of the people on the other hand.
- DCP ensures an integrated development of the district as it takes care of all linkage effects in preparing schemes for financing. It will thus ensure simultaneous development of all sectors of the district's economy.
- DCP identifies the specific infra-structural requirements of each district. This results in better DDP of the district.
- DCP enhances demand for credit by taking up new schemes for financing. This improves the credit deposit ratio (CDR) in the less developed areas.
- Besides reduction in intra-district disparities of development, DCP helps in reducing the inter-district and inter-regional disparities as well.

On the basis of above mentioned advantages of DCP, it is crystal clear that the DCP is a useful document in so far as it provides basic facts/data/information organised according to regions or sub-regions within the district. It also provides a frame-work of how to proceed with formulations of a plan. This planning exercise is carried out in the district basically with the object of ensuring flow of scarce resources to the needy sectors and to ensure balanced development. Thus, district credit plan is prepared after a systematic study of the scope for development of different sectors of the district's economy taking into consideration of the available resources and requirements of the people.

REFERENCES

1. Krishnaswami, O.R. and Sashaih, K. : The lead bank scheme : An Empirical Evaluation (Rainbow Publication, Coimbatore, Tamil Nadu, 1985)
2. Arumugum, P. : Lead Bank System and Service Area Approach (UDH Publishing House, Delhi, 1991)
3. Jatana, Renu : Lead Bank Scheme (Rupa Books Pvt. Ltd., Jaipur, 1996)
4. Mehta, Basant : The organisation and working of Lead Bank Scheme in India (Vohra Publishers & Distributor, Allahabad, 1989)
4. Lead Bank Scheme : A New Horizon for Development (Discovery Publishing House, New Delhi, 1992)
5. Satya Sundaram, I : Rural Development (Himalaya Publishing House, Delhi, 1997)
6. Kulshrestha, U.C. : Lead Banks in India (Radha Publication, New Delhi.
7. Satya Sundaram, I. : 'Lead Bank Scheme : Problems and Prospects' in I. Satya Sundram, Ed. 1989, Rural Poverty and Area Planning (B.R. Publishing Corporation, New Delhi)
8. "Report of the Working Group to review the working of the lead bank scheme", Reserve Bank of India, RPCD, Mumbai, Dec. 9, 1982.
9. "Report of study group of National Credit Council", RBI, Mumbai.
10. Laxman, Govind : "Lead Bank Scheme - Some Observation", (Economic Times, August 24, 1985)
11. Bohra, T.M. : "District Credit Plan - Future Strategy", (Indian Bank Association Bulletin, April, 1984)
12. Pathak, S.M. : "District Credit Plans" (Bank of India Bulletin, April, 1984)
13. Joglekar, S.N. : "Lead Bank Scheme - Genesis and Resurrection" (Article in the Journal of the Indian Institute of Bankers, January - March, 1976)
14. Mello, L.D. : "Nature and Methodology of District Credit Plan" (Prajnan, January-March, 1975)
15. Ghose, B.K. : "The Lead Bank Scheme : Some Reflections" (The Journal of Indian Institute of Bankers, April-June, 1983)

16. Bal Krishna : "Lead Bank Scheme : Problems and Prospects" (The Journal of the Indian Institute of Bankers, Volume 55, July-September, 1985)
17. Sharma, K.K. : Reserve Bank of India and Rural Credit (Premier Publishing, Delhi)
18. Singh, Ajit : Rural Development and Banking in India (Deep and Deep Publications, New Delhi, 1985)
19. Narula, R.K. : Agricultural & Rural advances by Commercial Banks (UDH Publishers, Delhi, 1984)

□■□

Chapter 3

Service Area Approach : An Innovative Concept in Rural Lending

The Service Area Approach (SAA), which is an innovative strategy for rural lending, was launched with the basic objective of improving the credit delivery system and quality of rural lending in the country by the Government of India and Reserve Bank of India.This approach is in operation since April 1st, 1989. Basically, the SAA is based on three tier programme of linking villages with bank branches, economic survey of villages and formulation of credit plans at village level, block level and district level. The focus of SAA, which is also known as 'Command Area Approach', is to promote all round development of rural areas through productive lending.

A BRIEF HISTORY OF RURAL LENDING IN INDIA

The concept of rural development obviously implies the overall improvement in the living conditions of the rural people. As we know, no development can take place without the adequate institutional credit flow at reasonable cost. Thus, the credit forms the basis of balanced and speedy development. For mobilising and optimum utilisation of non-credit inputs for rural development, availability of credit input is not only important, but also becomes inevitable. In the absence of adequate amount of credit at reasonable rate, no one can even think of rapid development. Due to paucity of financial resources rural people are unable to exhibit their latent talent not only for their own benefit as well as for the benefit of the society as a whole. The share of institutional credit to rural sector was only 4 percent of total rural credit before the independence of the country. This shows the pitiable position of institutional credit before the independence of the country. After independence the expectation of people of from the government increased tremendously. This led to the launching of five year plans and acceptance of rural development as a prime national goal which cannot be fulfilled without proper extension and strengthening of rural credit system. Accordingly, the Government decided to develop co-operative credit societies as an exclusive agency of rural credit. Besides this, to assess the rural credit needs and to recommend measures to meet the needs, the **All India Rural Credit Survey Committee (AIRCSC)** was appointed in 1951. The AIRCSC in its report mentioned that as much as 92.7% of the borrowings of the farmers come from private sources, of which a major share of 44.8% was made available by the professional money lendess only 7.3% of the total borrowings of the farmers was provided by the institutional agencies - co-operative, Government and Commercial banks together. Out of this 7.3%,co-operatives credit amounted to 3.1% and commercial bank credit only to 0.9%. The committee observed that the flow of rural credit was not adequate as per the requirement of the rural community. The disbursement of credit was also not on correct lines as it did not reach to the needy people either due to lack of credit worthiness or due to inaccessibility of such people. Rural affluent class pick-pocketed the large share of rural credit due to socio-economic-politico influence and high credit worthiness. Therefore, the committee recommended a number of measures ensuring a fair deal to small farmers and integrating lending with marketing and warehousing for improving repayment rate. The AIRCSC also recommended to enable and develop co-operative credit institutions by creating one integrated, state sponsored commercial bank with an effective machinery spread all over the country which would provide finance to the co-operatives for lending in rural areas. The GOI by accepting the recommendations of the committee converted the Imperial Bank of India into a public sector bank named as State Bank of India (SBI) by merging eight other private commercial banks. Several other committees were also appointed during the sixties such as the committee on co-operative credit in 1960 and institutional arrangements for agricultural credit in 1965. The Government implemented some of the recommendations of the above mentioned Committees, which led to the sufficient improvement in the resource base of co-operative institutions particularly of those which had better management and organisation. Inspite of the improvement in the resource base of co-operatives, the sanctions and disbursement of the credit was very poor especially to small farmers and other borrowers. The co-operatives also failed miserably in integrating the credit input with the marketing and warehousing facilities in the rural areas. All India Rural Credit Committee (1966) observed the following :

- Overdues were heavy and rising continuously;
- Small cultivators were unable to get credit; and
- A large number of primary co-operatives were neither viable nor potential was sufficient there.

Due to the various shortcomings as depicted above the share of co-operative credit in total rural lending was very small and insignificant proportions. Inspite of pious intention and support of Government, the co-opertives could not succeed in enhancing their share substantially so as to felt their presence because of faulty perception and unpragmatic approach towards the problems and their solutions.

The emergence of green revolution in late 60's based on HYV seeds and the concomitant input such as increased use of fertilizers, irrigation facilities, pesticides and mechanisation of agriculture-all together considerably increased the need for higher amount of credit to the farming community. This initiated the change in the norms of lending from credit worthiness to purpose-worthiness, so that the requirement of the farm credit could easily be met with. The need for change in approach for rural lending was a logical conclusion of the development which was taking place in the economy. The co-operative credit institutions failed to respond to the new challenges thrown up before them as they did not change their approach towards rural lending as per the need of the hour.

Such irretrievable state of credit co-operatives compelled for critical assessment of the exclusively single agency approach to rural lending. Already in 1950, the **Rural Banker Enquiry Committee** felt the necessity of encouraging commercial banks to finance productive schemes in agriculture directly in order to compliment the role of co-operative credit societies. But neither the banks were eager to implement the suggestion nor the government was keen to do that and so the inadequacy and improper deployment of rural credit lingered on, besides the mounting overdues that assumed disturbing proportions since the mid sixties. Therefore, in this context GOI established **National Credit Council (NCC)** a study group on "Organisational framework for the implementation of social objectives" under the Chairmanship of Prof. D.R. Gadgil in 1968. This study group strongly recommended the involvement of commercial banks in supplying of rural credit. The government then decided to nationalise 14 major commercial banks to ensure their effective participation in rural lending. Till then the banking system was predominantly urban-oriented and mainly catered to the needs of organised trade, commerce and big industries.

After the nationalisation of 14 major CBs the campaigning for opening up branches in rural areas was started vigorously. Though the development of rural areas also received greater attention of the GOI, but the nationalisation of banks gave it a real push. On the basis of the Gadgil study group recommendations, the most important structural change in the commercial banking system was made by introducing the **'Lead Bank' Concept**. The RBI launched this scheme in December, 1969 to give a concrete shape to the **'Area Approach'** for development. The detail of this scheme has been mentioned in the Chapter II. The subsequent period of the present study was marked by a phenomenal expansion of the network of CBs branches particularly the rural and semi-urban branches. Before the nationalisation of the banks in 1969, single agency approach to rural lending was in force, but it was thought after nationalisation of CBs to replace it by a multi-agency approach. For this purpose banks were forced to expand their branch network in rural and semi-urban areas.

In the mid seventies, it was felt that despite the efforts of co-operative banks over the last few decades and the spectacular progress shown by the commercial banks during the post nationalisation period, there was a vast gap in the areas of rural credit requirements. Moreover the CBs were basically urban oriented and to have their active participation in rural areas, their methods, procedures, training and orientation shall have to be shifted to rural environment, which was not easy to achieve. Further the cost of operation of commercial banks was high due to their high salary structure, staffing pattern and high establishment cost, hence they were not able to provide credit at lower cost to weaker sections of the rural areas.

Keeping in view all the facts mentioned above, a committee was appointed under the chairmanship of Shri M. Narasimhan to suggest measures to reduce the gap in rural credit. This committee recommended the establishment of a new category of bank - Regional Rural Banks (RRBs) in selected districts where co-operatives were weak and CBs were not active. It was thought that these banks will combine the merits of commercial banks and co-operative banks without inheriting their drawbacks. In other words, logistically the RRBs were intended to be rural oriented and commercially organised institutions. With the setting up of RRBs on October 2, 1975 the multi-agency approach got a further boost. Thus, the number of institutions, which were engaged in the sphere in rural lending, increased and also started extending credit to rural people in a big way.

In this regard, with a view to avoid scattered lending, to ensure better supervision of credit and to develop the village economy in all respect in a phased manner, another variant of area approach the 'Village Adoption Scheme' was adopted. This scheme was initially adopted by the SBI in 1977. Besides this, in order to sharpen the focus of assistance to the weaker among the weak, massive poverty alleviation programmes linked to bank credit with subsidy from the Government were also introduced. These measures were supported by modifications where necessary and enlargement of insurance coverage both for the loans extended and assets financed through the Deposit Insurance and Credit Guarantee Corporation of India (1981). This scheme was known as Crop Insurance and Cattle Insurance Scheme. The impact of all these measures and policy changes were favourable in the sense that more amount of credit flown to the rural sector, but the problem of recovery arose. Due to this the recycling of credit to priority sector became difficult to maintain the proper recovery of loans basically due to unproductive use of one hand and lack of effective check and supervision of the end use of credit on the other hand. This initiated the fresh efforts by the RBI to improve the supervision of credit.

Due to many inherit drawbacks in the multi-agency system in concept and in practice initiated the necessity of introducing some alternative, innovative and better approach for rural lending. After the field survey of rural areas and serious deliberations at high level the new approach to rural lending, which is popularly known as Service Area Approach, (SAA), was launched on April 1, 1989 aimed at bringing about an improvement in the quality of lending, optimising the use of credit, establishing improved linkages with production, productivity income and proper recycling of bank credit.

GENESIS AND ORIGIN OF SERVICE AREA APPROACH

The strategy of the GOI for rural development includes provision of credit for increasing production, productivity and income in rural economy, particularly in agricultural sector and for self employment ventures. Although since 1904, co-operative credit societies were in operation in the rural sector, but these were not adequate for enormous task of rural development. In this context, commercial bank's credit was also not adequately available to rural borrowers till the late 1960's.

For balanced and rapid growth of the country, a strategy based on the development of grass root level should be followed. Keeping this view, GOI and RBI adopted several policies/approaches and programmes for rural lending and ultimately for rural development. In this context, the main steps taken by GOI and RBI from time to time can be described briefly as follows :

- Social control on banks in 1968;
- Nationalisation of 14 major commercial banks in July, 1969;
- Introduction of 'Lead Bank Scheme' in December, 1969;
- Establishment of Regional Rural Banks in October, 1975;
- Nationalisation of 6 other commercial banks in April, 1980;
- Implementation of 'Village Adoption Scheme'; and
- RBI directive for banks to serve population residing with in 10 miles radius.

Thus, the CBs were increasingly deploying credit in rural areas through their rural and semi-urban branches. This was confirmed by the National Sample Survey, 1982. According to this survey, the share of commercial banks to total rural credit increased from 0.9% in 1951-52 to 28% in 1981-82; while the share of moneylenders declined from 69.7 % in 1951-52 to 16.9% in 1981-82.

Though the CBs had enlarged their rural credit and the strategy of area approach, which was adopted by them, was laudable, but the methodology in use was, however, not satisfactory. There was still scattered lending, no planned lending covering every sector and every section of the rural community in the area of operation. Even for the villages adopted for intensive lending, there was no planned intensive lending schemes for them in practice. The existence of multiple financial institutions which resulted into the problem of double financing, which involved duplication of efforts, mis-utilisation of credit and unplanned disbursement of credit. Since the village adoption scheme was voluntary, hence many villages remained out of the preview of this scheme. Thus, village-wise credit requirement neither assessed nor fulfilled.

Problems of Rural Lending

Leaving apart of the above, the Indian rural Credit system was affected by many other problems also, which made the Government to ponder over it. The main problems, which prevailed in the credit system at that time, were as follows :

- Recovery of agricultural advances have been declining year after year.
- District level credit planning introduced through lead bank scheme did not stabilize.
- Regional imbalances in distribution of agricultural credit were on the increase.
- National priorities for agricultural production inter-woven with the lending discipline of banks were ineffective except target achievement.
- Only a few rural branches have been working effectively. Majority of them did not do substantial lending for development.
- Qualitative aspects of credit deployment has not received due attention.
- Co-ordination machinery built-up at the block level did not result in effective linkages between development and credit agencies. It helped merely in target chasing.

All these problems were due to lack of knowledge on the part of banker of his area of operation and clientele; the area of operation being too large and many a time undefined and bound by local pressures. Hence, it was felt imperative to (i) make all branches in rural and semi-urban areas functionally effective; and (ii) prescribe certain rational boundaries for their area of operation.

The problems mentioned above and besides these, the problem of double financing and sectoral imbalances in credit deployment necessitated revision of the strategy and methodology to ensure (i) supply of credit in each and every village and (ii) deployment of credit in every sector and to weaker sections of a village and (iii) to check the problems accompanying multiple lending approach combined with area approach.

Due to all these problems, the RBI was deeply concerned with the mis-match between the quantum of credit to the agricultural sector and the rate of agricultural production, in particularly of foodgrains production. To ascertain reasons of stagnancy in production/productivity of agriculture produce, RBI advised the top executives of public sector banks to conduct study of their banks, at least in two lead districts and one non-lead district of the country. At the instance of the RBI, the Chairman of Public sector banks undertook a country-wide study on rural lending in November/December, 1987. The findings of these studies disclosed major deficiencies in the rural credit system, *viz.* Weak link between bank credit and production, productivity and income levels. Scattered lending over large areas diluted the quality of lending. Post disbursement supervision was paid little or no attention. The findings of these studies were discussed in a seminar on rural lending on 9th and 10th January, 1988. It was attended by the chairman of Public sector banks and senior officials from the GOI. It was felt by the delegates that with the establishment of large network of branches the time was opportune to adopt a system of assigning specific area to each bank branch in which it can concentrate on focussed lending and contribute to the development of the area. It was basically aimed at planned and orderly development of a command area/service area. Strengthening the existing rural credit delivery system with a view to improving the quality of lending and ensuring that the bank credit should be channelised for increasing production, productivity and income level and to bring about a visible development in the rural sector, were some other important suggestions of the seminar. The recommendations of the seminar on Rural Lending was accepted by the GOI and RBI. To examine the operational aspects of these recommendations, the RBI set-up a committee under the chairmanship of Dr. P.D. Ojha, the then Deputy Governor and Chairman of some public sector banks as its members.

The terms of reference for the committee were as under :

- To consider the modalities of a system of area allocation to rural bank branches within which they will operate for deploying credit.
- To examine and recommend the necessary procedures for effective co-ordination among the three institutional agencies viz. Commercial banks, RRBs and co-operative banks under the new approach.
- To examine the modifications if any, that may be necessary in the exercise of credit planning under LBS in the light of new approach.
- To examine and recommend measures to improve co-ordination with development agencies at the district/block/village levels with a view to improving the quality of lending.
- To examine mode of disbursement of loan and subsidy for Integrated Rural Development Programme (IRDP) and other subsidies based programmes and recommend modifications if any, for improving the utilisations of resources in an optimum manner.
- Any other aspect related to above terms of reference.

After considering the recommendations of the committee, the RBI introduced 'Service Area Approach' on April 1, 1989 for giving a new thrust to rural lending.

CONCEPT OF SERVICE AREA APPROACH

The SAA, which is also known as 'Branch Command Area Approach', is a new policy initiative under which a designated bank branch is given the responsibility of shouldering the burden of planned development of a cluster of villages located in a specified area which is known as 'Service Area'. Under the SAA, each rural and semi-urban bank branch has been allotted a well defined area of operation of around 15 to 25 villages for the purpose of financing, which is known as 'cluster of villages' for planning by the bank branches. Infact, the SAA is an extension of the earlier adopted 'Village Adoption Scheme'. The only major difference between these two is that the former was voluntary in nature, while the latter was obligatory.

The new concept of SAA is a modified version of LBS as in this new approach, the most important structural change has been incorporated in the form of cluster of villages allotted to a particular bank branch in lieu of area approach adopted by banks for all round development of the rural economy. The LBS was essentially an area approach to economic development through banking expansion; while the SAA is a modified version of area approach as concerted attention is given under it on 'Location area specific measures'. In other words, the SAA is an "Intensive area approach". The concept of SAA is based on the hypothesis that the 'trickle down theory' has its own limitations in bringing about balanced growth with social justice. Therefore, it is essential to adopt 'area specific planning' in a developing country like India keeping in view the need and resources of that specific area. Thus, the 'planning from below' is the right strategy of rural development. The SAA is a right step in this direction as the unit of planning under it is the village. The essence of this new approach is, therefore, compactness in the area of operation for lending with a view to making access to credit easier for the clientele and credit planning and close monitoring of the end use of funds at the grass-root level.

The crux of the SAA is demarcation of service area and preparation of credit plans for systematic administration of credit in the assigned area. For the economic development of rural areas in a phased manner, the bank branches are expected to play a pioneering role at 'Micro' level by surveying the villages in the allotted areas for assessing potentials for identified beneficiaries for assistance, preparing credit plans on-an-annual basis and monitoring the progress of the beneficiaries under different schemes. In this way, the SAA is a micro level credit planning or an exercise of credit planning at the grass root level, hence far-far better concept of rural lending and also a commendable scheme for rural development. Finally, the concept of SAA is perhaps a modified version of the area approach strategy with logistics much refined, more elaborate and with a commitment to meet more challenges both existing and emerging in the sphere of rural development.

OBJECTIVES OF SERVICE AREA APPROACH

The primary objective of the SAA is to improve the quality and productivity of lending so that the qualitative change in the life of rural people could take place. The main objectives of SAA are listed below :

- To make rural lending more productive by relating it intimately to local conditions and genuine needs of villagers;
- To forge a meaningful linkage of credit with production, productivity and generation of income;
- To revamp the rural credit delivery system by imparting development thrust to bank credit;
- To promote deposit mobilisation to augment resources for rural lending and improving the recycling of credit;
- To increase co-operation between bank local officials and local development agencies;
- To enhance field orientation and motivation of bank officials;
- To shoot out the snags of institutional financing like double/ multiple financing and wrong choice of beneficiaries;
- To rationalise rural lending and to reduce cost of supervision by reducing the number of villages in which the branches operate; and
- To avoid duplication of efforts in lending in a village by more than one bank.

In brief, we can say that ultimate aim of launching this new approach was to take lead bank scheme to the rural people and to improve the quality and productivity of rural lending by forging a meaningful linkages of credit with production, productivity and generation of income.

TENETS OF SERVICE AREA APPROACH

There are two tenets of such a big and ambitious scheme like SAA:

- Demarcation of area among commercial banks, RRBs and Co-operative banks;
- Village-wise planning;

Competition among different credit agencies is a healthy feature for privileged clientele, which enjoys the choice of agencies, but for less privileged classes particularly those coming from below the poverty line, there is no such choice. Under the SAA, by demarcating the area, the branch is made accountable for both privileged and non-privileged clientele in the allotted villages.

There are three main agencies in the formulation and implementation of DCPs and Service Area Plans (SAPs). These are banks including RRBs, Co-operative credit institutions and government agencies. It is an important point that if the banks have to prepare village-wise credit plans for their Service Areas, it is implied that government agencies have to plan village-wise.

Infact, the SAA has become a grass-root unit of LBS as LBS has been brought down to the grass-root level, i.e. at the village level. Movement to the villages is the explicit agenda of SAA. Infact, people's participation is a pre-requisite to any development process and credit planning for rural development. The National Institute of Bank Management (NIBM) has already initiated an action credit planning for development of villages with people (PDV), which aims at building an organic link between rural branches and the people and involve latter's participation in village credit planning.

As the faith was posed in Lead Bank Officer (LBO) when LBS was launched, the same faith is reposed in the Branch Manager (BM) under the SAA. In a way, BM becomes a LBO and represents the consortium of all credit agencies operating in his service area. Branch Manager is also empowered to negotiate with the relevant government agencies which have their schemes in the service area.

RATIONAL OF SERVICE AREA APPROACH

The rational of SAA is to avoid duplication of efforts and scattered lending over wider areas. The compactness in the area of operation will make it easy for the clientele to approach the bank for credit. It would also ensure proper credit planning and close monitoring of the end-use of credit.

The report of the committee to examine certain operational aspects of rural lending headed by Dr. P.D. Ojha has pointed out two following basic rationales for the SAA.

- The operational difficulties experienced in the erstwhile multi-agency approach to rural lending leading to spatial imbalances in credit flow in favour of the relatively more lucrative and competitive areas to the neglect of the other areas, where the opportunities were not considered adequate. In this regard report of the committee to examine certain operational aspects of rural lending reveals that : "The DCPs and AAPs prepared by the lead banks are yet to acquire the full status of operationally relevant plans for implementation, primarily on account of the absence of DDPs of the government, on one hand, and non-alignment with branch performance budgets, on the other. The lack of involvement of BM_s in the preparation of DCPs/AAPs was yet another factor for the plans not becoming meaningful to them. Incidentally, a snap opinion survey of BMs participating in the training programmes of NIBM also expressed identical views on the problems of AAPs. Report of the committee to examine certain operational aspects of Rural lending further states that "with the increase in bank branches/operations and with the concept of village adoption redefined, keen competition developed among the bank branches for business in areas with a good potential to the neglect of other areas where the opportunities were not considered adequate" and
- Certain inconsistencies and limitations affecting implementation of AAPs and DCPs under the LBS, emerging owing to both absence of government development plans and credit plans, non-alignment with banks performance budget and the non-involvement of the BMs at the planning stage.

STAGES/ASPECTS/CONTENTS OF SERVICE AREA APPROACH

Regarding the stages of SAA the detailed guidelines have been issued by the RBI in March, 1988, which were modified from time to time on the basis of experience gained and suggestions received from the field level functionaries. In brief, the SAA involves the following five major stages :

- Identification and allocation of service area for each rural and semi-urban branch of CBs , RRBs and Co-operative Credit Institutions for purposive and planned lending;

- Survey of villages on-an-on-going basis in the service area for assessing the potential for lending activities and identification of beneficiaries for assistance;
- Preparation of credit plan on an annual basis for the Service Area by each branch;
- Co-ordination between different credit institutions, on the one hand and the field level development agencies on the other on-an-on-going basis for effective implementation of credit plans; and
- System of continuous monitoring of progress achieved in the implementation of the plans branch-wise / bank-wise through Block Level Bankers Committee (BLBC).

A detailed description of each stage / aspect of SAA is given below:

IDENTIFICATION AND ALLOCATION OF SERVICE AREA

Identification and Allocation of a specific area for each bank branch was the first step in the implementation of the SAA. Specific areas were identified and allocated to each rural and semi-urban branch of CBs and RRBs. Earlier the co-operative banks were excluded from this approach. The RRB branches will cover only the target groups. Non-target groups would be assisted by the allotted CBs branches. The allocation of the service area to each bank branch was done by a committee headed by the Lead District Officer (LDO) of the RBI, the LBO of the concerned district and an officer of NABARD as its member. The concerned BDO was also invited to the meetings of the committee. The allocation was done in consultation with the concerned bank branches. Each rural / semi-urban branch of the CBs/RRBs have been allocated a certain number of villages ranging between 15-25, which is known as the 'Service Area'. The RBI has prescribed certain norms for allocation of villages to a particular bank branch for its service area. They are as follows :

- ***Proximity :*** The villages allotted to a particular bank branch should be near to the branch or within a manageable distance from the branch so that people need not to cover much distance from their village.
- ***Contiguity :*** The villages adjoining each other should be allocated to the same branch so that more people could have access to the branch with distance convenience.
- ***Cluster :*** Cluster approach should be followed in selecting the villages for service area meaning thereby that the villages in

the same Gram Panchayat should be allotted to the same branch to the extent possible,so that the supervision of credit becomes cost effective.

- Wherever a particular village has qualified for allotment to more than one branch on the basis of above norms, the allotment was made to that branch which was having dominant share in financing that village in terms of number of accounts.

Thus, it was ensured that the service area for a particular bank branch should typically comprise 15 to 25 villages as per the norms prescribed by the RBI. The service area allocated to a branch should be generally compact, accessible, proximity to the branch and contiguity of area. It was also ensured that service area of a branch was not intercepted by service area of another branch. Subject to the above criteria, the existing allocation of villages to different branches for the purpose of implementation of IRDP may also be kept in view while designating areas to different bank branches. The non-target group beneficiaries in the service area of a RRB branch will be financed by the branch of the concerned sponsor bank and, if it is too far away, then it will be financed by the nearest branch of any other commercial bank designated for the purpose.

In order to have a complete list of villages covered by each bank branch the lead bank is required to maintain block-wise records containing the following details :

(i) Name of branch and bank.

(ii) Village / Town in which it is located.

(iii) Names of villages allotted to it as its service area.

(iv) Names of villages for which the branch has been identified as 'designated branch' for catering to the credit needs of non-target groups in the service area of RRBs.

(v) Name of the convenor bank branch for the BLBC.

As and when there are changes in the villages allotted to branches on account of opening a new branch, the lead bank should make the necessary changes in its records.

For effective implementation of SAA, RBI had liberalised branch licensing policy for rural centres, so that each branch should have reasonable service area alongwith requisite business and profitability. At present BLBC allocate service area to new branches to be opened in the block.

With regard to the existing loan accounts among different banks/ branches may be transferred on their mutual understanding. Wherever this is not possible, the loan accounts may continue with the existing branch till they are liquidated. Normally, fresh financing should be done by the concerned service area branch.

Identification and allocation of villages was to be completed in a time-bound manner by the end of June, 1988. It is happily noted that the exercise of identification and allocation of service areas in the whole country was completed within the stipulated time period. Thus, all villages of the country numbering 6,18,216 including ward-wise sub-division of villages in the State of Kerala have already been allocated amongst 42,185 rural and semi-urban bank branch alongwith few urban branches which are having sizeable rural lending. Thus, each bank branch has been allotted approximately 15-25 villages under its area of operation.

Table no. 3.1 depicts the allocation of villages for SAA according to the category of banks. The table reveals that the highest number of villages were allotted to the public sector banks (3,66,382), which was followed by RRBs (2,36,692) and private sector banks (15,242) respectively. The table also reveals this fact that the average no. of villages per branch at national level was 14.66 as against the established norm of 15 to 25 villages, which could be termed as 'Satisfactory'.

Table No. 3.1

BANK GROUP-WISE ALLOCATION OF VILLAGES FOR SAA

S.N.	*Category of Banks*	*No. of Branches*	*No. of Villages*	*Average No. of Villages per Branch*
1.	Public Sector Banks	2,60,16	3,66,382	14.08
2.	Private Sector Banks	2,489	15,242	6.12
3.	RRBs	13,663	23,66,92	17.33
	TOTAL	42,168	61,83,16	14.66

SURVEY OF VILLAGES

After the allocation of service area, each branch was to undertake an economic survey of the allotted villages and prepare village profile in respect for each village in its respective area. The village profile provides details regarding following important aspects :

- Population and occupational data;
- Land uses;

- Types of economic activities undertaken and potentialities for expansion or for undertaking new activities;
- Skills of families for different activities to be undertaken;
- Coverage of rural families by credit agencies operating in the area;
- Infrastructure and linkage available in the area and those required to be developed to support bank credit; and
- Details of schemes/programmes being operated by the government agencies/institutions in the service area wherever necessary should be incorporated and made use of.

The survey was not intended to be a household survey. Village profiles need to be prepared by undertaking survey of the service area, hence the BM should have intimate knowledge of villages in his service area.

A proforma of the survey and a desk guide were given by the RBI to BMs containing guidelines for compilation of villages. The BM should make use of the data available with other agencies such as DRDA, DIC, block and village records etc. for the purpose of the survey. To help the BMs in this regard, the LBO of the district concerned should ascertain the availability of data with various agencies and the modalities for obtaining the same. The manager of each bank branch was to complete the survey within four months from the date of allocation of service area to it. Here, it is important to mention that the RRB branches conducted the economic survey for the allotted villages with the help of sponsor bank personnel.

The village profile is to be updated periodically usually once in a year taking into account the developmental changes and other factors which have taken place. The BMs were expected to keep themselves abreast of developments taking place in their service areas by periodical visits to the villages and establishing a continuous contact with the extension and developmental agencies. Therefore, it is quite obvious that under the SAA, branch manager have been assigned important responsibility of conducting economic survey of villages allotted to their branches for identifying the economic activities in the villages both existing and potential.

In preparation of village profile and conducting village survey, the role of NABARD is also very significant. The NABARD has decided to open up District Development Office (DDO) in each and every district of the country. The background papers are prepared jointly by DDM of

NABARD and LBO and are circulated among the BMs. Potential linked credit plans (PLPs) prepared by NABARD and background papers are very useful for updating survey of villages and preparation of realistic village credit plans.

To ascertain potential of different activities in the service area, the branches should be aware of different ingredients required to assess potential of technically feasible and economically viable activities in the area. On the basis of village survey, it is possible to formulate realistic and proper credit plans and to chalk out bankable schemes which could generate income, employment and help in developing the area concerned. The PLP represents an effort at making realistic and easy implementable projects of potentials of growth in different sectors in the district. The main objective of the PLPs is to explore the potential for development and evolve an appropriate mechanism through which such potential could easily be exploited over a period of time. Such plans represent credit projections taking into account various aspects like development potential, infra-structural facilities, credit absorption capacity, marketing support, availability of raw material and key critical constraints etc.

The identification of beneficiaries of such plans can be made either in public meetings in village or by contacting the representatives of village communities such as panchayats. The families selected under any government sponsored programmes are an integral part of identified beneficiaries.

Utility of Village Profiles

The more crucial stage in the implementation of the SAA is the preparation of village profiles for each of the villages allotted to a branch. The village profiles are expected to serve as the basic and essential documents for assessing the vital aspects of credit planning such as potential for development, skills of the population, schemes suited to the area, critical constraining factors affecting the action plan and the back-up support available from government departments and agencies for bank credit.

The unit of survey or planning as envisaged under SAA is 'village' therefore, the credit planning should start from the village. The banking and non-banking financial institutions have to prepare village-wise credit plans based on the village profiles and the data available in the 'Background Paper'.

Thus, prepared village-wise credit plan should be consolidated to arrived at branch level credit plan and by consolidating the branch-level credit plans, the block level credit plan could be prepared. Similarly, by consolidating block level credit plans district credit plan is prepared. It is thus crystal clear that the village profiles, which form the basis for preparation of credit plans are, infact, the backbone of whole credit planning exercise. These are required to be updated from time to time in the interest of formulation of realistic credit plans.

How to conduct Village Survey

From the foregoing analysis, it is evident that without the complete and updated village survey, it is not possible to prepare realistic and need based village credit plan which contains various technically feasible and economically viable schemes, popularly known as 'Bankable Schemes', for the overall growth of the specific village. Therefore, in view of this fact, the task of undertaking the village survey is most vital for fruitful exercise of credit planning. For conducting comprehensive and accurate village survey *the BM should :*

- read the survey format thoroughly and carefully.
- read the chart for sources of data given/ to be collected.
- identify for all service area villagers, the data has to be collected from institutional sources.
- plan his visits to the villages and should inform the Village Sarpanch/ Patwari/ Panch/ Gramsevak in advance to help so that he can seek his help.
- identify data which can be collected at the village level itself.
- identify all institutional sources from which the data has to be collected for all villages in the service area of his branch.
- go to the village/villages/and should stay the whole day in the village/villages and should discuss with as many sections of people as possible.
- club the information collected at the village level and at the institutional level to complete the format of survey. He should make sure that no data is found wanting for the plan formulation purpose.
- not much bother about the accuracy of data available and its reliability. He can also make use of the data and information available in ACP and DCP for making schemes depending on the environment of the area concerned.

Keeping in view the above mentioned points, the survey of villages should be completed. It is heartening to mention here that the survey work of villages in all four districts of the Hadoti region was completed within the stipulated time period of four months from the date of allocation of service areas to different bank branches. The detailed district profiles of Baran, Bundi, Jhalawar and Kota districts have also been prepared just after the completion of survey work of villages without loss of time.

PREPARATION OF CREDIT PLANS

The SAA is a blue-print of systematic credit planning for the integrated development of the service area assigned to each branch. BM and LBO have, therefore, to give due emphasis to this scheme of credit planning. The background paper supplied by the lead bank and the village profiles compiled by the branches themselves form the basic and serve as essential documents for preparing of the branch credit plans. Thus, the first stage in credit plan exercise is to update the survey of villages allotted a branch for its service area.

The next stage in credit plan exercise is the preparation of realistic credit plans for disbursement of credit in a phased manner to all villages and villagers as per already drawn bankable schemes for the service area. The credit plan should reflect the potentialities and the needs of the service area on the basis of the intimate knowledge gained by the branch managers through the survey and the availability of other information, on the basis of environment scanning.

The credit planning exercise has two parts *viz.* (i) The formulation of area specific credit schemes for the villages, blocks and districts; and (ii) The number of units which can be financed in the service area of the branch. While the LBO does the former, the latter will be done by the BM_S themselves. Each branch should prepare ACP for a financial year (April to March) on an ongoing basis. For this purpose the credit plan is first prepared for each village and then the VCPs aggregated to formulate the SAPs of the branch.

The credit plan preparation involves identification of technically feasible and economically viable activities, estimating potential number of units under each identified activity estimating the number of units which would require bank credit and determining non-credit inputs such as raw material supply, infra-structural facilities etc. In this exercise the LBO is assisted by NABARD whose District Development Manager (DDM) prepare the PLPs and circulate background papers to the bank branches.

The RRB branches should prepare credit plans only for the target groups. The preparation of credit plan for non-target groups in their service area will be the responsibility of the designated commercial bank branch. The co-operative sector will continue to operate in the service area of commercial bank branches as hitherto. Hence, the latter should take into account the lending programme of the PACS/ LAMPS/ LDBs, while formulating their (commercial bank branches) own credit plans.

The credit plans thus prepared also serve as the performance budgets of the branches. The activities proposed for inclusion in the credit plan of each branch in the block and the number of units to be financed should be discussed in a meeting with the BDO and his supporting staff before finalisation of the credit plans. This co-ordination with the field-level government officials is expected to ensure smooth and successful operation of the schemes and availability of non-credit inputs and other infra-structural support required.

The ACPs prepared by all the branches in block together with the lending programmes of the co-operatives are consolidated into the BLCP. This work is done by the main branch of the lead bank in the block. In exceptional cases where the lead bank may not have a branch at the block level, the work of consolidation of BCPs is done by another bank, which has the maximum presence in the block, with the assistance and guidance of the lead bank. The lead bank is supposed to designate the name of the bank which will perform this task. The LBO aggregates the credit plans of all agencies into BLCPs and send such aggregate plans of each block to the convenor of the respective BLBC. The aggregation of BLCPs constitute the District Credit Plan (DCP). The aggregation is done by the lead bank block-wise, bank-wise and sector-wise. Thus, there are four credit plans at different levels *viz.*

(i) Village Credit Plan - by aggregating the family-wise / activity-wise credit needs of the people living in that particular village;

(ii) Branch Credit Plan - by aggregating the village credit plans of allotted villages in a service area;

(iii) Block Credit Plan - by aggregating the branch credit plans of the concerned branches; and

(iv) District Credit Plan - by aggregating the block credit plan of the concerned blocks.

A typical credit plan prepared as per guidelines of RBI should consists of the following chapters :

(i) Updated profiles of blocks in the district and the list of service area allocations with necessary code number thereof;

(ii) Review of previous year's performance;

(iii) Developmental programmes in the district;

(iv) Arrangement for supporting facilities and infra-structural gaps as indicated in Service Area Credit Plans; and

(v) Bank-wise, activity-wise credit plan for the priority sector lending including physical targets.

CO-ORDINATION

As several agencies are involved in the rural development, therefore, it is necessary to have proper co-ordination among them. The need for proper co-ordination between different agencies involved cannot be overemphasised for the realistic formulation and effective and smooth implementation of credit plans. Co-ordination between credit institutions and field level development agencies on-an-on-going basis is not only important, but also essential. For this purpose LBS has been evolved and various meetings are conducted at Block, District and State levels. In this context, DLCC, Standing Committee (SC) of DLCC and District Level Review Committee (DLRC) co-ordinate the activities at district level. Similarly, State Level Banker's Committee (SLBC), Steering Committee of SLBC and State Level Co-ordination Committee (SLCC) co-ordinate the activities at State level. Besides these, with the introduction of SAA, Block Level Banker's Committee (BLBC) has been constituted in each block to co-ordinate the activities of block level.

Block Level Banker's Committee

To ensure better and effective co-ordination among the activities of banks and with block officials, a Block Level Banker's Committee (BLBC) has been constituted at each block level. All the banks operating in the block, including the district central co-operative banks and RRBs are the members of the committee. The Block Development Officer (BDO) and other technical officers in the block such as extension officers of agriculture industries and co-operatives are also its members. The chairman of the committee is the LBO and if, for any reason, he is unable to attend the meeting of the committee, the senior most branch manager of the Lead Bank presides over its meetings and he will also be the convenor. If the lead bank has no branch in the block, another bank which has maximum presence in the block and designated by the lead bank shall act as the convenor.

The functions of the BLBC can be summarised as under :

- Discussion on the credit plans of different bank branches and their aggregation in to block credit plan.
- Consideration of operational problems in the implementation of credit programmes of banks particularly.
- Review of the progress in implementation of government sponsored schemes;
- Review of the progress in implementation of the block credit plan and the provision of other inputs required so that bank credit becomes more productive.
- Allocation of service area to a new branch to be opened in the block.
- Monitoring the recovery programmes and the adequacy of the steps taken in this regard, including the support available from the State Government machinery.

The meeting of BLBC may be held at least once in a quarter. The representatives of Panchayat Samities may also be invited to attend the meetings of the BLBC at half-yearly intervals. They may be invited in the meetings held in the month of February for finalisation of block credit plans and in September when a mid-term review of the block credit plans is made. The chairmanship in these meetings may be decided by the members attending the meetings. With a view to achieve the objectives of the meeting, it is necessary that the discussions in the BLBC meeting are held in accordance with the structured agenda items already circulated to its members. The notes are prepared for each such items and circulated among members in advance.

MONITORING OF PERFORMANCE

The last stage/aspect of SAA is the proper monitoring of the credit plans with a view to ensuring the adequate flow of credit in the desired direction. The purpose of monitoring is to locate the gap in implementation and apply timely corrective measures. As per guidelines of RBI, there is scheme-wise monitoring for the service area as a whole.

To ensure the smooth and adequate flow of credit to different sectors in the service area on desired lines as per the provision of credit plans, the monitoring (performance review) is necessary at following four levels :

(i) At the branch level - by the branches themselves for each of the villages in their service area in relation to village credit plans.

(ii) At the controlling office level - by the controlling offices of the respective banks.

(iii) At the block level - by the block level bankers committee.

(iv) At the district level - by LBO/DDM of NABARD.

The performance of credit plan in respect of both priority and non-priority areas is monitored by the branches and their controlling offices. The monitoring at the BLBC level is done with reference to priority sector lending. The branches should endeavour to maintain village-wise data on disbursement of credit activity-wise/scheme-wise etc. The monitoring at district level is done by the DLRC. For effective monitoring at district level, it is essential to have a complete and clear picture of all credit programmes operating in the district. The LBO accordingly has to collect full information on all credit related activities and furnish the same to DDM of NABARD in form of computer printout/floppy disks. For the monitoring purpose of credit plans four types of returns (LBR-2, LBR-U2, LBR-3 and LBR-U3) are prepared by the branches and they are required to submit them to the LBO.

Exemption of certain Regional Rural Banks from Service Area Approach

While introducing the SAA it was made applicable to RRBs also and villages were allotted to them. It was also decided that the non-target group beneficiaries in the service area of RRB branches may be financed by the designated branches of the CB_S. However, it was observed that some of the RRBs have not been in a position to finance even the target group of beneficiaries within their service areas on account of their weak financial position and poor operational efficiency. Therefore, in order to ensure un-interrupted flow of credit to the rural sector, the RBI has been directing designated branches of CB_S in the areas of weak RRBs to concurrently take-up target group financing also. Inspite of this, it has been observed that the beneficiaries in the service areas of weak RRBs were not getting the required financial assistance. The matter has been reviewed by the RBI and it was decided in December, 1993 to relieve 70 RRBs, having disbursal of less than Rs. 2 crores in 1992-93, from the obligation of SAA. The said number of RRBs were freed from the obligation of financing even the target groups in their service areas. As a result, villages which were allocated to such RRBs for the purpose of the target group financing are now considered to have been allotted to designated branches of CBs who have been already financing the non-target group beneficiaries in their respective service areas. The RBI had again advised CBs in April 1994, to ensure that the service areas of the above referred 70 RRBs should be covered by designated branches of CBs without delay for extending credit facilities as part of their command areas.

As a result of this policy change as mentioned above, the borrowers have now two options for meeting their credit requirements in a specific service area. Firstly, they are free to seek credit from the erstwhile RRB within its service area and secondly, they may approach the designated branches of the CBs concerned. In order to remove dual financing, it is necessary for borrowers to get a no dues/no objection certificate from such RRBs on the basis of which the service area branch of the CBs may extend financial assistance.

Self-Help Groups and Service Area Approach

In recent years, Self-Help Groups (SHGs) have become significant institutions for enabling the poor to participate in the process of development. In India, NABARD introduced this approach in respect of poverty alleviation programmes and launched a pilot project in 1991 for linking 500 SHGs with banks for extending credit input to them.

With a view to study the functioning of SHGs the RBI constituted working group in November, 1994 under the Chairmanship of Shri K. K. Kalia, then Managing Director of NABARD. The working group in its report recommended that the linking of SHGs with banks is a cost effective, transparent and flexible approach to improve the accessibility of credit from the formal banking system to the rural poor to whom getting credit from formal lending system was a distant dream. The working group was of this opinion that SHGs may also provide solution to the twin problems being faced by the banks, viz. recovery of loans in the rural areas and the high transaction cost in dealing with small borrowers at frequent intervals. Therefore, the group suggested that the banks should encourage formation of SHGs for providing credit to the poor through them and improve the economic condition of the rural poor.

By accepting the recommendations of the group the RBI issued guidelines to CBs in April, 1996 with the request for linking SHGs with the banks and to promote and finance them liberally. Further, the RBI advised banks to implement SHG approach on regular basis as part of their business activity and review it periodically. However, it may be borne in mind that the SHG linkage with banks is an innovation in rural credit rather than an orthodox targetted credit programme.

Inclusion of Self-help Groups in Service Area Approach

The scope of lending to SHGs in a particular service area of a branch depends on number of factors, such as the nature and extent of poverty, the type of economic activities which are being operated by SHGs, number of Non-Government Organisations (NGOs) operating in the area and the need and awareness among the rural poor for forming SHGs for uplifting their well being. Banks may identify branches having potential for linkage and provide necessary support services to such branches for inclusion of SHGs for lending purpose within their SAPs. Keeping in view the potential available for this purpose, the service area branches may fix their own programme for lending to SHGs on the lines of other activities under the priority sector. With a view to forge linkages by banks with SHGs, the services of NGOs should be utilised to the fullest extent possible. For this purpose, the names of NGOs operating activity in the area should be given in the background paper prepared for SACPs, so that banks operating in that area can easily establish rapport with them.

The service area BMs are supposed to have constant dialogue and rapport with the NGOs and SHGs of their area of operation for effective linkage with them. If any NGO or SHG is willing for some reason or the other, to obtain finances from a particular bank branches other than the service area branches, in such a situation the NGO or SHG should be allowed to do so freely and such loans should be included in the LBR reporting system of the banks and also be reviewed periodically.

ADVANTAGES OF SERVICE AREA APPROACH

The SAA is most important policy initiative taken after 1969 to improve the credit delivery system in India, thereby enabling bank branches to operate effectively as an instrument of rural lending. The SAA, in seeking to provide a rural credit delivery system more conducive to increase production, productivity and income level so as to achieve the social objectives of banking, makes vital departure from the earlier system of LBS. SAA is one of the most striking and innovative feature in the history of banking development in India. The SAA has several distinct advantages inherent in it. The main advantages claimed by its exponents and supporters are as under :

The first advantage of SAA is the concentrated attention of the BM towards the development of service area allotted to him. This approach gives ample opportunity for the BM to concentrate his full efforts for extending productive lending to the needy people in the area as he has the specific operational area under his command. The essence is the compactness in the area of operation.

As a result of the vast expansion of rural branches network of banks, the average number of villages served by the service area branch has declined substantially and is between 15-25 villages against over 300 in 1969. Thus, it is now possible for the BMs to pay personal attention to such a manageable number of villages. This has made possible the **'Intensive Development Care'** at the micro level, which was unheard earlier.

The SAA has eliminated the problems of multiple financing and duplication of efforts which were more pronounced in the earlier system. Under the village adoption scheme the banks could fulfil the credit requirement of only 1,11,808 villages upto the end of June, 1981, whereas under the SAA banks are fulfilling the credit needs of all 5,57,149 villages of India. Thus, the entire villages of the country has been covered by credit institutions for the purpose of extending institutional credit without the problem of multiple financing and duplication of efforts. This approach helped in avoiding the unplanned, un-co-ordinated and competitive lending pattern of various financial institutions and also helped in getting freedom from the clutches of village money lenders and non-institutional sources of credit.

With the introduction of SAA it has become possible now to eliminate scattered lending over wide areas in order to ensure planned and organised manner.

The implementation of SAA has made possible to keep close monitoring of the end use of credit and to assess the impact of lending on production, productivity and generation of income. This ensured the fixation of responsibility and accountability of the BM as he himself is responsible for the planning and implementation of the credit plans. The credit planning under SAA begins from grass root level *i.e.* at the branch level, therefore, the planner and the implementer of credit plans is the same person.

Before introduction of SAA, there was a mis-match between the preparation and implementation of the credit plans, but after launching the SAA this problem could be overcome as under it the BM knows his exact operational area being well defined area of operation.

The LBO also assist the BM in preparing credit plans for the branch by extending his expertise, skills and experience. Thus, credit plans prepared under the SAA are more realistic and match with ground realities of the area concerned.

Under the SAA, the work of identifying the bankable schemes is being performed by the bank manager with the help of survey conducted by himself. On the basis of potentials for development of each village, the bankable activities for the beneficiaries are identified. The beneficiaries of scheme are also taken into confidence by consulting them before finalising the schemes. Whereas the work of identifying the bankable activities for the beneficiaries was formerly performed by the BDO and the village level worker and it was imposed on the banks. The BM on his part is supposed to study the village data and programmes of development being undertaken in the villages and in consultation with the village level staff, decides, the schemes and viable number of units there under, which he will be able to finance in a given time period.

Under the SAA, credit planning starts from the grass root level i.e., at the village level, hence credit planning under it is decentralised in the real sense of the term at the micro-level and moves upward from village level to branch level, branch level to block level and from block level to district level. Under the old LBS credit planning was done at the district level and then segregating it for block levels. The SAA has made possible the credit planning more effective on the one hand and also minimising scope of spatial imbalance in credit disbursement as the branch is 'nucleus' for the development in the command area.

The SAA, will also help banks in recovery of their dues as under it the credit input is linked with production, productivity and generation of income and also control over the end use of credit is possible. Under the SAA, BM has personal link and liaison with the borrowers which improves the credit recovery position and reduces the wilful default on the part of borrower.

It also ensures meaningful sponsoring with gainful activities. For this, the bank branch develops a detailed and thorough knowledge of the general environment, infra-structural facilities and economic activities in each of the villages in its area. In the light of such information and keeping in view the various governmental programmes and activities, the branch draws a systematic plan for assisting productive economic activities keeping in view the financial and other resources available. Mobilisation of savings with a view to augmenting the resources available for credit expansion is also important. The village and bank credit plan envisages provision of credit support to bankable schemes in the villages in the area in an organised manner. Thus, the branch functions as a catalytic agent promoting development in the area.

The concept of performance budgeting, which was introduced in 1973, could not percolated down to the grassroot level and planning and budgeting were remained more or less form filling exercise in most of the branches till 1989. With the implementation of SAA, the credit plan formulated constitutes the performance budget of the branch concerned as the monitoring and evaluation of performance will be done on the basis of this plan. Infact, credit plans prepared under the SAA are action plans of the branch, hence can also be termed as its 'Performance Budget'

SAA develops a sense of pride, motivation and involvement of the BMs in the success of his own plans and thus bringing about an improvement in the quality and productivity of lending, optimising the use of credit and establishment of better linkages with production and productivity. In other words, assigning the cardinal role to the BM in bringing about an orderly development of villages in the designated area through well directed and planned efforts at credit expansion is a significant feature of the SAA.

In the light of above mentioned advantages in the new approach of rural lending, it can be said that the SAA is much refined and better strategy of rural lending. The SAA is expected to overcome the many shortcomings of earlier lending approaches experimented for rural poor as it combines the beneficent aspects of both the LBS and VAS, introducing the concept of concentrated micro level credit planning for systematic development through productive lending. Thus, we can summarise by saying that the SAA is a consistent and logical approach which tries to establish an organic link between rural branches and rural people.

PERSPECTIVE

The concept of SAA was evolved after a lot of soul searching and was basically a result of considerable and serious thought, deliberation and discussion at the highest forum of bankers. Undoubtedly it is a noble concept and new horizon for giving a new thrust to the rural development. As the SAA combines the beneficent aspects of both the LBS and VAS, therefore, it is much better and refined credit planning at the village level. It is considered as a unique experiment in the sphere of rural lending evolved out of the credit planning efforts made by the banks under LBS. The SAA is a well thought out programme for extending rural credit on more sound footing and rational basis.

It was expected by the framers of SAA that the 'planning from bottom' approach would go long way in the orderly credit deployment in the target area and help in the increased supervision of credit utilisation, recovery of loans and harmonising the efforts of banks in providing credit for rural development activities with those of other development agencies which are active in the area.

The successful implementation of SAA is expected to bring about a radical transformation in the credit planning process in theory and practice at the grassroot level and forge better links between credit and production, productivity and income in rural and semi-urban areas of the country. As and when the credit planning and development planning are integrated in a proper manner, the credit planning under SAA could become more meaningful and effective, thus will prove to be a vehicle for rapid and orderly development of rural India.

The SAA is still considered as an 'evolutionary phase' in rural lending, but it is not a magic stick which can solve all problems of rural lending. It is merely an approach to rationalise rural lending, reduce cost of supervision by avoiding duplication of efforts in lending and also by reducing the number of villages in which the bank branches operate. It is a step in the direction of micro-level planning with 'village' as the unit of planning. It also ensures meaningful sponsoring with gainful activities. The focus under SAA is to develop productive and qualitative lending and promote integrated rural development.

Keeping in view the above facts, there should be no doubt and hitch in accepting the policy part of SAA. Indeed, conceptually SAA is a noble idea in bringing about speedy and continuous development at the grassroot level. But due to some reasons, its implementation part has remained weaker, eg. Problems of management, poor recovery of loans, political intervention in sanctioning of loans, non co-operation of other related institutions etc. have brought down the credibility of financial institutions. This apart, the rural staff is not adequately motivated and they do not have any commitment, involvement in activities for upliftment of their area. Hence, these problems are creating hurdles in the way of successful implementation of SAA.

Pre-requisites for Success of Service Area Approach

For effective implementation of SAA, the following conditions should be fulfilled:

- There must be a full sense of dedication and involvement in the all round development of the villages on the part of all concerned in both government and banks;
- There must be perfect harmony in the functioning of credit institutions and the government departments concerned, so that a co-ordinated approach to development could be evolved.
- There should be an active and meaningful participation of people for whom the credit plans are prepared and implemented. The change in attitudes and behaviour of all participating agencies and individual is also necessary to take the credit planning to its logical end.

The expertise and skills of BMs in plan formulation and its implementation should be improved through suitable training and orientation so that realistic and pragmatic credit planning could be prepared and implemented successfully.

The system of timely interactions with present and prospective beneficiaries of credit should be evolved in such a manner that it is able to create the personal link between the banker and borrower. This will help not only in assessing and meeting the credit requirement for all bankable schemes as well as in better recovery of loans and recycling of funds. In this context, the bank branches should be well-equipped in terms of both skilled and adequate staff and with information and resource-base.

At the end, it can be said that the SAA can really transform the rural lending system and thereby rural life successfully only when sincere, skilled and dedicated bank officials are posted in service area branches of banks, proper dovetailing of credit plans with development plans is ensured and active participation of people is promoted. There is also need to evolve a realistic data bank which may form the basis for formulation of realistic credit plans. The NABARD can help in creating data bank and in chalking out bankable schemes for the service areas.

REFERENCES

1. All India Rural Survey Committee (1954), Reserve Bank of India.
2. Study Group on organisational framework for the implementation of social objectives (1969), Prof. D.R. Gadgil, Chairman.

3. Committee on Branch Expansion (1969), Reserve Bank of India (Shri F.K.E. Nariman, Chairman).
4. Working group on Multi-agency approach in Agricultural Finance (1976) RBI, (Shri C.K. Kamath, Chariman).
5. Committee to review arrangements for institutional credit for agricultural and rural development (CRAFICARD), 1981, RBI.
6. Committee to examine certain operational aspects of rural lending (1988), RBI (Dr. P.D. Ojha, Chairman).
7. G. Krishan, "Service Area Approach : Some neglected aspects; proceedings and papers of bank economist; conference, 1990, January 4-6-1990, Himalaya Publishing House, Mumbai.
8. Joshomayee Devi, "Service Area Approach : Some reflections on the concept and the approach, "Proceedings and papers of bank economists, conference, 1990, Himalaya Publishing House, Mumbai.
9. R.N. Malhotra, "Banking in 1990's", Southern Economist, Volume 29, No. 6, July 15, 1990.
10. K.K. Ammannaya, "Service Area Approach - A new challenge for Banks", Southern Economist, Vol. 29, No. 6, July 15, 1990.
11. Ghulam Gouse, "Changing emphasis in lending", The Hindu Survey of India Agriculture, 1989.
12. Dr. K. Dinker Rao, "Service Area Approach and the grass roots", IBA bulletin, January, 1993.
13. A.C. Chug, "Service Area Approach : A new dimension in credit planning", from Trends and Portents in Banking - edited by - Khandelwal, Batra and Sharma, Pointer Publishers, Jaipur)
14. R.N. Malhotra, "Rural Credit : Issues for 1990", from Trends and Portends in Banking, Edited by - Khandelwal, Batra and Sharma, Pointer Publishers, Jaipur.
15. D.J. Kanvinde, "Service Area Approach - A new strategy for Rural Development", from Indian Banking in Rural Development, Edited by - B.L. Mathur, RBSA Publishers, Jaipur.
16. Service Area Approach for Rural Lending : How close to welfare banking concept, Editors column - The Banker, January, 1989.
17. Reeta Mathur, "New strategy for rural lending - Service Area Approach", from Emerging Perspectives of Indian Banking, Vol. II Edited by B.L. Mathur, Arihant Publishing House, Jaipur.
18. Basant Mehta, "Service Area Approach - A new horizon for rural development", from Trends and Challenges to Indian Banking, Edited by - S.S. Hugar, Deep & Deep Publications, New Delhi.

19. P.R. Upadhya, "Service Area Appraoch and its Jargon", from Trends and Challenges to Indian Banking, Edited by S.S. Hugar, Deep and Deep Publications, New Delhi.
20. Alok Kumar Jain, "New Dimensions of the Mass Banking : Service Area Approach, from Indian Banking Vol. I, Social Banking and Profitability, Chief Editor - C.R. Kothari, Arihant Publishers, Jaipur.
21. Pradeep K. Saxena & Mukesh Mathur, "Service Area Approach in Banks", from Indian Banking, Vol. I, Chief Editor - C.R. Kothari, Arihant Publishers, Jaipur.
22. Bindal, G.S., "Service Area Approach", The Journal of the Indian Institute of Bankers; Vol. 60, No. 4, Oct. - Dec. 1989.
23. Dr. Jayant Joshi and Prof. D.N. Tulapurkar, "New Dimension of Branch Licensing Policy - Service Area Approach for Rural Lending", from Changing Profile of Indian Banking edited by Sushil J. Lalwani, Radhi Publications, New Delhi.
24. H.S. Dua : Social Banking for Economic Development, Deep & Deep Publications, New Delhi.
25. Jag M. Chona : "Rural lending : Focus on Service Area Approach", The Hindu Survey of Indian Agriculture, 1991.
26. Rajendra Singh, "Service Area Approach : A Rejoinder", The Economic Times, March 2, 1989.
27. Natabar Khuntia : "Service Area Approach : Rural Area Financing", The Economic Times, November, 1989.
28. Kanhaiya Singh : "Rural Development : Service Area Approach", The Economic Times, January 2, 1989.
29. B. Ramachandra Rao : "Service Area Approach : Manpower Planning for Rural Banks", The Economic Times, December 1, 1988.
30. N.A. Shanbhag : "Challenges and Opportunities", The Economic Times, November 1, 1989.
31. Keya Sarkar : Service Area Approach : Onus on Branch Managers; Business India, 13-26, June 1988.
32. T.N. Anand and B.K. Narayan Swami, "Service Area Approach to Rural Development", Agricultural Banker, July - Sept., 1992.
33. Bandi Ram Prasad, "Service Area Approach, Need for a streamlined monitoring system", Financial Express, January 16, 1989.
34. K. Elumalai, "SAA - A Myth, Financial Express, January 16, 1989.
35. Juneja, N.K. : "Service Area Approach", Manans Publication, Delhi, 1992.

36. Kumar, Ashok : New Approach in Rural Development , Anmol Prakashan, New Delhi.

37. Arumugum, P. : Lead Bank System and Service Area Approach, UDH Publishing House, Delhi, 1990.

38. Sarada, D.P. : Hand Book on Priority Sector Lending, Govind Prakashan, Jaipur.

39. Sundram, I. Satya : Rural Development, Himalaya Publishing House, Delhi, 1997

40. Desai, Vasant : Indian Banking, Himalaya Publishing House, Delhi, 1991

41. Singh. G. : Rural Credit Planning, RBSA Publishers, Jaipur, 2000.

□■□

Chapter 4

Methodology for Formulation of Credit Plans under Service Area Approach

Formulation of realistic credit plan is the basic challenging task of service area approach. Allocation of resources based on national plan priorities is fundamental to the process of credit planning. After nationalisation of major commercial banks in 1969 the principal objective of country's credit policy has been the allocation and disbursement of credit based on broad sectoral and regional priorities (national plan priorities) keeping in view the constraint of resources available with the financial institutions. Therefore, the credit plans should be formulated in accordance with national economic policy goals. For this, there is need for proper and suitable methodology for formulation of credit plans. Under the LBS, the prime duty of lead bank was to formulate the DCP for the district concerned. The DCP provides the basis for different participating financial institutions to draw the concrete programmes which were to be taken up by them for financing purpose. DCP was supposed to be a means for financial institutions to deploy their resources according to national plan priorities. DCP encompasses the wise range of activities chosen by financial institutions treating them as bankable schemes for financing purpose. DCP prepared by the lead bank was not merely a derivation of post trends based on historical data only of few activities, but it was an elaborated process which involved identification of new bankable schemes which can be operatinalised on sustainable basis in the district concerned. Thus, DCP was prepared after careful and systematic study of the scope for development of different sectors and activities of the district's economy.

Formulation of DCP requires a strong and reliable data base, availability of planning skill and technical knowledge. The tasks in the process of formulation of DCP were collection of statistical data, information relating to on-going schemes and proposed developmental programmes/schemes, impressionistic surveys of various blocks, assessment of developmental potential and local aspirations. The knowledge of the topography of the district was the first essential condition for proper formulation of DCP because without the knowledge of topography sufficient and reliable data/information could not be obtained for meaningful formulation of DCP. Formulation of bankable schemes is an integral and essential part of any credit planning exercise which include those schemes/activities which are technically feasible and economically viable and also have some motivational input on-an-on-going basis. Thus, sound DCP consists of several such schemes/activities which are not only technically feasible and economically viable, but also area specific based on the local resources and need of the people. Infact, DCP is a blue print (compendium) of all bankable schemes which can be/will be taken-up for financing by the financial institutions. The DCP places emphasis on technically feasible and economically viable schemes rather than on the methodological excellence in the academic sense. The formulation of DCP involves simultaneous formulation of a development plan of the district because a DCP may be regarded as the financial framework of a district development programmes/plan. In this context, the approach for the formulation of the DCP is outlined as below :

- Critical appraisal of the present level of development is made based on a thorough economic survey of the whole district with regard to its physiographical conditions and natural resources in the context of the pattern of agricultural and industrial activities.
- On the basis of knowledge and data/information gathered from economic survey technically feasible and economically viable schemes are formulated covering all sectors of the economy, which could be taken-up for financing by financial institutions with is the framework of the present infra-structural and other facilities.
- The credit requirements for all bankable schemes are estimated in a rationale manner and then the exercise of estimated credit gaps is undertaken with the purpose to find out the difference between the present requirement of credit and the capacity of financial institutions to meet it.

- In order to meet the credit required by different sectors, an assessment of the savings potential is done considering different modes of savings such as bank deposits, insurance premium, post-office savings etc.
- In the last, all participating financial institutions (commercial banks, co-operative banks and RRBs) are entrusted with specific responsibilities of bridging the credit gaps and financing the bankable schemes which are mutually agreed upon and accepted by them in DLCC meeting.

There are three main stages in the formulation of DCP which are as follows :

- Identification of economic activities which can be financed by various credit institutions.
- Collection of data with a view to formulating bankable schemes covering these activities.
- Estimation of credit needs likely to arise under each bankable scheme for different sectors and different blocks in the district.

While formulating the DCP the following factors are taken into account :

- existing number of banks and dispersal of their branches in different blocks of the district;
- deposits and their growth rate of different banks in various blocks of the district and also their likely growth rate of deposits;
- personnel structure of the participating banks, particularly the structure of their field staff;
- existing level of advances and credit deposit ratio of the banks functioning in the district;
- infrastructure of different government departments having impact on the development of the district, both economic and social;
- future plans of the government departments functioning in the district;
- availability of development plans of various blocks in the district so that financial requirements may be marked out and funds made available as per requirement;
- availability of loanable funds with the financial institutions operating in the district keeping this fact in view that the credit deposit ratio should be at least 60%; and

- fixation of responsibilities of the banks and government departments for development plans to remove the obstacle, if any, in the smooth and timely implementation of the plans.

The objective of DCP is to make available the necessary credit input needed for development at the grass root level for all productive activities. To ensure the availability of credit input needed by all financial institutions operating in the district including the lead bank have to be actively participate in the whole exercise of credit planning at the district level. Formulation of DCP is a joint venture of lead bank and other financial institutions of the district. Lead bank acts as a leader of the team. To formulate a DCP, a taskforce is constituted. The taskforce consists of the representatives of all those departments and institutions of the district which are directly or indirectly involved in the process of development of the district.

The scheme of formulation of DCP by lead banks covering activities in the priority sectors was mooted by the RBI. In pursuance of the recommendations of "The study group report", December, 1975 on the working of LBS in Gujarat and Maharastra. From time to time detailed guidelines were issued to lead banks by RBI, covering the objective, contents, methodology, modalities of preparation of credit plans and fixation of responsibilities for different implementation items of work. It was emphasised that LBS should ensure the alignment of DCP with the credit based development programmes of Government and other development agencies operating in the district. So far lead banks have prepared four rounds of DCPs. The fourth round of DCP covered the period 1988-90. Description in brief of each round of the preparation of DCP is given below:

FIRST ROUND OF DISTRICT CREDIT PLANS

The first round of DCPs was maiden venture of banks due to absence of specific and elaborate guidelines by RBI to lead banks and also due to lack of experience and expertise in the credit planning exercise as the formulation of DCPs was altogether a new task for the lead banks. These DCPs were based on different methodologies in the absence of clear-cut and uniform guidelines from the RBI to lead banks, therefore, there were several serious deficiencies in them such as lack of uniformity in coverage, contents and period, lack of alignment with DDPs and lack of adequate attention to agriculture and its allied activities. Due to these deficiencies, RBI advised the lead banks to terminate the first round of DCPs at the end of 1979 and formulate the new DCPs.

SECOND ROUND OF DISTRICT CREDIT PLANS

RBI advised lead banks to formulate second round of DCPs for the duration 1980-82 and action plans for each calendar year accordingly on the basis of new guidelines issued by it. This round of DCPs was co-terminous with the sixth five year plan together with annual action plans (AAPs) prior to the commencement of each year. Although five year plans were based financial year basis (April - March), banks were advised to prepare credit plans on a calendar year basis so as to facilitate inclusion of the yearly commitments accepted by banks under the DCPs into their own annual branch performance budgets which are prepared on a calendar year basis. In short, in the guidelines issued by RBI for the preparation of the second round of DCPs suggested that the DCP should be dovetailed into the District Development Plan (DDP) so that the DCP will aim at the same plan priorities as the DDP.

The main objectives of the RBI guidelines in the second round were:

- to finance labour intensive schemes which generate employment;
- to assist weaker sections of the population for productive purpose to the maximum extent possible; and
- to help increase productivity of agriculture and other allied activities so as to reduce unemployment and increase income levels.

The essential features in the formulation of DCP introduced by the guidelines of RBI were as under :

- The lead banks should ensure alignment of the credit plan with credit based development schemes, both on-going and potential of Government and other development agencies operating in the area;
- With the shift in emphasis to the block as the unit of planning, DCPs should be prepared on a block-wise basis;
- Credit planning should be participative, involving all concern agencies through the mechanism of the district level task-force; and
- Since DCP is a broad framework for credit programmes therefore a separate action oriented plan should be drawn-up annually and implemented during the year.

The second round of DCPs were definitely an improvement over the first one. The lead banks had also gathered useful experience of preparing credit plans earlier and uniformity was brought about in respect of period and the contents both due to specific guidelines issued by the

RBI. In brief, dovetailing DCP with DDP, constituting standing committee for preparation of DCPs, introducing AAPs as an operational component of DCP, block-wise dis-aggregation of DCP outlays, providing formula for estimation of crop loan requirements, uniform chapter scheme and annexures were the noteworthy contributions of second round of the DCPs.

Annual Action Plan

Annual Action Plan (AAPs) are being prepared from 1980 and onwards continuously. AAPs are formulated by the standing committee for which a lot of preliminary exercise has to be done by the LBO.

While DCP is a perspective document regarding the direction to be given to the lending activities of the financial institutions in the district, AAP indicates the short-term annual operational goals to be achieved. Unlike the DCP which gives detailed information about the block, governmental programmes, marketing arrangements etc., AAP confines itself to presenting credit allocation for different activities /schemes. In other words, AAP concerns itself with the actual shares of the commitments of different financial institutions area-wise. These also take care of the changes that have taken place after the preparation of DCP such as increase in the cost of inputs, marketing arrangements etc.

THIRD ROUND OF DISTRICT CREDIT PLANS

The third round of DCPs were formulated on the basis of fresh guidelines issued by RBI in February, 1982, so that they would be co-nterminous with the balance of the sixth five year plan. In this round preparation of DCPs,covered the period between the January, 1983 to March, 1985. The idea was to switch the DCPs calendar year to financial year (April - March). So that necessary co-ordination between the banks and governments and between five year plans and DCPs could be ensured.

The objectives of third round of DCPs were more or less the same as that of the second round of DCPs. The objectives of the RBI guidelines for the third round of DCPs were :

- making the AAP operationally more meaningful to the banks and government agencies;
- reducing avoidable bulk of the documents without removing the essential data or information; and
- focussing attention on the more important schemes for the development of weaker sections such as IRDP, so that these could be monitored effectively and better results could be achieved through the mechanism of AAPs.

While finalising deployment of credit under various sectors for different sections of population, care has been taken to the various directives issued by the Government of India and RBI, which were as follows :

- Attain by 1985, a level of 40 %of total lending of priority sector;
- Attain by 1985, a level of 40 % advances to priority sector of the total advances and also to attain 16 % of advances to agriculture of the total advances given by banks.
- In respect of their total direct advances for agriculture and allied activities; provide by March, 1985 to less than 50 % to weaker sections (i.e. small and marginal farmers with land holdings of 5 acres and landless labourers and persons engaged in allied activities whose credit limits for such activities do not exceed Rs. 10,000); and now the total advances to weaker sections should reach a level of 25% of total priority sector advances or 10 % of total bank credit by March, 1985;
- In respect of advances to SSI attained by 1985, a level of 12.5% of such advances should go to weaker section (comprising of artisans, craftsmen, cottage and village industries and SSI, with credit limits in each case upto Rs. 25,000);
- Attain by March, 1985 a credit deposit ratio of 60 % in respect of semi-urban and rural branches;
- Disburse at least one percent of their total advances as at the end of previous year under the DIR scheme at an interest rate of 4 % and ensure at least 40 %of such advances to SC/ST and further that at least two third of DIR advances are made through rural and semi-urban branches;
- Pay particular attention to the credit needs of SC/ST under special component plan and tribal plan and make special efforts to prepare bankable schemes for them.
- Give special emphasis to sub-sectors/ activities listed under the new 20 point programme.

The major noteworthy features incorporated in the third round were as follows:

- The state government had to provide essential data for DCP.
- Only bankable schemes should be taken in DCPs.
- To ensure the participative nature of the exercise and the active involvement of the standing committee of DLCC, DRDA, DIC etc. in the formulation process.

- While the state government provides infra-structural support and other assistance for development programme, the lead banks should indicate in the DCP document the implementing agencies for the development programmes.
- The new set of credit plans have laid specific stress on implementation of the relevant points of new Twenty Point Economic Programme (TPEP). Banks were expected to extend credit support particularly to beneficiaries under IRDP and other rural poor in consultation with district authorities particularly DRDA, DIC and KVIB etc. set up in the district.

Thus, the third round of DCPs had shown a vast improvement over the previous rounds of DCPs in the sense that the DCPs had a definite target for achievement with the help of Government departments and the on-going anti-poverty programmes. The stress in the third round of DCPs was on the national plan priorities like removal of unemployment and under-employment.

The third round of DCPs attempted to establish meaningful linkages between:

- Bank's lending for priority sector activities on the one hand and Government subsidised programmes for such activities on the other hand.
- Bank's lending outside the Government subsidised programmes on the one hand and their overall commitments for priority sector/ sub-sectors lendings as part of the corporate plans, on the other hand.
- Government's programmes for providing infra-structural support on the one hand and bank's lendings which require such support for ensuring their viability on the other hand.
- Besides this, the third round of DCPs presented inter-block, inter-sectoral allocations of credit and inter-institutional sharing of responsibilities as already been stated earlier.

The third round of DCPs comprised the following chapters :

1) District and Block Profile;
2) Review of the second round of DCPs;
3) Development programmes in the district;
4) IRDP and other special programmes;
5) Arrangements for infra-structure and other supporting services;
6) Bankable schemes and assessment of credit demand;

7) DCP 1983-85/

8) Resources - financial and manpower; and

9) Implementation - responsibilities of different agencies.

The third round of DCPs ended on March, 1985 and thereafter year-wise Annual Action Plans from 1985 to 1987 were prepared and implemented. These credit plans included a vast range of economic activities that could be taken up for financing by financial institutions in the districts. These DCPs met the national priorities and guidelines from the GOI/RBI from time to time. The schemes taken up in the DCPs were selected on the basis of resources, demand factors and existing supporting facilities in the district.

FOURTH ROUND OF DISTRICT CREDIT PLANS

In March, 1987, RBI issued guidelines for the formulation of the fourth round of DCPs covering three years period from 1988 to 1990 and AAP only for 1988. The objectives of the DCPs continued to be the same as spelled out in previous DCPs. The data regarding the implementation of DCPs for 1985 and 1986 were compiled within the stipulated time period, i.e. by the July, 1987. The identification of bankable schemes, estimation of credit demand and preparation of the draft district credit plan was circulated to all financing agencies and development departments by October, 1987 for their comments.

The revised plan discussed by the DLCC and the shares were allotted to the participating banks. By December, 1987 the final DCPs were circulated to all the participating banks for working out branch-wise break-up and the implementation of DCPs from 1988.

While the DCPs were prepared for three years, some of the schemes drawn from the plans of various departments have been prepared only for one financial year. For further improvement in the methodology, some blocks were selected for formulation and implementation of block level planning. The main features of the fourth round of DCPs were as follows :

- Grass-root level participation in the formulation of DCPs;
- Formulation of village-wise targets and identified activities to arrive at realistic targets for the block based on needs and potentialities of the area;
- Time schedule for implementing various stages of the schemes;
- Periodical review of physical and financial targets of the schemes to clear bottlenecks, ensure proper linkages etc;

- Frequent visits to villages, contacts and discussion with beneficiaries by the bank staff and extension agencies to ensure proper utilisation of funds and smooth implementation of the schemes; and
- Demonstration effect of the schemes implemented in few villages and benefits derived by some persons in the initial stage.

While preparing the fourth round of DCPs the banks had taken into account their past experience of financing certain schemes and those involving local resources to enhance the income of the area. Poverty alleviation programme and certain activities coming under new TPEP are also be financed as a part of DCP. While formulating new bankable schemes more stress is attached to minor irrigation, dry farming, oil-seeds development, waste land development etc.

while formulating the fourth round of DCPs following points have also been kept in consideration by the lead banks. They were as follows:

- A level of 40 % of total lending to priority sector has been estimated;
- A level of 18 % of the total advances had been envisaged for direct financing to agriculture;
- Advances to weaker sections i.e. small and marginal farmers, landless labourers and borrowers belonging to SC/ST has been envisaged at the level of 10 % of net bank credit;
- Programme for waste land development, oil-seeds development and dry land farming had included in the plan.
- Severe drought is a common feature in Rajasthan, therefore more emphasis was given on non-farm sector activities viz. small scale industries, rural artisan, craftsmen and service sector to reduce the burden on farm sector activities.
- AAP 1988 included various farm sector activities including the drought relief action plan. Stress was also laid down on financing the digging of wells, deepening of wells, buying and developing milch cattle, bullock pair, sheep rearing, cultivation of fodder etc.; and
- Massive package of programme and other schemes like IRDP, SEPUP and SEEUY for removal of unemployment has been included in the plans.

Thus, the DCPs formulated in the fourth round under the LBS indicated the volume of credit demand likely to arise under the various bankable schemes in a block and in a district.

As per the RBI guidelines the fourth round of the DCPs comprised the following chapters :

1) Profile of the district;
2) Review of the performance;
3) Development programmes of the district;
4) Bankable schemes and assessment of credit demand;
5) DCP for the coming three years and Annual Action Plan of the present calendar year;
6) Resources for the plan.

The RBI after a period of two decades of bank nationalisation introduced a revolutionary scheme and an innovative concept of 'command area' from April 1989 in the area of rural lending for rapid and all-round rural development. The main objective of this approach to make rural lending more productive and meaningful by relating it intimately to local conditions and genuine needs of villagers, promote deposit mobilisation to augment resources for lending and improving recycling of credit. Indirectly it means that not only rural credit covering agriculture, industries and services would flow on a large scale in each and every village, but thereby optimising the use of natural, physical and biological resources lying un-exploited in villages through bank credit, but also imbalances within block, district, state and region would be minimised in terms of flow of credit.

Methodology for Formulation of Credit Plans

The district credit plans are prepared for the financial year (April - March) every year by all branches of credit agencies viz. Commercial banks, Regional Rural Banks (RRBs), District Central Co-operative Banks (DCCB), Primary Land Development Bank (PLDB) and non banking financial institutions like Rajasthan Finance Corporation (RFC), Khadi and Village Industry Board (KVIB) etc. operating in the district. The unit of planning under service area approach is 'village' and therefore the credit plan starts from the village and aggregated at the branch, block and district levels.

Keeping in view the information available after preparation of village profiles with regard to potentialities for lending and the resources available or to be mobilised for financing them, the branch manager proceeds with drawing up the Annual Credit Plan (ACP) for each village. In drawing up such a credit plan, he also keeps in view essential aspects such as the extent to which the credit deposit ratio (CDR) should be improved during the year, number of units to be financed under different activities, the availability of required physical inputs, linkages and infrastructure available.

The major steps involved in the formulation of a credit plan are as follows :

- Confirming the technical feasibility of the activity;
- Establishing the economic viability of the activity;
- Estimating the potential number of technically feasible and economically viable units;
- Estimating the number of units which would require credit and the quantum of credit available from the banks (credit plan); and
- Determining the non-credit inputs i.e. raw material supply, marketing arrangements, training and extension services, infrastructural facilities etc.

Detailed description of each step involved in the formulation of a credit plan is given below :

Confirming the Technical Feasibility of an Activity

The first step in the formulation of credit plan is to confirm the technical feasibility of an activity. The knowledge of relationship between resources and resultant probable production and income levels is essential for identifying technical feasibility of an activity. This task, which is technical in nature, normally falls within the perview of concerned government department or other agencies. For example, suggesting the cropping pattern taking into account the soil and climatic conditions, indicating the ground water potential, suitability of a particular breed of cattle development in the area etc. are accepted functions of technical personnel in the concerned departments of Government.

The question of technical feasibility may not be relevant to all the activities. For example, trade and most types of industrial processes are physically possible anywhere. Therefore, technical feasibility would be required in case of agriculture, its allied activities and resources based industries.

The existing activities, which have been carried out for quite sometime successfully, may be taken as an indication of their being technically feasible. Therefore, while preparing credit plan, it may not in all cases be necessary to test the technical feasibility of such on-going activities. But in case of new activities, the concerned government departments at district level and NABARD would certify their technical feasibility. It is the duty of LBO to keep the branches informed about the technical feasibility of the new activity/activities.

Establishing Economic Viability of an Activity

The second step in the formulation of credit plan is establishing the economic viability of an activity. As all technically feasible activities are not economically viable, therefore testing the economic viability is necessary. This requires data regarding :

(i) necessary inputs and their costs and

(ii) output and prices.

While former would help to work out the cost aspects, the latter facilitates calculating the income aspect. These data have to be realistic having local relevance and applicability.

Estimating the Number of Units of Technically Feasible and Economically Viable Activity

The third step in the formulation of credit plan is estimating the volume (number of units) of technically feasible and economically viable activity. The crucial step of credit plan can be divided into two parts. Part A explains the basic idea and approach for estimation of volume of any activity. To enable the branch managers to understand the approach, it is illustrated by the RBI with the help of dairy and crop activity. Part B focuses on the practical aspects of application of this approach by the branch managers in the live situations. These two parts have been discussed below in detail :

Part A - Having ascertained technical feasibility and economic viability of the activity, it is necessary to work out number of units which can be sustained in the specified service area. Obviously, volume of an activity would depend upon supply of resources needed to carry it and the market for its output. Hence, either of them can act as constraints in determining the volume of operation. Thus, interplay of supply of resources and market for the produce determine the volume of an activity. It is, therefore, important to identify the critical constraining factor, either on the resources side or as marketing factor which restricts the size of the activity.

Generally, the supply of resources is the critical constraining factor in determining the volume of activity. For instance, ground water potential in case of wells, infra-structural facilities such as veterinary services in respect of dairy / poultry / technical / extension services with regard to propagation of high yielding variety crops. Experience gained in respect of same type of activity financed in the service area can also be helpful.

In case of trade service and demand based industries, which have to depend on local demand, the size of the marketing facilities is a crucial factor in case of those activities of which market may be outside the village.

Part B - In this context, the question arises, how far is it possible to operationalise the idea of identifying the critical constraining factor in a real life situation at the branch level? Is the branch manager in a position to get relevant data on supply of resources and market of the produce to identify correct critical constraining factor? Here the moot question is to know how the BM should proceed on for adopting this approach.

For knowing the critical constraining factor, it is not necessary to list all the resources/items on supply side and then quantify their capacity. The simple method of identifying the critical factor is that the branch manager should ask himself with reference to an activity– what is the major obstacle responsible for restricting its size or which is a major problem coming in the way of increasing its volume? Answer to this question will reveal him to correct critical constraining factor. Likewise, branch manager can judge it for different activities in vogue in his service area.

Generally, the critical constraining factor may not vary from village to village in the same service area. However, once branch manager identifies the critical factors for all relevant activities he may, on the basis of his knowledge and understanding of different villages, see whether a critical constraining factor identified for an activity is relevant to all villages or not. In case it is not, then for such villages, he may have to identify separately. Generally, any manager who has spend six to twelve months at the branch should be able to perform the job of identification of the critical constraining factor without any difficulty.

The BM, however, would not be able to perform this job alone. After completion of this home work of identification of the critical constraining factor, he should consult NABARD, the government functionaries at village level and make inquiries from other knowledgeable persons including village level worker, Panch and

Sarpanch of village panchayat, village doctors, co-operatives, school teachers, post master etc. There are two basic advantages of this cross consultation : (i) the branch manager gets an opportunity to cross check and confirm that his identification is correct, and (ii) he involves the government functionaries and other concerned persons in the plan preparation process right from the beginning.

Thus, in order to know the potential volume of any activity, it is necessary to identify the critical constraining factor so as to estimate the extent up to which it is possible to expand an activity during the credit plan period. The main difficulty in this regard is the availability of futuristic data.

The BM is also supposed to utilise the knowledge and experience of the block level staff, who are well conversant with the conditions prevailing in different villages and limitations and shortcomings obstructing the growth of various activities, about the extent to which critical constraining factor is likely to be mitigated in terms of number of units and the rational underlying (a) This would assist in estimating the volume of special activities that could be taken up in different villages immediately and in the near future. A clear cut picture about what is feasible in the short run and medium run will emerge. The LBO should assist the BM in this regard.

This approach enables the Branch Manager in identifying the 'critical constraining factors' and then quantifying potential volume of activities. It also ensures consultation and involvement of government agencies which are expected to extend vital support to activities covered under village credit plan by providing 'non-credit inputs'.

In nutshell, potential volume of the activity to the extent feasible in the village environment either from supply side or from market side is the prime consideration behind the approach. Particularly, with regard to supply side, it takes into consideration the availability of all requisite resource items by keeping the size of an activity confined to the level of 'critical constraining factor'.

Estimating the Number of Units which would require Credit and the Quantum of Credit available from the Credit Plan

The branch manager should visualise the following possibilities while estimating the number of units which will demand credit from all agencies including banks and co-operatives :

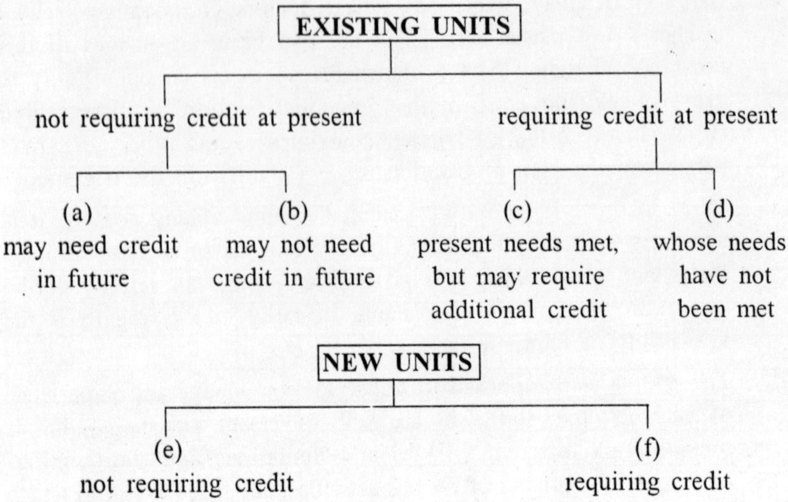

Total number of units classified under (a), (b), (c), (d), (e) and (f) indicate the number of units which may require credit. It may be pointed out that working out exact number of units which would require credit may be neither feasible nor required. The purpose would be served if a range specified lower and upper limit is indicated while estimating the number of units under SSI, rural and cottage industries, artisans etc. their volume of operation and size distribution of units may be taken into consideration. It is important that units are arranged in terms of activities.

After arriving at an estimate about number of units which may require credit under different activities, it would be the decision of the BM about the number of units to be included in the credit plan. Various important factors such as corporate objectives, his past experience of lending to different activities, concentration on certain target groups and their skills which may vary from village to village and activity to activity etc. may be some of the factors influencing his decision. In this exercise he should be guided by what positive steps are needed on the part of all concerned to increase the level of activities/production/ productivity/ income in the service area of the branch.

Steps in Service Area Credit Planning

There are three steps in service area credit planning exercise. These include:

- Physical potential plan;
- Credit potential plan; and
- Credit action plan.

Physical potentials of a credit plan have to be arrived at on the basis of village profile data and information relating to development programmes. But these data are not readily amenable to translation into potentials. For instance, cattle population in the area and capacity of insemination centres do not indicate the number of animals in the breedable age available in the market. Ground water potential for a group of villages has to be translated into village-wise potential for wells. This exercise needs certain assumption of technical nature.

There are certain activities such as dairy, poultry etc. where an external market/ material source has to be shared by a number of service areas. In this regard the higher levels (state or district) are in better position to plan and apportion the share of market/ material supply for various service areas. For this reason and also to provide a perspective, erstwhile block-wise planning exercise done by LBO needs to be continued. In other words, 'bottom-up' planning implied in SAA should not be taken literally, on the other hand, it has to be multi-level planning exercise involving all types of people at different levels as per the nature and scope of credit planning.

Preparation of Credit Plans

The branch manager should prepare annual credit plans in a phased manner for deployment of credit in each of the village in the service area. The annual credit plans should be prepared in such a way that they should reflect the potentialities and needs of the service area concerned.

The RRBs branches are to prepare credit plans for the target groups only in their service areas. Similar credit plans for the non-target groups to be prepared by the designated commercial bank branch. The branch managers are expected to take note of the lending programmes of PACs/ PLDBs while finalising their credit plans. They are required to obtain a list of borrowers from the PACs/PLDBs to ensure that double financing is avoided.

Preparation of credit plan is a challenging task for the service area BM as it needs lot of skill in the sphere of plan formulation which was generally lacking in BMs in the beginning of such credit plans. In the absence of such skills, the BMs in the beginning kept in view the present DCPs/AAPs prepared under the LBS, which broadly identify schemes relevant for different areas of the district. It is important that the branch managers should exercise their own judgement in choosing activities relevant to their service area and determining the number of units feasible to be taken up for financing in the light of village-wise surveys conducted by them, the demand for credit for productive schemes in their service areas and the information which they might gather from local development agencies alongwith their own perception and vision based on environment scanning.

Presently, programmes such as Swarnjayanti Gram Swarozgar Yojana (April, 1999), Prime Minister Rozgar Yojana (October 2nd, 1993) and Swarn Jayanti Shastri Rozgar Yojana (December, 1997) are included in each credit plan (with the coming into force of above mentioned programmes the earlier programmes viz., Integrated Rural Development Programme, Training of Rural Youth for Self Employment, Self Employment for Educated Unemployed Youth, Jawahar Rozgar Yojana, Development of Women and Children in Rural areas, supply of improved tools to rural artisans, Ganga Kalyan Yojana, Million Well Scheme are no longer in operation).

The activities proposed for inclusion in the credit plans of each branch in a block and the number of units to be financed are discussed in a meeting with the Block Development Officer (BDO) and his supporting staff before finalisation of the credit plans.

The annual lending programme drawn by each branch is aggregated into the annual credit plan for the block. The priority sector activities proposed to be financed in the semi-urban areas by the branches located in these centres in the block is also added for the purpose of the block level credit plan. Aggregation at the block level is done by the main branch of the lead bank. This branch also collects details of lending programmes of the co-operatives for the purpose of consolidation of block-wise plans. The block credit plans are then aggregated into the annual credit plans for the district by the lead bank. A detailed description of each step involved in the formulation of DCP under service area approach is given below :

VILLAGE CREDIT PLAN

The unit of planning as envisaged under the SAA, is the 'village,' therefore the credit plan is prepared for each of the villages and aggregated into service area credit plan for the financial year *i.e.* from April to March. The commercial banks/RRBs/DCCBs/LDBs/non-banking financial institutions like SFCs are also prepare annual village-wise credit plans based on village surveys and other information gathered from developmental agencies/government departments/lead banks/ NABARD etc.

The commercial banks and RRBs will procure village-wise lending programmes of co-operative/PLDBs/non-banking financial institutions in their service area before finalisation of village credit plan.

The village credit plan includes :

- Financial assistance activity-wise outlay under priority sectors;
- Financial assistance outlay under non-priority sectors in aggregate; and
- Quarterly break-up of plan based on seasonality and targets fixed quarterly.

For the formulation of realistic village credit plan, the BM requires following information of each village in his service area :

a) Infra-structural support inclusive of extension work for different technically feasible and economically viable activities in the area. The information on existing as well as additional (quantified) infra-structural support from identified major inputs providing agencies during the plan period for each activity is also required.

b) Potential of each activity.

c) Existing on-going (incomplete) units.

d) Mandatory targets :
   - Swarnjayanti Gram Swarozgar Yojana (SGSY)
   - Prime Minister Rozgar Yojana (PMRY)
   - State sponsored schemes
   - Special food grain production programme

e) Demand : Activity-wise from public, other than mandatory targets.

f) Past Experience :
   - From personal feed back.
   - Number of accounts disbursed under each activity.
   - Minutes of BLBC / DLCC.
   - Interaction with concerned development agencies.
   - Total resources at the disposal of financial institutions.
   - Staff capacity in terms of number of accounts to be handled.

The branch can collect the data village-wise as mentioned above, but the staff and resources at the command of the branch are common for all villages and urban areas in case of semi-urban area branches. The format for the village credit plan is the same as the one prescribed for the service area credit plan in LBR-1. While making allocations potential should be first utilised for incomplete units, mandatory targets and thereafter for the eligible demand. Ensure that allocations under each activity do not exceed the respective potential. The aggregated number of accounts and amount of allocations should match the total number of accounts and amount earmarked for the same village. While making the allocations past performance of the activity should be considered. Where the past performance of the activity is poor, the reasons for poor performance should be ascertained and kept in view before fresh allocations are made. It is quite essential in the interest of formulating realistic credit plan. If the demand for credit for an activity is low in a particular village due to less potential for development, the earmarked amount of such an activity should be transferred to another village where the potential for development as well as demand for credit exist. This fact should be brought to the notice of district administration so that necessary steps may be taken for the development of infra-structure and other extension facilities.

SERVICE AREA CREDIT PLAN

First the village credit plans (VCPs) are to be prepared for formulating SAPs. The VCPs are presented in format LBR-1. The VCPs once finalised are aggregated at the branch level to arrive at SAPs. The SAPs are also presented in the format LBR-1. The finalised plans are segregated into four quarters in format LBR-1 based on considerations like seasonal variations, credit requirements and other aspects. The SAP of the branch of commercial banks includes lending programmes/ activities of the branch. The bank branch prepare credit plans as under :

(i) First of all branch has to prepare credit plan for its own service area by aggregating village credit plans.

(ii) Secondly, branch has to prepare credit plan for non target groups in the service area of RRBs, if any

(iii) Thirdly, branch has to prepare credit plan for villages in service area of other commercial banks/RRB, a service area-wise basis, if any.

It is worth mentioning here that the RBI has also given some relaxation to branches to consider extension of credit assistance outside service area. These relaxations are as follows :

- In case of partly disbursed term loans, the service area branch may either take back the outstanding amount from the branch which disbursed the loan or alternatively the branch which disbursed earlier instalments may continue to disburse the remaining instalments. In the latter case, fresh crop loans may continue to be provided to the borrowers by the concerned (predecessor) branch till term loan outstanding is repaid. Subject to above, it has ensured that branches lend only to borrowers in their respective service area.

- The branches may extend / sanction fresh crop loans to a borrower residing in the service area of another branch it has outstanding term loan including medium term loan / conversion loans from the borrower.
- Additional term loan/ crop loans can also be sanctioned to the borrowers residing in the service area of another branch according to their eligibility and provided security by way of mortgage of immovable properties as primary or as collateral security has already been given to the financing branch. Borrowers requiring large amount of credit and other subsidiary services from urban/semi-urban/metropolitan branches and also certain other banking facilities which the branches in the service area may not be able to provide, may borrow from other branch where such facilities are available, likewise, if a borrower has activities spread over or has landed properties in the service area of different bank branches, option may be given to him to have credit arrangements with one or more of the bank branches within whose service area he/she resides or activities are carried on or landed properties are located. In these cases, there should be proper co-ordination among financing banks ensuring that there should be no double financing to the borrower. The activities carried out with such financing should be reflected in the block plans and monitored closely for the end use of funds.
- Rural and semi-urban branches located in places like airports, defence establishments, educational institutions etc. as also urban branches which have not been allocated service area, should not lend in the service area of other bank branches.
- At present rural and semi-urban branches are also extending credit to borrowers located in industrial estates may fall in the service area of any one branch, it is suggested that existing arrangement for financing the borrowers in the industrial estates may continue.
- Credit from banks routed through co-operatives may continue to be given by the same bank as hitherto even if the co-

operatives are located in the service area of another bank branch. However, the activities to be financed through such credit should be part of block plans and monitored closely.

- Advances are being granted by banks to state level corporations whose borrowers are spread over the service area of different bank branches. In all such cases the existing financing arrangements may continue. However, the activities to be financed should be reflected in the block plans and monitored closely for the end use of funds. In case of projects for which NABARD refinance has been obtained, the concerned bank may continue to finance the beneficiaries till the project is completed. Banks should in future ensure while submitting schemes for refinance to NABARD that their lending under such refinance schemes are confined to the service area of their bank branches.
- Sick industrial units enjoying credit facilities under nursing programmes may continue to be financed by the concerned bank.
- In case of second instalment of IRDP loans, it will be more desirable that the same branch should disburse the second instalment which has already disbursed the first instalment.
- If any of the RRB is not in a position to adequately meet the demand for credit even to the target group of beneficiaries in its service area, the designated branch of the commercial bank concerned may extend financial assistance to these beneficiaries in addition to non-target group beneficiaries, as an interim measures.

The RRB branches prepare service area credit plans for :

a) Villages of their own service area.

b) Lending to be made outside their service area, service area-wise as per aforesaid RBI relaxations.

The RRB branches send one copy of their credit plan to the commercial bank branches which are financing non-target groups around 15th December every year so that the commercial bank branches can plan for non-target groups beneficiaries in their credit plans.

If the service area of commercial bank inclusive of RRB spreads over two or more blocks/districts the concerned branch prepares separate credit plans for the village/service area pertaining to each block for submission to the respective LBO/convenor of BLBC for aggregation into block credit plan.

Sector-wise/Activity-wise, priority sector lending programmes of all semi-urban/urban branches in the semi-urban/urban areas are prepared on computerised format LBR-U1. The non-priority sector lending programmes are mentioned in aggregate lump-sum in the above said format LBR-U1. The branches club activity-wise/sector-wise allocations under priority sector and non-priority sector lending programmes from LBR-1 and LBR-U1. Such aggregated plan can be termed as branch credit plan.

In the cases of DCCB/LDB branches/non-banking financial institutions their rural area of operation might extend to more than one service area/block. As such, they prepare their credit plans village-wise/ service area-wise on LBR-1 on the same lines as mentioned earlier in this chapter.

a) The copies of the village-wise/service area-wise credit plans are sent to the relevant branches of commercial banks inclusive of RRB which have been allocated that particular village/ service area, so that these branches can consider the plans prepared by the DCCB/ LDB while arriving at their own projections.

b) Lending programmes in semi-urban/urban area, including financing through Primary Agricultural Credit Society (PACS) to weavers / other societies located in semi-urban / urban areas will be reflected / included in their credit plans under priority sector and non-priority sector in lump-sum / aggregated figures on the format LBR-U1.

c) The aggregation of sector-wise / activity-wise allocations from LBR-1 and LBR-U1 gives branch credit plan for the respective branches of DCCB/ LDB and non-banking financial institutions.

The above mentioned co-operative and non-banking financial institutions are required to obtain approval of their branch credit plan from their controlling offices keeping in view various constraints such as resource position, state of development including poverty and unemployment situation etc. in respect of their credit plans. The tentative allocations of different financial agencies as given in their LBR-1 and LBR-U1 are placed in BLBC meeting specially convened for preliminary discussion and for inter-service area adjustments of the potentials. Keeping in view the deliberation of the BLBC meeting, LBR-1 and LBR-U1 are adjusted accordingly, if necessary. Credit plans on LBR-1 and LBR-U1 shall be got approved from controlling offices and thereafter a copy of approved plan shall be submitted to concerned convenor BLBC as per time schedule.

The credit plan also serves as performance budget of the branch for credit deployment. The LBR-1 and LBR-U1 duly approved from controlling offices is placed in the BLBC to be held in the month of February every year. The plans should not be changed in the BLBC, unless there is overlapping of allocations. If there is any change in the plan due to overlapping, the corrected plan should be finalised in BLBC.

BLOCK LEVEL CREDIT PLAN

A Block level credit plan is the sum total of the service area plans of all agencies including co-operatives in the block, which covers all villages in the block plus non-service area plans within the block which cover all the semi-urban and urban areas in the block. The block credit plans is however, supposed to cover credit in respect of priority sectors only. In other words, the Block Credit Plan is the aggregation of LBR-1 and LBR-U1 drawn for the block in respect of priority sectors. (For preparation of the credit plan LBR-1 covers all villages and LBR-U1 covers all priority sector lendings in semi-urban and urban area). It is the responsibility of the LBO to aggregate the credit plans into block credit plans and send such aggregate plans in respect of the bocks to each of the BLBC convenor at the earliest and in any case not later than February 28/29 of every year.

The priority sector lending programmes of villages and urban/semi-urban area of respective credit agencies are finalised at BLBC and aggregated sector-wise / activity-wise / programme-wise into the Block Credit Plan, by LBO on proforma of LBR-1. In other words, the block credit plan can be presented in LBR-1 format itself because format LBR-U1 is the prototype of LBR-1.

DISTRICT CREDIT PLAN

The DCP represents the aggregation of block credit plans of all credit agencies operating in the district. Aggregation is being done block-wise / bank-wise / sector-wise by the LBO concerned for all the branches of each bank, making use, wherever available, of the computer facility.

Besides these, sectoral aggregated credit data, the DCP includes four other chapters. Thus, a typical DCP consists of the following chapters:

(i) Updated profile of blocks in the district and the list of service area allocations with necessary code numbers thereof;

(ii) Review of performance;

(iii) Developmental programmes in the district;

(iv) Arrangement for supporting facilities, responsibilities of different agencies/ departments and infra-structural deficiencies as indicated in SAPs; and

(v) Bank-wise and activity-wise credit plan for the priority sector lending including physical aspects of the plan.

Time Frame for the Formulation of Credit Plans

The entire credit planning process under the SAA is required to be completed prior to the commencement of the credit plan year i.e. from April to March according to the time-frame stipulated below :

ACTIVITY	*Date by which to be completed*
(a) Supply of background paper	31, October
(b) Preparation of service area credit plans by co-operative bank branches (SLDBs/PLDBs/DCCBs)	
(i) Initiation	1, November
(ii) Completion	30, November
(c) Preparation of service area credit plans by CBs/RRBs	
(i) Initiation	1, December
(ii) Completion	31, December
(d) Finalisation and approval of service area credit plans by controlling offices	31, January
(e) Aggregation of service area credit plans and credit plans of semi-urban and urban areas into block credit plans and approval by BLBCs	28/29, February
(f) Aggregation of Block credit plans into district credit plans	15, March
(g) Launching of credit plans	1, April

ASSESSMENT OF POTENTIAL

Potential Linked Credit Plans (PLPs) and the background paper are the instruments for the assessment of potential. Description in brief of each is given below :

Potential Linked Credit Plans

The PLPs are being used by the branches for the formulation of VCPs/SAPs. The PLPs are prepared by NABARD for each district of the country since 1988-89 and are updated in each financial year. It is a comprehensive documentation of potential for rural economic activities in a district, both in physical and financial terms. It also gives assessment of gaps in infra-structural support, which needs to bridged to facilitate development of the reliable potential. In other words, PLPs represent at making realistic and exploitable project of potentials exist in different sectors in the district. PLPs are prepared by District Development Manager (DDM) of NABARD in the district. The objectives of PLPs are:

- To enable various organisations in directing their efforts in a planned manner in accordance with the available potential for rural development which are engaged in this task.
- Optimum utilisation of scarce financial resources by channelising them towards sectors with high growth potential.
- To assess the gaps in infra-structure support, which needs to be taken care of for developing the potential and segregating the same into commercial infra-structure and developmental infra-structure.

In brief, the main objective of PLPs is to explore the potential for development and evolve an appropriate mechanism through which such potential could be exploited over a period of time.

The PLPs represent credit projections taking into account various aspects like development potential, infra-structure, credit absorption capacity and marketing support. As the service area plans are prepared based on potential of development and demand for credit, the branches of financial institutions are required to take into account projections made in the PLPs prepared by NABARD for each district.

In other words, the PLP is a essential reference document which is used by bankers and other credit agencies for preparing their own credit plans because PLP indicates broad perspective of the service area plan. The information / data contained in the document can be utilised by the lead district managers / officers while preparing the background paper for the service area plans. This document is also significant for different government departments and development agencies at the district level because it contains useful information concerning with them.

Background Paper

Background paper is used as an important tool for credit planning exercise. The format and guidelines for the 'Background paper' have been supplied by the NABARD to all its DDMs(wherever posted) as also to the LBOs. These guidelines followed with such modifications as may be deemed necessary to suit local requirements. Systematic and purposeful presentation of data may, however, be ensured while preparing the background paper for the respective districts.

On the basis of the PLP projections and the information gathered by lead bank office, background papers are prepared jointly by BM, LBO and DDM of NABARD and are circulated among the branch managers of the service area branch.

The background paper should broadly cover the following aspects:

(i) District / Block profile;

(ii) Sector-wise review of performance in the block for each category of credit agencies for the previous year;

(iii) Estimated credit requirements based on potentials in the district for the credit plan year for various sectors, including crop loans;

(iv) Block-wise projections of item;

(v) Infra-structural development programmes on going and proposed for future;

(vi) Bankable schemes (block-wise);

(vii) Projections of Government sponsored programmes (block-wise);

(viii) Details of on-going / new schemes in the district;

(ix) Specific agencies responsible for the development of district / block;

(x) Approximate share of financing agencies (category-wise and block-wise) for credit programmes keeping in view the relative strengths and weaknesses of the credit agencies in the district and ground level exigencies;

(xi) Commitment of development agencies for infra-structure / linkage-support; forward and backward both;

(xii) A list of code number allocated to villages, service areas, blocks and the district.

The background paper may also include details relating to other priority sector activities such as :

(i) Transport operators
(ii) Professional and Self-employed
(iii) Education loans
(iv) Rural housing and
(v) Other activities

Thus, the DCP is prepared in the manner mentioned above under the service area approach.

Though the preparation of DCP is a joint endeavour of all concerned authorities and departments, but the BM of a branch and LBO both are the key functionaries for formulating the DCP. Therefore, it becomes necessary to elaborate / discuss the role of BM and LBO in this context. The main tasks of BM and LBO in the formulation of the DCP have been discussed separately in subsequent pages of this chapter.

Main Tasks of Branch Manager

The task of the BM is not merely confined to collection of village environmental data. The data so collected is only an aid to understanding the potential for loaning in various activities relevant to the village. The ultimate objective is to enable him to work out a programme of lending which, in course of time, should cover all viable schemes and exploit the full development potential of the village with credit support from commercial banks and co-operative institutions.

The service area approach has the thrust on the BM for his three dimensional role as mentioned below :

- He has to prepare the village credit plan for his service area and also the branch credit plan, which is treated as performance budget for his branch.
- He has to take into account while preparing credit plans, the inter-linkages between the various economic activities sought to be financed and the resultant generation of income and employment.
- He has to do constant dialogues and liaison with various government officials and households of his service area.

In the context of his three dimensional role the main tasks of BM can be summarised as follows :

- The BM is the key person at the grass-root level and has to play a vital and participative role in successful implementation of various bankable schemes given in the plan;

- The work of BM starts right from the stage of formulation of credit plan for the villages in his service area.
- The BM should study the environment and infra-structure of the block and put forward his views well in advance when the lead district manager/block level authorities undertake the work of preparation of DCP/AAP;
- In case any difficulties in implementation of plans are foreseen, the BM should boldly put forward his views;
- The BM may, if found necessary, suggest opening of a new branch in the nearby unbanked centre for effective implementation of DCP/AAP;
- The BM should bear in mind that lead district managers/ district co-ordinators are representatives of the bank, therefore he should extend utmost co-operation to them in providing them with the information / statistics called for and also by financing under various programmes and schemes accepted by the bank for the district;
- The BM should ensure timely submission of statistical information, (LBR) and information about subsidy claims etc. required by various offices;
- The BM should attend all block level meetings / recovery committee meetings and act as "Bank's representative at Grass-root level" by actively participating at such meetings;
- It should be noted that once targets under DCP/AAP are accepted by the banks, it becomes their prime responsibility of BM to achieve the sector-wise, scheme-wise and physical targets for his service areas;
- For achieving the targets laid down in credit plans, the BM should have his whole hearted involvement for successful implementation of the scheme by utilising the staff at the branch to the maximum extent;
- The BM should be vigilant and at the same time, give adequate importance to various schemes particularly the advances to weaker section of society, advances to SC/ST persons, DRI scheme by the government and other government sponsored schemes;
- Being the first person to deal with the borrowers, BM should be careful while lending. He should avoid instances of mis-utilisation by proper scrutiny of the cases sent to him and periodical inspections as per stipulation;

- Any instances of mis-utilisation both existing and suspected should be brought to the notice of higher authorities/concerned authorities;
- The BM should not hesitate to take guidance from his immediate higher authorities in case of any problem faced while implementing the DCP/AAP;
- The BM is required to contact and assist the government officials in discharging their duties particularly in processing applications received under various government sponsored schemes.

Thus, the BM should combine in him all skills of a planner, public relation officer and implementor of his own credit plans.

For preparation of branch credit plan, the BM requires details in regard to :

- On-going development schemes and schemes which are proposed to be implemented, infra-structure and other facilities available and proposed to be created.
- Potential for lending in the service area.
- Lending programmes of other agencies such as co-operatives.
- Resources available and likely to be mobilised by the banks themselves to sustain their credit plan.

In short, under SAA the branch manager should be considered by the villagers as a 'friend-in-need' who is genuinely interested in the betterment of grass root level of living.

The Main Tasks of the Lead Bank Officer

Under the service area approach LBO has a vital role to play as a friend, philosopher and guide to branch managers. He has to act as a vital link between the banks and the district development authorities. His role is also crucial being the convenor of the DLCC. He has to also act as the credit planner for the whole district. Thus, the LBO is the kingpin in the process of formulation of credit plans in his district. The main tasks of the LBO in formulation of credit plans have been discussed below:

- To collect data regarding the profile of the blocks.
- To collect block-wise details of the development programmes of the various government departments and agencies operating in the district.
- To collect block-wise data regarding the arrangements for supporting facilities/ services from various developmental departments/ agencies.

- To ascertain from the NABARD the details of the projects being refinanced by it in the district.
- To ascertain from the banks :
  - (a) Details of their performance in implementation of schemes included in the DCP;
  - (b) Details of the schemes in the priority sector area, apart from those included in the DCP, being financed by them;
  - (c) Details about their existing network of branches and plans for opening up new branches;
  - (d) Details of the various categories of the staff of the branches ; and
  - (e) Their existing and estimated financial resources during the credit plan period.
- To review critically the scheme-wise and institution-wise implementation of DCP, with a view to draw lessons for the formulation of a realistic credit plan.
- To make a general assessment of the scope for development in the various blocks of the district under the various sectors/sub-sectors of the block economy on the basis of resource inventory collected.
- To study the bankability of various schemes/projects drawn-up by the various government departments/agencies and specialised bodies so as to formulate schemes for inclusion in DCP.
- To prepare bankable schemes for inclusion in DCP in respect of those sub-sectors/activities which have scope for development in the block and which have not been covered by the development programme of the existing agencies.
- To assess the scope for lending under the bankable schemes included in the DCP taking into account the market for products/services, availability of programme specific and general infra-structure and estimated demand for credit in the light of the past experience of the credit institutions.
- To consider the overall feasibility and size of the credit plan after carefully studying the various assumptions underlying and the estimates included in the credit plan.
- To decide :
  - (a) The share of the various participating financial institutions in the financing of the DCP; and

(b) Responsibilities of the various financial institutions in providing the supporting facilities for the success of the credit plan in consultation with individual institutions/departments/agencies concerned.

- To draft the DCP according to the chapter scheme included in the RBI guidelines.
- To get the draft of DCP approved by the DLCC and to get it Cyclostyled/ Xeroxed/Printed.
- To circulate the DCP to the concerned institutions/ agencies/ departments/ authorities as per the directives of the concerned authorities.

The above mentioned tasks of LBO themselves highlight the importance of LBO as a planner, co-ordinator and evaluator of credit plans prepared for the district. Thus, his leading role is multi-facet in nature as a friend, philosopher and guide.

Bankable Schemes and Assessment of Credit Demand

CRAFICARD has rightly mentioned about the nature of schemes which should be incorporated in DCP in these fine words that "For all its importance, the DCP is a broad framework. It becomes operationally only to the extent that it is translated into technically feasible and economically viable schemes with reference to location specific realities or in the popular phrase, 'Bankable Schemes'. The term 'Bankable Schemes' indicates, whether it will be possible to recover the principal amount and interest thereon." In other words, the scheme must be self-generating so that the borrower can pay back his loans with interest and earn also an assured income afterwards.

The role of the lead bank as the leader of consortium of financial institutions consists of preparing the bankable schemes and seeking the co-operation of other financial institutions in meeting the credit demands without reliance on outside agencies for the purpose of preparing the DCPs. In this context, it is essential that out of the various development programmes / schemes presented in Annexure-II only those schemes are to be included in the DCP/AAP which are bankable in nature.

Once the basic data relating to resources inventory, infra-structure facilities, socio-economic profiles of the blocks, development programmes of government departments / agencies etc. are collected, the next stage is (i) to assess the bankability of the various schemes prepared by the various agencies; (ii) to on-going schemes; and (iii) to prepare new schemes which have not been covered by the development programmes. For the purpose of preparation of bankable schemes, the LBO may have to undertake sample study of the activities proposed to be included in the credit plan. If certain areas show marked variations in 'cost benefits'; separate schemes can be prepared for such areas. In case of those which are to be formulated, the criteria adopted testing their bankability should be discussed.

A further aspect of DCP formulation relates to the implementation of CRAFICARD recommendations. In pursuance of an important recommendation, NABARD was set-up in 1982. NABARD provides re-finance assistance not only for agriculture and allied activities, but also for the rural industries artisans etc. on the basis of viable programmes. Therefore, schemes prepared by NABARD are / should also incorporated into the DCPs.

Under the SGSY only those schemes are included in DCPs which are found to be economically viable and technically feasible. The same is also applicable to schemes sponsored by DIC and KVIC. At the time of inclusion of various schemes prepared by NABARD and the state government / lead bank makes use of related information available with the state governments. This helps in ensuring the establishment of mutual linkages of various economic activities.

For estimating the credit demand, the lead bank prepares a representative project profiles of activities covered by the schemes which give basic economic and technical data and may also helpful in the actual extension of credit. The representative project profile are also helpful for DLCC and finalising the credit plans.

The economics of a particular scheme pre-supposes the availability of necessary inputs, supporting services like marketing etc. in the desired dimension and at the desired time. After tracing out the bankable schemes the credit needs for various activities should be worked out keeping in view the manpower position, availability of financial resources, infra-structural facilities and the availability of extension services in the district alongwith the willingness of the beneficiaries to undertake risk for different venture.

Assessing the Scope for Lending

After the schemes to be financed under the DCP are finalised, the LBO proceeds to make an assessment of the scope for lending in terms of number of units which can be financed under each activity during the period of credit plan. In assessing the scope for lending, following facts should be considered judiciously:

(i) Volume of market and arrangements for marketing;

(ii) arrangements for supplying services like extension, input supply etc.; and

(iii) likely demand for credit that is expected to arise taking into account the development consciousness of the people and extension efforts planned during the credit plan period.

The scope for lending under various activities should be determined in detail under each activity particularly those which benefit the weaker section. On the basis of the number of units expected to be financed under each activity and the corresponding scales of finance, the extent of credit disbursal, which will be required, for each activity is calculated.

Finalisation of Credit Outlays

After these estimates are over, draft DCP is prepared. This is discussed in the standing committee in detail and circulated to all members of the DLCC and discussed in District Level Review Committee (DLRC). DLRC takes a close look at the draft and suggest such modifications as it feels necessary. Once overall schemes and the size of the DCP is approved in the DLRC, standing committee decides tentative allocations of the DCP to various participants of the DCP and fixes the responsibilities of various government departments / agencies. The details of the shares / responsibilities of individual agencies is then circulated to them and their confirmation is obtained. On the receipt of the confirmation from the individual of their respective shares, the LBO prepares final credit outlays as per Annexure-IV of the RBI guidelines. The LBO, then, convenes a meeting of DLCC for the formal approval of outlays by it. This meeting should be invariably attended by senior officials of the banks and other institutions who can accept commitment on behalf of their respective institutions.

Role of Standing Committee

The standing committee was constituted under the DLCC in 1980 for associating it in credit plan formulation process. In this regard the RBI guidelines suggest that the standing committee should be closely associated with the formulation of DCPs. The standing committee meets every month and help the LBO in preparing the DCP. The role of standing committee in the formulation of DCP is given as under:

- To assist the data collectors;
- To approve the identified activities and the schemes formulated for these;
- To decide about the scales of finance;
- To approve the estimates regarding the number of units which can be financed under each scheme;
- To prepare background papers for the DLRC;
- To finalise the allocation of the DCP in consultation with the individual participating institutions/agencies;
- To determine specific responsibilities of and action points for development departments/agencies;
- To approve the final draft of the DCP;
- To ensure that the time-table relating to the plan work is adhered to and to render all assistance technical as well as administrative such as provision of typing support and copying facilities wherever needed to the LBO to succeed in doing so.

To assist the standing committee in playing its role effectively, four sub-groups of the standing committee may be formed. Each of the sub-groups will cover one of the following sectors /activities:

(a) Agricultural Activities;

(b) Activities allied to agriculture;

(c) Industrial activities; and

(d) Tertiary activities.

The LBO is the convenor for all the four sub-groups. Officials and experts associated with the respective fields like District Agriculture Officer, District Veterinary Officer, District Animal Husbandry Officer, representative of development agencies in the district etc. constitute the sub-groups. The group is responsible for its respective sector.

Drafting the DCP Document

It is well established and accepted fact now that as a part of the overall process of directing the credit policy towards planned development, the credit plan is a significant step forward. Therefore, DCP should be clearly worded and devoid of unnecessary descriptive material. All assumptions should be clearly spelt out. Necessary support for implementation from other agencies should be specified. It should clearly indicate the roles of all participating financial and developmental agencies/ institutions.

Methodology for Estimation of Credit Demands for Various Sectors

DCP is a blue-print of various bankable schemes which will be taken-up for financing by financial institutions, hence the methodology for estimation of credit demand for various sectors/activities is an essential step in the formulation of credit plans to facilitate realistic goal setting by banks.

The utility of these estimates is to know to what extent and in which areas credit organisations need to be strengthened to meet existing credit needs. These credit demand estimates guide the banks to develop their organisation to meet developmental credit needs of an area. Such exercises are an essential input in planning and directing the development of credit institutions.

The credit demand estimates are also necessary to match the flow of existing resources of financial institutions with the actual credit needs of the people; i.e. to match the credit demand with available resources with the participating financial institutions.

In terms of the methodology for estimation of the credit demand, programmes of development prepared by developmental agencies/ departments are studied against the background of the potential for development existing in the district after assessing the economic viability of individual schemes. The goals of development included in the programmes are studied in the context of prevailing development consciousness and the expansion efforts envisaged to estimate the credit demand, credit estimation is in terms of standard schemes included in the credit plan, prepared on the basis of a study of 'cost-benefit analysis' of the activities and their need for credit. Credit demand is expressed in terms of the number of units and total credit required for setting up these, calculated with the help of estimated investment per unit less owner's equity of margin. In regard to other activities for which development programmes are not available, extent of their likely development is estimated on the basis of the 'Linkage-effects'.

Keeping this fact in mind that the credit is a critical input in any development planning, the effectiveness of area development planning will ultimately depend on how accurately the credit needs of the area are identified and estimated. Estimating credit demand for various sectors/ activities belonging to priority sector contributes an important element in the process of preparing of district credit plans. Such an estimation helps the financial institutions and governments functioning in the district to understand the pattern and dimensions of the credit demand pertaining to the activities covered under DCP. It facilitates the process of realistic acceptance of targets by financial institutions for various priority sector activities in the district. Estimation of credit demand begins with the identification of beneficiaries under SGSY-1999or Govt. sponsored schemes. The public meeting are organised between the March and June every year in the blocks to identifying the prospective beneficiaries of SGSY. After the identification is completed in all the villages, the BLBC is convened to approve the schemes considering the demand and supply of various schemes on the basis of their merit and needs of the block. Primary Agriculture Credit Society (PACS) estimate the credit needs of its members after taking into consideration their productive requirement of credit. DIC and DRDA select the beneficiaries after screening the applications and interviewing the applicants at the appropriate period for their schemes which fall under their jurisdiction.

Panchayat samities and other agencies related to the task of rural development also estimate the demand for credit for various schemes before the end of the financial year. The estimates of credit demand made by these institutions are discussed in the DLCC meetings before approving them in the month of December and then they are apportioned among the participating financial institutions for implementation.

The schemes formulated by the Government, NABARD and the individual banks are also incorporated into the credit plan for implementation. Before convening the DLCC meeting the credit plan, which is supposed to be the 'performance budget', is sent to the standing committee for critical analysis and meaningful observations, so that the plan could become more realistic and feasible.

Thus, the conglomeration of all the credit estimates of schemes formulated by the Panchayat Samities, Government, NABARD and the individual banks for all the blocks make up the district credit plan.

The actual methodology followed at the time of formulation of various DCPs in regard to major activities is need not merit here to mention in detail However, a brief mention of this fact is given below :

In the first round of DCPs, some banks prepared estimates of credit demand likely to arise under bankable schemes in a given period and presented these in credit plans. The credit demand estimates were, no doubt, sought to be made as realistic as possible, taking into account the development potential, infra-structure support available, plan programmes and development consciousness of the people in the area. Even so that network of bank branches and the strength of co-operatives was not adequate to meet the estimated credit demand in full. Hence, financial shares under the DCPs and the 'Operational Credit Plan' or the plan for actual deployment of credit accepted by financial institutions was smaller than the initial credit plan. Sometimes pressures were built up in the DLCC on the banks and the lead bank in particular to accept the credit estimate in full, which was often beyond their organisational strength.

In the second round of DCPs, the process of discussions with the participating agencies on the basis of the credit estimates prepared by the lead bank preceded the finalisation of the credit plan and only the 'accepted commitments' were presented in the document at the 'credit plan'. This was a welcome procedural refinement as credit plans were presented as the 'Operations plans' and not merely as estimates of credit demand.

In the third round of DCPs, the same procedure/practice is applied as adopted in the second round of DCPs. This round also explained the very important fact that the "DCP is more of an exercise for planning of credit deployment than one of estimating credit needs". All the same, an assessment of the credit needs for supporting different activities under DCP becomes necessary so that the size of the different programmes/ schemes (in terms of physical units and financial outlays) can be related to the estimated resources.

While preparing the fourth round of DCPs, the estimate of credit demand is presented sector-wise *i.e.* for crop loans, agricultural term loans and for meeting the working capital and term loan requirements of industries in a district. While estimating the credit demand, the credit needs of tertiary /service sector comprising transportation, retail trade, community services, production schemes for helping the weaker sections were also taken into account.

For operational facility, area planning for the service area of a branch can be visualised in the following broad sectors :

- Agriculture;
- Allied Activities;
- Rural Artisans, Cottage Industries, Small Scale Industries; and
- Trade and Services.

Agriculture

Even after five decades of planned development, agriculture still plays a dominant role in the Indian economy and is the backbone of the rural economy of our country. Therefore, financing to agriculture sector constitutes an important ingredient of any credit policy. The BM should chalk-out the strategy for financing agriculture in his area of operation on the basis of the profile and survey of village in the service area and after prudent estimation of credit demand for agriculture.

- Extensive agriculture : brining more land into production through crop husbandry, horticulture etc.;
- Increase in the area under irrigation and commensurate change in the cropping pattern;
- Changing over to more remunerative cropping pattern in irrigated and un-irrigated areas;
- Increase in yields through optimum dosage of inputs, more applicable in assured rainfall or irrigated areas;
- Improving the yields through better cultivation practices and moisture preservation strategies in dry lands; and
- Providing storage facilities to take advantage of remunerative prices.

The rural BM should have a thorough grasp of the operation of agricultural sector in his service area. There are certain areas where the BM can act on its own such as extending crop loans. In this regard, he is required to develop close co-operation with co-operative societies working in the area. Collaboration with Government agencies and NABARD would be necessary in certain other areas, such as new cropping pattern, waste land development or dry land farming which require sustained extension efforts, increasing irrigation facilities, improving the regularity and adequacy of supply of existing irrigation facilities, water management and optimising the use of existing facilities.

The Government agencies have a number of scheme for development of agriculture. With his enlightened understanding of agriculture of the service area, the BM should contact various functionaries at the local level to elicit their information on schemes which are under operation in the villages covered by the service area. The important aspect is to know the major developments in agricultural sector which are on-going and likely to continue. Identifying those spheres where credit can play an important role, the BM should prepare an action plan for the year.

While preparing the credit plan, the branch manager should also give due consideration to the resources position of the branch. An estimate of the financial resources should include the expected growth in deposits besides present level of deposits refinances likely to be available from NABARD, SIDBI etc. and recovery performance of the branch.

Activities Allied to Agriculture

Major activities allied to agriculture are dairy, poultry, goatery, sheep-rearing, pigery etc. The data/information relating to these activities could easily be obtained from the village profile. Where such data are not available, rough estimation can be made on the basis of the knowledge of the area. It is necessary to distinguish the size and the number of animals/birds of improved/standard varieties which can be considered for financing under bankable schemes.

For agriculture basic inputs such as HYV seeds, fertilizers, insecticides etc. are usually supplied from outside the service area and for more than one service area and the supply source may be the same for all. Therefore, once the service area plans are prepared rationally, the BM should assess the demand in relation to supply for making necessary adjustments in targets and allocations. In case of allied activities, where marketing, infra-structure or veterinary facilities or even supply of green fodder are critical factors, dependence on the same source by many service areas may restrict the scope for expanding such activities. In such cases, dialogue among managers and concerned government agencies is essential before finalising the targets.

Rural Artisans, Cottage Industries and Small Scale Industries

Almost in all villages of a service area, generally we find a few artisans of different categories, such as cobblers, blacksmiths, carpenters etc. The schemes for the development of rural artisans can be classified into following two categories:

- To rehabilitate a few artisans within the village giving them proper training and design to produce comparable substitutes which are in market.
- To form collective ventures of artisans from one or more villages for setting up common unit/work places and help them in ensuring supply of raw material and link with marketing outlets in the nearby semi-urban and urban centres.

In above mentioned both categories the role of development agencies such as DIC/KVIC/KVIB etc. is very crucial in formulating the credit plan.

Cottage Industries

Cottage industries include all khadi and village industries, handloom carpet and dhurry weaving etc. which depend on traditional schemes and craftsmanship can be classified under this category.

There are certain products of cottage industries which are of artistic nature and may easily be sold in the markets which are situated outside the service area. But there are some common products, such as handloom clothes, leather products, bamboo-work etc., which are being produced by the cottage industries of two or more than two service areas. In case of such products, marketing is a critical constraining factor. Performance of cottage industries basically depends on the quality and facilities of training, the capability of change in product, designing, innovations in products and improvement in operational skills. Besides these, the most significant factor is the proper linkages with concerned Government departments and other marketing channels and/or penetrating into the new markets.

Small Scale Industries

SSI, generally, embraces modernised manufacturing activities which usually requires certain minimum infra-structural facilities for growth. Certain special categories of SSI such as agro-processing activities and other units based on local natural resources are usually found in rural areas. It should not be difficult for the BM to assess the potential of growth for such units for arriving at their actual credit needs. Similarly the semi-urban areas generally have sufficient scope for demand based industries. The estimation of credit needs of such industries may be done on the basis of existing and potential growth. The potentialities for development of ancillary industries situated are also estimated. For the healthy development of SSI in the area, the BM should utilise the information available with the DIC.

Trade and Services

In the absence of official registration facility of units engaged in petty trade and services in rural areas, the data/information relating to them may have to be ascertained village-wise on the basis of local knowledge and environmental scanning of the villages. Nature and size of various constituents comprising the tertiary sector depend and vary according to the size of population and business activity in the village. The number of villages in any service area alone is not adequate to give a fair idea of the nature and size of tertiary activity. It will, therefore, be useful that the managers should discuss the composition of tertiary activities in their service area and scope for their expansion on a viable basis in BLBC meeting.

In brief, it can be said on the basis of forgoing analysis that the credit plan should reflect the village-wise outlays for credit under different activities including both priority sector and non-priority sector credit. The credit plans prepared for the service area should reflect the capabilities of borrowers to undertake various bankable activities identified for them. There is also need to initiate positive steps for improving the participation of borrowers in economically viable and technically feasible activities, so that production, productivity and levels of income of the people in villages could be raised to a reasonably a good standard. The main aim of the credit plans should be to increase the low level of economic activities/ incomes of the people to their high levels.

Factors Influencing the Formulation of District Credit Plan

Although, DCPs are formulated by lead banks as per the guidelines laid down by the RBI and availability of scale of finance from the NABARD for various bankable schemes, but even then there are some important factors which also influence the nature and size of DCPs in practice. These are as under below:

- Present resource position of the financial institutions operating in the district concerned and likely growth during the credit plan;
- Financial assistance likely to be received from refinance institutions such as NABARD etc.;
- Manpower position of the financial institutions operating in the district concerned;
- Infra-structure available in the respective district;
- Performance of the previous annual action plans;
- Arrangement for supporting facilities available and likely to develop in near future;
- Backward and forward linkages of various schemes;
- Existing credit portfolio of financial institutions operating in the concerned district;
- Recovery position of financial institutions;
- Involvement, co-operation and co-ordination amongst the financial institutions operating in the district concerned;

- Co-operative attitudes and availability of extension services provided by various development agencies;
- Credit-absorption capacity of the beneficiaries and their general socio-economic attitudes; and
- Overall development policies and attitude of Government officials.

Finally, it can be said regarding the formulation of DCPs that the lead bank is the kingpin in the whole process and for refinement in the process of formulating realistic credit plans, the LBO is expected to develop the following things :

a) Skills of analysing the economic environmental data;
b) Insight into the process of development planning; and
c) Understanding of the dynamics of growth based on mutual linkages of various sectors and of the process of planning at the grass root level.

It is well established fact that credit is one of the essential inputs for any development programme, therefore, credit planning assumes great importance. For formulating realistic credit plan, the correct and accurate exercise for estimation of credit demand is of immense importance. The need of hour is that for attaining fruitful result from the credit planning exercise, the credit demand estimation should be properly linked with development plan that is dovetailing of credit planning with the physical planning of the district. For this the credit planner has to use his own judgement and that in turn depends on the insight and skills of the credit planner. The credit planner has to accurately assess not only the technical aspect of various activities, but also their cost benefit analysis before taking them up for financing purpose.

To sum-up, it can be said that the formulation of the credit plan will serve its true purpose only when its targets are realistic and achieved in letter and spirit within the stipulated time frame. Besides this, the benefits accruing from the credit plan should reach ultimately to the people for whom the credit plans are formulated and implemented.

REFERENCES

1. Guidelines for the formulation of Third round of DCP, Rural Planning and Credit Department, RBI, 1982.
2. Udeshi, J.J., District Credit Plans - Fourth Round, The Economic Times, Sept. 1, 1988.

3. Service Area Approach, Formulation of credit plan, Rural Planning and Credit Department, RBI, May, 1988.
4. Revised Guidelines on credit planning and Monitoring under Service Area Approach, Rural Planning and Credit Department, RBI, March, 1991.
5. Kanvinde, D.J., "Methodology for estimation of credit demand under DCPs", SBI monthly review, August, 1981.
6. Committee to review arrangements for Institutional Credit for Agriculture and Rural development (CRAFICARD) 1981, Reserve Bank of India.

Chapter 5

Implementation and Monitoring Machinery under Service Area Approach

The Government of India introduced the social control on banks in 1968 and nationalised 14 major commercial banks in 1969 with the purpose to improve credit delivery system in the rural areas. After the nationalisation of major commercial banks, the lead bank scheme was launched on the recommendation of Gadgil Group, but many problems could not be tackled especially the problems of fulfilling the credit gaps, multiple financing and linking the credit with the production, productivity and the generation of income. Later on many flaws in the LBS cropped-up. Therefore, to overcome them and to forge link between the credit and production, productivity and level of income, the Service Area Approach was launched in April, 1989. SAA is a new scheme of rural lending meant for the purpose of rapid rural development by linking the credit with the production, productivity and generation of income. This scheme can be only significant contribution in achieving its objectives only when its implementation and monitoring is done in an impeccable manner. For any sound planning to be a grand success proper implementation and effective monitoring are two basic conditions, therefore the implementation and monitoring machinery becomes all the more important.

The implementation of SAA involves two vital aspects. The first and foremost aspect is availability and proper utilisation of funds and the second is the achievement of pre-determined objectives and set targets. The monitoring aspect pertains to the timely availability of adequate and reliable information with the planning and controlling authorities for assessing the progress of implementation and to help in taking correct and timely decision to ensure that the credit plans are implemented in letter and spirit as per the scheduled time frame.

Ultimately, the success of any plan depends upon how well and impeccably it has been implemented and what has been its system of monitoring and the follow-up action. If the implementation and monitoring system is scientific and sound, then the plan is bound to be a thumping success and becomes worth all accolades. But at the same time any good plan can fall flat on its face, if the implementation and monitoring system is full of blemishes and flaws, obviously the plan is bound to be flop-show because the obstruction of any kind in implementation and monitoring may prove to be a stumbling block in the path of its success.

Fixation of Responsibilities - Joint Efforts

Joint efforts of the various participating agencies in an integrated and synchronised manner with optimum utilisation of available resources can only ensure rapid and balanced district development. While the credit, being one of the essential components required for development, is extended by the credit institutions, other components like infra-structural facilities, supporting services including promotional and extension services, being even more important than the credit component, are to be made available by the concerned government and other development agencies with proper integration with the credit component.

It is, therefore, desirable that while the financial institutions adhere to the credit programmes as envisaged block-wise, sector-wise and scheme-wise in terms of financial outlays and physical targets under DCP, a detailed programme be also chalked out for the various development agencies giving individual responsibility expected out of each of these agencies. This means that the development agencies and credit institutions should synchronise their efforts so that the backward and forward linkages of development can be achieved. The RBI had pointed out this very fact at the time of formulating of second round of DCPs in these nice words: "One of the features of new DCP/AAP is that it should be an action oriented plan which may be fully operational and responsibilities of the agencies are pinpointed.". Thus, the DCP/AAP besides other details, should also indicate (a) what individual financial institution will accomplish during the plan period and (b) what was expected of government departments by way of specific action on infra-structural facilities, supply of inputs etc.

If only infra-structural facilities, inputs, services and credit were not limited and ubiquitously available, the more accessibility and stressing the roles of different agencies would have induced the priority sector beneficiary to use them and achieve the critical integration. Since the resources are limited and infra-structural facilities are scarce, the beneficiaries have to be chosen and full package has to be ensured. A step to this inevitable objective is to move towards 'Location Specific Commitment'. For this purpose joint efforts of development agencies of the government and the financial institutions are needed. For example, without credit facility small and medium farmers often find it difficult to take up the cultivation of high yielding variety crops. However, supply of credit, by itself, is not enough for the success of the programme, unless simultaneous supply of other inputs is also ensured. This pre-supposes that the extension agency involved at the village level co-ordinates its activities with the credit agency in such a manner that both credit and other inputs supply are provided together.

Responsibilities of Financial Institutions

The implementation process commences with the credit share allocation among various financial institutions operating in the district. At the time of finalisation of DCP, the standing committee of DLCC finalises the allocation of DCP in consultation with the participating credit These credit institutions accept their share after taking into consideration of their existing and potential network of branches and resources position both financial and manpower. Later on, at their own level, the individual credit institutions allocate the total accepted share to their branches in definite proportion looking at their capability and strength for the actual implementation of the DCP.

Thus, the actual implementation of the financial aspect of DCP rests on the shoulders of the individual branches/units of the various participating financial institutions. But the real success of the credit plan depends upon the various departments/agencies of the government which provide the supporting facilities without which the process of rapid development cannot be initiated.

Modalities of Evaluation of Performance of Banks

At the meeting of the finance ministry with the chief executives of the public sector banks on the 6th March, 1980, it was decided to raise the proportion of advances granted to the priority sectors to 40 percent by March, 1985 and allocate a significant portion of the overall target to the beneficiaries of 20 point programme. Accordingly, the RBI set-up a working group to work-out the modalities for the implementation of these decisions. The group considered the question of evaluation of the performance of banks in lending to priority sectors and assistance programmes to the beneficiaries of the 20 point programme and recommended some criteria to be taken into account for such evaluation. The recommended criteria of the working group includes the following main points:

- Compliance with the targets and sub-targets fixed;
- Number of additional beneficiaries financed during the reporting period under each category like agriculture, small scale industries, etc.;
- Extent of lending to 'weaker sections' under each of the categories like agriculture and small scale industries;
- Performance of the banks on the basis of disbursement of outstanding as appropriate; and
- Quality and recovery position of advances-overall as well as for different categories.

The group felt that the individual bank should conduct studies of the specific schemes financed by them and also in specific areas covering all schemes in the area on a continuous basis by multi-institutional teams. At the district level the DCC and at the State level the SLCC reviews the bank's performance in lending to priority sectors including assistance to beneficiaries under the 20 point programme.

Responsibilities of Development Departments/Agencies

The standing committee of DLCC determines specific responsibilities of and action points for development departments/agencies in consultation with individual department concerned. The support from the various development departments/agencies in respect of the following is needed :

- strengthening of certain infra-structural facilities;
- supply of necessary inputs;
- provision of supporting services;
- provision of subsidy;
- carrying out extension work; and
- identification of potential borrowers.

This is actually, worked out at the time of finalisation of DCP in DLCC meeting. Thus, the responsibility of the implementation of the non-financial aspect of the plan remains with the various departments/agencies of the government. The fixation of responsibilities of different agencies/authorities is shown in the following schematic chart :

Schematic chart showing fixation of responsibilities

S. No	*Loan Category*	*Essential Components of the Programmes*	*Agency/Authority Which has to take action*	*Remarks*
1.	2.	3.	4.	5.
1.	Croap Loan	1 Evolving modern cropping pattern.	District Agriculture Officer/ Project Authorities, BDO.	
		2. Organising demonstration frames.	- do -	
		3. Supply of inputs: (a) Seeds (b) Fertilisers	BDO/Project authorities. Fertilisers dealers/co-operative societies, pesticide dealers/ co-operative societies.	DLCC should review the supply position vis-à-vis requirements indicating sources of supply block-wise.
		(c) Pesticides	Projects authorities	
		4. Spraying operations and spraying equipment.	Co-operatives	
		5. Issue of no-dues certificates		
2.	Irrigation and equipment loans	1. Technical feasibility certificate for exploration of groundwater resources	Groundwater department.	
		2. Ascertaining/ guiding the dimension of the well and depth to which it has to dug.	Ground water department and Civil Engineer/Irrigation Engineer of the District Administration	This will help in standardising the cost and improving the viability of the scheme.

		3. Organising group of small farmers.	DRDA	This will help small farmers to optimally utilise the irrigation facilities in their fragmented holding.
		4. Energisation of pumpsets by drawing programme of village electrification.	Rural electrification corporation and state electricity board.	This will help credit agencies to finance the beneficiaries of these specific villages so that the electric pump sets may not remain idle. Repairing facilities (work shop to be set-up at the strategic places).
		5. Pump sets /electric motors of suitable size and quality.	Dealer/ Manufacturers District Administration	- do -
		6. Provision for after sale service and training in operation and maintenance of pump sets etc.	- do -	
		7. Regular supply of diesel oil.	District Administration	Made available at economic price so that the viability of the scheme is not adversely affected.
		8. Construction of wells and repairs, therefore, supply of cement and steel.	- do -	
		9. Counselling service for co-farm developing works.	Field staff of banks and project authorities.	Since a majority of the beneficiaries are illiterate, they should be made

				aware of optimum use of scarce and costly inputs.
		1. Procurement of quality animals at reasonable prices.	DRDA, District Animal Husbandry Department Livestock officer.	Cattle fairs to be organised.
		2. Provision of additional quantities of fodder and concentrate.	District administration block authorities through Milk Unions/ Societies.	Arrangements to be made for support programme for fodder cultivation and supply of concentrates will have to be planned on time.
		3. Veterinary facilities/ services including setting-up of additional dispensaries at convenient centres.	Veterinary officer stockman.	With the increase in the livestock population; proportionate increase in vet. Facilities including supply of medicines have to ensured through increased budgetary allocations. DLCC should review the position periodically.
		4. Charting Milk routes.	DRDA/ Block Authorities.	In consultation with District A.H.O. Credit agencies and Milk Union.
		5. Disposal of surplus milk.	Dairy Development Corporation.	This will help the milk producers to get remunerative prices.
		6. Insurance cover for animals.	District A.H.O./ General Institution. Corporation and credit institutions.	These authorities should arrange for through discussing with beneficiaries for removing the misgivings.

4.	Sheep and Goat Rearing	1. Effective vaccination and health care. 2. Collection and marketing of wool and linking of recovery of loans with the sale proceeds. 3. Breeding, feeding and management aspects.	Husbandry Officer/ Veterinary Officer. Sheep and wool development department. DRDA, District Animal Husbandry Department.	This is essential since sheeps are prone to disease. In absence of arrangements for organised collection and market benefits of the programme middle men. This may adversely affect the viability of the scheme. Results of the research should be passed on to the sheep breeder for improving their income.
5.	(a) Rural and Cottage Industries (b) Village Industries	1. Identifications. 2. Imparting training etc. Identification of borrowers, their input require-ments marketing training.	D.I.C. DRDA/Khadi and village Industries Board / DIC	Training should be given to the weavers, institution of new designation coupled with adoption of mixed fibre would enhance their earnings.
6.	Small Scale	1. Sponsoring of entrepreneurs providing technical know-how and raw material marketing facilities. 2. Supply of power/water	District Industries Centres. State Elect. Board DIC/RAJCON.	There is a need for working out tie up arrangements between banks and KVIB which will have to undertake sponsoring technical know-how and training and arranging retail outlets for the products.

		3. Training of entrepreneurship development		There is need for arranging technically feasible and economically viable projects to enable the entrepreneurs to run the project successfully.
7.	Truck	Availability of trucks	District Administration	
8.	Gobar Gas Plant	1. Selection site, provision of cement, steel and necessary equipment and installation of plant.	DRDA	As sizeable number of milk animals and bullocks are being introduced under DCP, it is advisable to link this with Gobar Gas Plants to provide fund and fertiliser in village itself.

Responsibility of Branch Manager under Service Area Approach

The SAA is based on this hypothesis that the BM working in rural areas will develop the requisite skills to scan the socio-economic environment of villages, the resources potential available, the needs of farmers and other productive communities, potential for development of technically feasible and economically viable activities. It has also expected from him that he shall be capable in chalking out lendings programmes for his service area based on the locally available resources potential and skills, infra-structure and development linkages. Thus, the success of implementation of SAA depends mainly on the in-depth and intimate knowledge of the BM about the economy of villages and talents of the villagers which will enable him to ensure the proper end-use of credit and improvement in quality of lending, thereby linking the credit input with the increase in production, productivity and level of income in rural areas.

The BM, while being sympathetic to the villagers, should also ensure that the credit extended by him reaches to bankable schemes and ultimately to income and employment generating activities. The intimate knowledge of service area economy and the skill of BM to scan environment properly can enable him to resist the pressure of accepting non-viable activities for lending purpose. Close collaboration of branch staff and village level workers during the village surveys would lead to a better understanding of the mutual needs and help remove the cobwebs of mis-understanding, thus leading to more harmonious relationship between the various developmental agencies.

The responsibilities of BM under SAA is to study the village data and programmes of development being undertaken in consultation with the village level staff, decide the schemes and the viable number of units there under which he will be able to finance in a given time frame. The annual lending programmes drawn up by each bank will then be aggregated into an annual credit plan for the block. The annual credit plan so emerging will improve in its coverage and realism. The Branch Manager's commitment to fulfilling the branch credit plans will also improve, since they would be implementing the plans prepared by themselves.

Calendar of Activities and Action Points

Action calendar of planned activities/programmes can help in fixing the responsibilities of different development agencies and credit agencies at the time of planning and implementation both. The action calendar can be more instrumental in the effective implementation of credit plans, if these are got approved in DLCC forum also and sent to the concerned development agencies through District Collector by LBO. The action calendar will also improve the quality of credit planning and quality of lending.

The calendar of activities and action points are discussed in BLBC and DLCC meetings and the final decisions taken about them are recorded in the minutes of these two committees. It is expected from the participating credit institutions and development agencies to implement them. These points of action are evaluated in the next meeting of BLBC and DLCC with a view to what extent these have been implemented or not. If these are not implemented, then reasons for failure are ascertained and measures to overcome them are suggested, which are to be implemented in remaining period of the credit plan.

SAA is to bring about a major change in the quality and productivity of rural lending. Since the service area plan is to serve as 'Performance Budget' of the branch for credit deployment, the primary responsibilities of ensuring that the credit is being properly utilized will be of the relevant credit agency, which has extended the credit. To develop the activities at a particular level, the role of different developmental agencies and financial institutions become very important in providing credit and non-credit inputs.

Infra-structure

For the same or different activities the infra-structure shall be provided by the different government departments such as Agriculture Land Development, Marketing Board, irrigation Department, State Electricity Board, Animal Husbandry Department, Public Works Department, Railway, Radio, Television Centre, State Warehousing Corporation, District Industries Centre, State Industrial and Investment Corporation etc.The availability and development of sound infra-structure should be ensured before implementing the credit plans.

Non-credit Inputs

Non-credit inputs like subsidy, improved technologies, fertilizers, HYV, pesticides, extension services (besides infra-structures) etc., shall be arranged by the concerned agencies namely DRDA, Command Area Development Authority. DIC, KVIB, Milk Plants, Agriculture and Animal Husbandry Department etc.Timely arrangement should be made for the availability of non-credit inputs.

Credit Component

Credit component will be provided by the financial institutions. The above mentioned credit and non-credit inputs should be provided in the requisite proportion to optimise the returns from investments. The requisite proportion of credit and non-credit inputs is decided at the time of finalisation stage of credit plans in BLBC meetings, which is held in month of February every year. These ought to be provided by concern departments/agencies at appropriate time.

Organisational Set-up for Implementation and Monitoring of Service Area Approach

It has rightly been said by the famous management scientist Koon'tz and O'Donnel regarding the importance of organisation that the "Good Organisation will attack the problems as they arise, excellent organisation will anticipate them and their occurrence."

As many financial and developmental institutions are engaged in the formulation and implementation of credit plans, therefore, the organisational structure in SAA is of a consortium nature. Being a joint effort, credit planning and its implementation could not succeed without the active involvement and positive co-operation of all participating agencies. The organisational set-up of SAA is more or less the same as of the old LBS except with a major difference of BLBC, a forum created at block level.

Now, it is well-established fact that the banks, being a kingpin in the whole exercise of credit planning, have to shoulder the multiple and complex responsibilities under the new scheme of rural lending. Therefore, it has become imperative for them to develop an appropriate organisational set-up and design a suitable procedural frame-work for effective implementation of the SAA. It was also felt necessary to establish the liaison between the financial institutions and other developmental agencies functioning at block, district, state and national levels. So that, accordingly different committees have been set-up at various levels, not only for brining about appropriate changes, but also for studying the problems which have cropped-up in the banking sector in the wake of SAA. A specific committee have also been constructed to probe into the deficiencies of reliable statistical data, banking legislation etc. and to suggest necessary corrective steps required for the successful, implementation of the SAA. The organisational set-up for implementation and monitoring of SAA at different levels is shown in the chart given below :

Organisational Set-up for Implementation and Monitoring of SAA

At Block Level	At Sub-Divisional Level	At District Level	At State Level	At National Level
1. BLBC 2. BLCC	Sub-divisional Recovery Committee	1. DLCC 2. Non-Lead DLCC 3. Standing Committee 4. DLRC 5. District Recovery Committee (DRC) 6. Sub Committee of DLCC 7. Case group for improvement of C. D. Ratio.	1. SLBC 2. Steering Committee 3. SLCC	1. High Power Committee (HPC) 2. Regional Consultative Committee (RCC)

The main tasks and the composition of different committees / forums have critically been discussed below :

Block Level Bankers Committee

With the introduction of SAA, BLBC has been constituted in each block to ensure better and effective co-ordination among banks and with block level officials. BLBC is constituted with the purpose to have a constructive dialogue and co-ordination amongst the participating credit and non-credit institutions. It also serves the purpose for facilitating the collection of information and passing it on to the different functionaries so that proper formulation, implementation and monitoring of credit plans become easier.

Composition of Block Level Bankers Committee

All financial institutions including the commercial banks, RRBs, PLDBs, SLDBs, DCCBs and other financial institutions which are operating in the block are its members. Besides the BDO and other technical officers of agriculture industry, co-operatives and animal husbandry department working at the block-level are also its members. LDO from RBI and DDM of NABARD are also the members of BLBC. They attended the maximum number of meetings of BLBC. The chairman of BLBC is LBO and the senior most BM (posted at block head-quarters) of the lead bank is the convenor of it. In those blocks where the lead bank does not have a branch or the branch located is far away from the block headquarters, the another bank branch at block head-quarters having largest operations in the block acts as a convenor of the BLBC. In case the LBO is unable to attend the meeting, the chairperson for the meeting is chosen by the members of BLBC. The Pradhan of Panchayat Samity may also be invited to attend the meetings of the BLBC, which are held at half-yearly intervals in February for finalisation of block credit plans and in September when a mid-term review of the block credit plan is done.

Functions Of Block Level bankers Committee

BLBC is the grass-root forum through which SAA is being implemented. The functions of BLBC have been mentioned below :

- The first and foremost function of BLBC is to hold discussion and to finalise the SAPs of participating branches after holding discussions.Further the BLBC is to aggregate the SAPs arriving at the BLCP;

- The second task of BLBC is the consideration of operational problems in implementation of the credit programmes of banks, particularly in regard to ensuring availability of inputs and linkages;
- The third task is to review o the progress in the implementation of Government sponsored schemes (SGSY, PMRY, SJSRY etc.), including their impact on the beneficiaries;
- The fourth function is to review of the implementation of the service area credit plan/block credit plan and the provision of other inputs required so that bank credit becomes more productive;
- The fifth function is the allocation of service area to a new branch which is likely be opened up in the block;
- The sixth function is to monitor the progress of lending target of priority sector/sub-targets; and
- The last function is to monitor the recovery programmes and the adequacy of the steps taken in this regard including the support available from the State Government machinery.

The meeting of BLBC is to be held at least once in a quarter. With a view to achieve the objectives of the meeting, it is necessary that the discussions in the BLBC meeting are held in accordance with the structured agenda items and the notes are prepared for each such items and circulated among members in advance.

Block Level Consultative Committee

Block level consultative committee meetings is convened by the BDO regularly on pre-decided dates and are attended by the majority of branch managers invariably. The committee reviews the progress under the Government sponsored schemes for poverty alleviation viz., SGSY, SJSRY, PMRY etc. The date of animal purchase camps or application for loans preparation camps and spot verifications arc finalised at the meeting in consultation with branch managers of respective bank branches. The problem faced by field staff is also discussed and if found necessary, are referred to DLCC.

Sub-Divisional Recovery Committee

The Chairman of this committee is Collector and the LBO is its convenor. All Tehsildars and BDOs are members of this committee. At the sub-divisional level, the role of Sub-Divisional Recovery Committee is very important. The main function of this committee is to review the recovery position of banks at the sub-divisional level and suggest corrective measures for improving the recovery position. It also reviews the cases of RODA act and hard core defaulters of Government schemes at the sub-divisional level.

District Level Consultative Committee

The District Level Consultative Committee has a crucial role to serve as useful and key forum for banks and government agencies seeking solutions to problems arising out of developmental activities under the SAA. The DLCC is the central point for implementing and reviewing the success of SAA. The standing committee of DLCC has an advisory role as an expert body to give valuable advice on the issues pertaining right from the formulation to the implementation and monitoring of ACPs.

Composition of DLCC

The overall strength of DLCC is generally maintained at the compact level of 20 to 25 members for sake of meaningful and result oriented discussions. The District Collector is the Ex-officio Chairman of the DLCC and the LBO is its convenor. Other important members of DLCC are :

(i) LDO of RBI

(ii) Representative of NABARD

(iii) District Co-ordinators representing 5-6 major banks operating in the district

(iv) Chairman of the RRB

(v) Managing Director of DCCB

(vi) General Manager of DIC

(vii) District Planning Officer

(viiii) Project Director/Officer

(ix) BM of insurance companies operating in the district

(x) BDO

(xi) Representative of KVIC

(xii) Incharge of SFC at district

(xiii) Incharge of the agriculture and animal husbandry department of the district, and

(xiv) 3-4 other development agencies may be made regular members and may be invited as special invitee as per need.

As per the guidelines of RBI, the meetings of DLCC is held quarterly in a year to review the progress of implementation of credit plan. The collector of the district, being the chairman of DLCC, presides over the meeting. His presence is supposed to ensure the co-operation of all the Govt. departments/agencies in the district. The LBO functions as a focal point being the convenor of DLCC. His main task is to consolidate the information for review of the progress under various schemes and prepare agenda papers for the meeting and its proceedings. The agenda papers of the meeting are circulated to all the members about 2 weeks in advance. The focus of meeting is to decide the action plan and the action to be taken by the various participating agencies. The committee also reviews the follow-up action taken-up by the concerned agencies / departments.

Functions of DLCC

The various functions performed by the DLCC are of great importance from the point of view of the effective and successful implementation of SAA. The DLCC is expected to perform the following main functions :

- To identify potential for bankable schemes and to formulate schemes for inclusion in the DCP/AAP;
- To finalise the DCP and to allocate shares of various institutions participating in it;
- To monitor the overall progress of DCP in the physical and financial terms in regard to its implementation;
- To identify unbanked centres for opening up of branches and to review the progress in this regard;
- To take-up such matters with the State Government/SLBC/SLCC which require attention of the higher level authorities;
- To monitor the recovery position of banks and rendering necessary help to them for recovery of overdues;
- To monitor bank-wise performance under various schemes against the targets given to them;
- To ensure smooth release of subsidies;

  To review the progress in disposal of loan applications;
- To ensure proper disbursement of loans sanctioned by the financial institutions;
- To review the progress in implementation of Government sponsored schemes (SGSY, SJSRY, PMRY);

- To monitor the support forthcoming from Government departments;
- To identify the problems and bottlenecks in the area of infra-structure,credit and non-credit inputs, credit etc and to take necessary steps to overcome them;
- To ensure that applications are sent to banks in a phased manner and not bunched in the last quarter of the financial year;
- To monitor bank-wise/sub-division-wise cases filed under the State agricultural operations (Removal of Difficulties act);
- To evaluate the benefits derived from various schemes and to suggest measures for improvement;
- To review the security arrangements and other infra-structural facilities required for rural branches;

On the basis of functions of DLCC as mentioned above, it can be inferred that DLCC is a crucial forum right from the stage of formulation of credit plans and ultimately to their implementation and monitoring. Thus, DLCC involves itself at all stages of credit planning in the district.

Non-Lead DLCC

While ensuring that DLCC becomes a compact forum for meaningful discussions, it is necessary to secure an arrangement for adequate rapport between the DLCC and those institutions which are not represented on a permanent basis. Therefore, LBO has to function as the link and liaison officer of such co-ordination by convening meetings regularly with the district co-ordinators of non lead banks. These meetings could be held well in advance of the DLCC meetings so that the problems thrown up in these meetings could be taken-up for discussion at DLCC meetings. LDO of RBI is also invited for such meetings. The special meetings of bankers convened for finalising the allocation of shares in ACP should also be attended by all participating financial institutions. In some of the districts, this meeting is named as Non-Lead DLCC meetings.

Generally, the Non-Lead DLCC is comprised of the following officials:

(i) Project Director of DRDA as its Chairman;
(ii) LBO as its convenor;
(iii) All non-member banks of DLCC;
(iv) General Manager of DIC;
(v) District Planning Officer; and
(vi) Any other Special Invitee;

The functions of Non-Lead DLCC are similar to that of DLCC.

Standing Committee

The DLCC by virtue of its constitution and its functioning may not be in a position to exercise proper supervision and control over the working of the SAA on an on-going basis and may not be able to attend the operational and procedural problems in length and depth. With a view to look in to these problems, an expert technical sub-committee of DLCC was constituted in 1980, which is popularly known as Standing Committee.

Composition of Standing Committee

The standing committee is chaired by the District Collector and convened by the LBO. Other members of the committee are the chief executive of the DRDA, LDO of RBI, representative of NABARD and other banks having major shares in SGSY earlier IRDP lending.

While DLCC meeting is held once in a quarter, the meeting of standing committee is held every month. As DLCC is the main body, the meeting of standing committee is generally not be held in the month in which the DLCC meeting is held, unless it is necessary due to some specific important reason.

Functions of Standing Committee

The standing committee acts as a task force. The main functions of the standing committee are as under :

- To identify the feasibility of newly formulated bankable schemes and to assist in reviewing the DCP;
- To look into the question of availability of necessary infra-structural facilities and supply of inputs etc. for proper implementation of the scheme;
- To examine the factors affecting flow of credit to priority sectors;
- To devise ways and means to ensure proper co-ordination among all agencies/departments;
- To follow-up closely the decisions taken by the DLCC;
- To sort out grass-root level operational problems in implementing various schemes;
- To prepare proper background notes for meaningful discussions at the DLCC meeting and circulate these to all the members well in advance;
- To act as an operative sub-committee and ensure better functioning of the DLCC thereby creating an effective impact on the development of the rural economy in the district.

District Level Review Committee

The meeting of DLRC is generally held in the second and fourth quarters of the year. A review of achievements against the targets of credit plans is done in these meetings. Problems in formulation and implementation of credit plans at various levels are identified and suitable remedial measures are suggested by the DLRC. Decisions taken in DLRC meeting are taken-up for approval in the DLCC. In addition to members of DLCC, non-officials (including local MPs and MLAs) may also be invited to get feedback on the implementation of various programmes.

Functions of DLRC

The following are the main functions of DLRC :

- To review critically activity-wise / sector-wise / bank-wise / block-wise performance under ACP;
- To suggest measure to overcome the deficiencies;
- To review critically the supply of non-credit inputs; and
- To raise any other related issues with the permission of the chair.

District Recovery Committee

DRC was constituted with the main purpose of improving the recovery position of loans and reducing the non-performing assets of banks, so as to improve their viability position. The Chairman of the committee is the District Collector and the Convenor is the LBO. The other members of the committee are Additional Collector (Development), all the regional managers of banks in the district, all block development officers, registrars of the co-operative societies, managing director of Rajasthan State Co-operative Bank and Chairman of Zila Parishad. The main function of the DRC is to review the recovery of loans under Government sponsored schemes and to give suggestions for improving the recovery position in the district. It also reviews the cases under RODA and hard core defaulters of government schemes at district level. The committee meets quarterly.

Sub-committee of DLCC

The sub-committee of DLCC is formed with the purpose of reallocation of service area of bank branches and shifting of RRB branches. The Chairman of this sub-committee is LDO of RBI and LBO is its the Convenor. The members of the sub-committee are the branch managers of all concerning banks, project director DRDA and DDM of NABARD.

Core Group for Improving the Credit Deposit Ratio

The District Collector is the Chairman of this core group and in the absence of the Collector the Additional Collector (development) will chair its meeting. LBO is the secretary and the incharge officers of DIC, RFC and bank managers are the members of the core group. The main function of this core group is to extend help in improving the situation of industrial development and also in improving motivates the new industrial establishment and improve the position of advances and deposits in the district, so that the norms of CD ratio is easily achieved.

State Level Bankers Committee

Co-ordination at the State level is achieved through SLBC. The meeting of SLBC is convened once in a quarter by the lead bank which has been designated as convenor bank at the State level. Representatives of Regional offices of major banks operating in the State, RRBs, State Co-operative Banks, SLDB, NABARD, NHB, SIDBI and RBI attend it. Representatives of Director of Institutional Finance and other concerned departments of the State Government are also attend it. Problems faced in implementation of credit plans are discussed in its meeting and efforts are made to find out an acceptable solution. The matters referred by DLCC are also discussed in it. The agenda of the meeting is prepared and circulated by the convenor bank well in advance of the meeting. It also prepares proceedings indicating the decisions taken in the meeting and action to be taken by various institution. The convenorship responsibilities of SLBC is entrusted to the specified banks on the basis of their lead responsibilities and also the spread of their network in rural areas. The Bank of Baroda has been designated as the Convenor of the SLBC of the State of Rajasthan.

Steering Committee

A sub-committee of the SLBC named as its steering committee has been formed in most of the states. It's meeting is held once in a month to review the progress of credit plans. It also discusses difficulties faced by the banks in implementing the various Government sponsored schemes such as PMRY, SGSY, SJSRY etc. and tries to find out the solutions to them.

State Level Consultative Committee

SLCC was constituted during mid-seventies to serve as a forum for co-ordination between the State Government and financial institutions and for reviewing the performance of banks particularly of the credit based development programmes of the Government. SLCC considers the problems requiring inter-bank co-ordination such as area demarcation of various schemes, uniformity in terms and conditions of credit under specific areas and removal of imbalances in availability of credit or / and filling the credit gaps.

The meeting of SLCC is convened by the State Government and presided over by the Chief Minister/ Finance Minister/ Chief Secretary of the State Government. It is attended by the registrar of co-operative societies other Government officials, representatives of banks, RRBs, SCB, SLDB, NABARD and RBI. The meeting of SLCC is generally held once in a year. However, there is no uniformity in the constitution of SLCCs and regularity in conducting such meetings as these meetings are convened by the State Government.

High Power Committee

On the recommendations of the study group on the working of lead bank scheme at the apex level, a high power committee was constituted by the RBI to provide necessary guidance on various matters pertaining to the LBS. The High power committee is presided over by the Deputy Governor of RBI. The Chairman of this committee is Deputy Governor of RBI and the other members of the committee are:

- Joint Secretary of Banking Division, Ministry of Finance, GOI;
- Managing Director of NABARD;
- Director of NIBM;
- Secretary / Director of Institutional Finance of four state governments;
- Chairman of SBI;
- Chairman and managing director of five major banks;
- Representatives of all India Federation of State Co-operative banks and State Land Development Banks.

The membership of lead banks and State Governments will be roated every two years with the purpose of giving opportunity to different banks and State Governments to associate them with the committee. The meetings of the committee are held, generally, twice in a year. The agenda for discussion in the meeting of the committee normally include the following :

- Problems faced by financial institutions in the implementation of credit plans and the measures to overcome them;
- Suggestions received from the various organisations pertaining to improvement of schemes;
- Policy matters regarding the improvement in the skills of formulation and implementation of credit plans.

Regional Consultative Committee

Regional Consultative Committee (RCC) is the highest forum for evaluating the functions of SAA. The meetings of RCC is convened by the Ministry of Finance, Government of India for each region separately, normally once in two years. The meetings of RCC are presided over by the Union Minister of Finance. The representatives, among others include the Chief Ministers of the concerned states supported by Senior Officers, Governor, Deputy Governor and senior officials of RBI, Chairman of NABARD and Chairman of other All India Financial Institutions, Chairman and Managing Director of Nationalised banks.

In RCC meetings, development of banking with reference to branch expansion, credit deposit ratio, investments, priority credit and problems relating to development of banking are reviewed. The minutes of the meeting are taken by the Union Ministry of Finance and circulated to banks, State Governments and RBI for follow-up and implementation purpose. Problems which are very important and generally remain unsolved at the state level are referred to this committee requiring decisions at the apex level.

The whole country has been divided into six regions covering two or more states for the purpose of constituting RCC for monitoring the performance of credit plans. The RCC assesses and reviews the performance of public sector banks specially to their lending operations to priority and hitherto neglected sectors.

The State of Rajasthan is the member of the Northern region RCC. The other members of this committee are Haryana, Himachal Pradesh, Jammu and Kashmir and Chandigarh.

Besides various committees as mentioned above, there are some other important institutions, Government departments / agencies and officials who play vital role in the process of implementing and monitoring the credit plans. The organisational set-up of such institutions and officials have been discussed below.

Reserve Bank of India

The overall responsibility of successful implementation and monitoring of credit plans under the SAA in the country is of RPCD of the RBI. It issues necessary guidelines and instructions regarding various aspects of credit planning under the SAA and lending to priority sector. The RPCD has regional offices to co-ordinate the activities of various banks and Government agencies at state and district levels. It deputes its Lead District Officer (LDO) to attend various meetings called at district level in his respective district and monitor the implementation of AAPs.

Role of Lead District Officer

The LDO is appointed by the RBI from its Rural Planning and Credit Department, who monitors closely the developmental activities in the allotted district to him. Generally, 3-4 districts are allotted to the LDO. If the geographical size of the districts are very large, hilly or backward, the number of districts allotted to him may be restricted to 2 districts only. Where the NABARD has opened up its office at district level the post of LDO has been abolished and the role of LDO is performed now by the DDM of NABARD.

The main responsibilities of the LDO are discribed below :

- Effective participation in the meetings of DLCC, SC and the other forums at the district level and lending support to LBO;
- Discussions with LBO, District Co-ordinators and concerned government development departments/agencies to identify problem areas and help in finding solutions;
- Monitoring the implementation of AAPs financial agencies and the government departments with special reference to poverty alleviation programmes namely SGSY, SJSRY, PMRY etc.;
- Visits to bank branches in the district to ascertain progress and problems;
- Monitoring of the implementation of procedures and instructions of RBI at the ground level;
- Acting as a link between the district and state levels on various matters connected with the credit plans under SAA.

NABARD

NABARD is an apex bank for the agriculture and rural development in the country which is responsible for planning, co-ordination and monitoring the rural credit delivery system at the district level. Accordingly, NABARD is gradually setting up its offices at the district level with a few technical experts keeping in view the predominant economic activities of the district. The district office of NABARD not only co-ordinates the activities of various credit agencies, but also keeps contact with the concerned development departments of the government. The LBO acts in close co-ordination with the NABARD district office. The DDM of the NABARD who is stationed in the district assists the LBO in formulating the DCP and formulates the PLPs.

Potential Linked Plans

NABARD has been preparing potential linked credit plans for each district since 1988-89. To facilitate development of available potential through credit, NABARD inter-alia, has been mapping/updating sector-wise potential and dovetailing credit plan with development plan of the Govt. through PLPs on an on-going basis. It is a comprehensive useful reference document which covers the priority sector financing of banks with emphasis on rural financing. PLP helps to various organisations involved in the process of rural development in directing their efforts in a planned manner in accordance with the available potential. It also assists in enabling optimum utilisation of scarce financial resources by channelising them towards sectors with growth potential. It also gives assessment of gaps in infra-structural support, which needs to be bridged to facilitate development of the realisable potential.

PLPs are used by bankers and other credit agencies for preparing their own credit plans. Since PLP indicates broad perspective of service area plan, it is expected that the information/data contained in the document will be utilised by the Lead District Managers / Offices while preparing the background paper for the service area plans. The document also contains many useful information for the government departments and developmental agencies at the district level.

Government Agencies

The involvement of the District Collector, being overall in-charge of the district administration, is imperative for the success of credit plans under SAA. The district collector acts as Chairman of DLCC, DLRC and

DRC. At district level, a separate organisation for looking after the task of district rural development has been set-up in each district, which is popularly known as District Rural Development Agency (DRDA). Though the overall in-charge of this organisation is the district collector, but in view of his business in other administrative work, the Additional District Magistrate (ADM), development or Project Director is designated as the incharge of the DRDA. The DRDA provides the necessary government assistance for the implementation and monitoring the AAPs. In order to ensure co-ordination at state level, a separate department 'Directorate of Institutional Finance' has been set-up in each state with a senior official of the rank of secretary as its incharge.

Organisation Set-up at Zonal Office and Head Office Level of Commercial Banks

The zonal office is responsible for effective and successful implementation of credit plans under the SAA not only in its lead districts, but also in non-lead districts too. It has also been assigned the task of monitoring the progress of credit plans alongwith their implementation. For this purpose, a representative of zonal office attends meetings of SLBC/SLCC and ensures implementation of the targets allotted to the branches in its zone. The zonal office also consolidates various data/ information at its level and submit them to the Head Office. The Head office keeps a watch on the implementation of the SAA in the entire country. On the basis of guidelines received from RBI, NABARD and GOI, the Head Office of a bank issues necessary instructions to branches through its Zonal/Regional offices.

Regional Rural Banks

RRBs have been set-up mainly with the purpose of creating an alternative source of credit and for making the accessibility of credit easier to the rural people. At present, RRBs have sufficient involvement and stake in the rural credit, therefore, they are active partners in the holy cause of rural development. For making their role effective in the development of rural areas, a special cell should be created at the head office level under the charge of some senior officer, who should not only co-ordinate the various activities pertaining to formulation, implementation and monitoring the credit plans under the SAA, but also take keen interest in the proceedings of the various meetings.

Co-operative Banks

As we all know that co-operative banks are playing a very significant role in financing agriculture and village/cottage industries, obviously they have sufficient involvement in the credit/savings process. A separate cell may be created at the head offices of DCCBs to attend to the work relating to the SAA. A representative from DCCB may attend the meetings called at district level and a representative from SCB may attend the meetings called at state level.

As far as LDBs are concerned, it is observed that jurisdiction of PLDBs/ branches of SLDBs may not necessarily synchronise with the districts. However, SLDBs have established regional offices covering a few districts. These regional offices may create a lead bank cell and represent LDBs at district level. A representative from head office of SLDB represent at state level meetings.

Role of District Co-ordinator of Non-lead Bank

Non-lead banks in the district have appointed district co-ordinators to represent their bank. The district co-ordinators should report directly to the Regional/ Divisional office which controls the branches in the district. Some of the banks have appointed the Regional Managers as District co-ordinators which help them to ensure implementation of the targets allotted to their banks. Following are the main responsibilities of the district co-ordinators.

- To attend all meetings convened by the lead bank of the district regularly. He should also attend standing committee meetings wherever he is co-opted as a member and other relevant forums created by the Government for lead bank in his capacity as a co-ordinator.
- To study the minutes of the meeting thoroughly and minutely and take follow-up-action with controlling office/branch managers wherever required.
- To help the branch managers in rural areas for timely submission of data/information required under SAA to RBI, lead bank, GOI and other Government bodies by guiding them suitably.
- To have acquintance of the various schemes that are in operation in that particular district and should also to have the complete understanding of the DCP/AAP prepared by the lead bank for

effective monitoring of the targets given to his bank. He should also report to his controlling office wherever there are difficulties in achieving the targets so that solutions could be found and implementation is done as per the plan.

- To maintain close rapport with all the branches of his bank in the district and should monitor the performance of each branch in relation to plan allocation under the AAPs.
- To maintain close liaison with the LBO, LDO, and various Government departments of the district connected with the implementation of various developmental schemes.
- To convey the important decision taken at the DLCC meetings to all the branches in the districts.
- To review constantly the performance of each branch with reference to the share allocation and provide necessary feed back to the lead bank regarding performance of the bank under the AAPs, including the special programme like SGSY etc.
- He should present the problems regarding the implementation of AAPs, if any, faced by the branches in the DLCC meetings.

In nut-shell, the district co-ordinator is expected to perform various functions as narrated above with deep sense of involvement and responsibility. In view of the multi-faceted role of the district co-ordinator, he is conceived as a 'District Officer'.

Role of Lead Bank Officer

The lead bank of the district concerned has to designate one of its officers as the lead bank officer. Thus, in all districts of the country one LBO is appointed by the respective lead bank of the district. The lead bank of the district is designated by the RBI after considering the spread of branches in the district concerned, besides many other factors. The LBO is the kingpin in the whole process of credit planning. Without the active participation and deep involvement of LBO, neither realistic credit plans can be formulated nor they can be implemented successfully.

In view of the importance of the LBO, some senior officer should be appointed as he has to deal with the other branch managers of his bank. As far as possible, his rank should not be lower than that of a branch manager of district headquarters and he should report directly to the controlling authority of the bank who supervises the branches in the district. He is assisted in his role by the DDM of NABARD and the LDO of RBI.

LBO is a catalyst in mobilising co-operation and co-ordination from other banks and government departments for achieving the objectives of SAA. Among others, the following are the important functions of the LBO :

- To carry the message of the new concept to managers functioning in his lead district;
- To convene DLCC/SC/DLRC meetings regularly in time as per RBI / head office instructions;
- To convene the meeting of DCOs of non-lead banks before the DLCC meeting as per the RBI guidelines;
- To circulate notice/agenda and detailed background papers for DLCC/SC/ DLRC/DCOs meetings among all concerned well in time;
- To preside over the BLBC meetings to sort out the bottlenecks with active assistance and co-operation of block level government agencies;
- To evolve strategy for fulfilment of commitments under DCP/ AAP/SGSY and other sponsored programmes by branches of his bank as well as other banks operating in the district;
- To regularly monitor the progress achieved by his bank as well as other banks vis-a-vis the targets allotted under DCP/AAP/ SGSY and other sponsored schemes, and identify the problems, wherever they exist, with reasons thereof and suggest suitable remedial measures to overcome them;
- To collect the compiled information and statistical data from all banks, concerned government agencies for circulation with agenda papers and presentation in various meetings to make the deliberation meaningful and result oriented;
- To prepare the minutes of DLCC/SC/DLRC/DCOs meetings and circulate them among all concerned in time;
- To follow-up the decisions taken in various DLCC/SC/DLRC meetings with the concerned financial institutions and government department/agency and to review the progress achieved in subsequent meetings;
- To monitor the progress of lead bank branches in the district vis-à-vis the budgets for priority sector advances and various sub-goals viz.,direct agricultural advances,advances to weaker sections, DRI advances, advances to SC/ST under DRI Scheme etc.;

- To help and guide the branches in achieving their targets under priority sector advances;
- To motivate poor performing branch managers to achieve deposit targets and priority sector budgets and to give greater emphasis to lending to weaker sections under priority sectors;
- To assist branches in the matter of recovery of loans particularly in respect of difficult accounts and also improving the recovery position for achievement of recovery budgets;
- To keep liaison with district/tehsil authorities for effecting recovery;
- To maintain liaison with the district Government officials connected with developmental activities;
- To acquaint himself with the latest economic development and poverty alleviation programmes being implemented in the district;
- Conduct evaluation studies to assess the impact of SAA;
- To utilise effectively the services of the technical field officer viz.; agricultural officers, SSI officers for formulation of new projects identified in the DCP/AAP, processing of loan proposals, recovery of dues etc.; and
- Any other responsibility related with SAA assigned by Regional Manager/ Zonal Manager/ Head Office.

Revised Monitoring and Information System under SAA

With the objective of effective monitoring of credit plans under SAA information system has been modified for collection of data. In order to facilitate expeditious compilation and analysis of data, the help of computer is also being taken for this purpose. In this context, revised monitoring and information system has been introduced from April, 1st 1991. A 'Management Information System' (MIS) consisting of LBR returns has been developed. With the help of these returns, data are compiled for monitoring purpose against the targets in the various meetings convened at block, district and State levels. In addition to the monitoring in various meetings under SAA, the controlling authorities of banks also continue to have an overall review of the priority sector advances in respect of the branches under their control.

In MIS, with a view to ensuring the smooth sectoral flow of credit in the direction of priority areas/ sectors under the SAPs the performance under these plans are continue to be monitored at three levels :

(i) at the village level - by the branches themselves (including co-operatives) for each of the village in their service area in relation to VCPs.

(ii) by the controlling authorities/administrative offices of the respective credit agencies; and

(iii) at the block level by the BLBC;

At the district level, monitoring is being done on bank-wise and activity-wise basis by the LBO/DDM of NABARD. For effective monitoring, it is essential to have a complete picture of overall credit related programmes in the district. The LBOs accordingly collect full information on all credit related activities and furnish the same to the DDM of the NABARD in the form of computer printouts/ floppy discs.

The monitoring of the progress of priority sector lending, activity-wise, pattern of flow of credit position of deposits and advances, number of cases suit-filed is done through the modified computerised format LBR-2, LBR-U2, LBR-3 and LBR-U3 in the credit plan by the branches and in the returns mentioned above, are proposed to be computerised at the district level. The consolidation of the data, through such computerised arrangements (service area-wise, block-wise and institution-wise) is the responsibility of the LBO.

The arrangements for computerisation in each district of the country have been made for quick and correct compilation of data and its analysis including in all four districts of Hadoti region, namely Baran, Bundi, Jhalawar and Kota.

There are four types of returns to be submitted by the branches to the LBO, DCO and focal point BM for onward submission to their respective controlling offices, as mentioned below :

S. No.	*Nature of Return*	*Return Number*	*Periodicity*	*Due date for submission by the branch*
A.	*For indicating the progress of disbursement of financial assistance periodically.*			
	(a) Service area credit disbursal scroll (SAS)	LBR-2	Monthly	Before 7th of the month to which the return relates.
	(b) Credit disbursal in semi-urban/ urban areas.	LBR-U2	Quarterly	Before 7th of the month succeeding the quarter to which the return relates.

B. For indicating the progress of recovery and position of outstanding credit.			
(a) Service area recovery and outstanding (SAR)	LBR-3	Quarterly	Before 30th of the month succeeding the quarter to which the return relates.
(b) Semi-urban/ urban area recovery and outstanding	LBR-U3	Quarterly	Before 30th of the month succeeding the quarter to which the return relates.

Description of returns LBR-2, LBR-U2, LBR-3 and LBR-U3 in brief is given below :

Service Area Credit Disbursement Scroll

The Service Area Credit Disbursement Scroll is also known as Service Area Scroll (SAS) in which there are two types of returns LBR-2 and LBR-U2. The information is given by the service area branch to its controlling offices and respective agencies. The main focus area of monitoring through LBR-2 and LBR-U2 are listed as under :

- Number of units to be completed;
- Number and aggregate disbursements for all on-going units; and
- Amount to be disbursed under each potential sector/ sub-sector/ category/ activity.

For indicating the progress of disbursement of financial assistance periodically all the credit agencies viz. CBs, RRBs, DCCBs, LDBs and non-banking financial agencies are required to maintain a SAS containing details relating to the villages, borrower, activity and disbursement, branch-wise. The semi-urban/urban branches with service area allocations are also prepare LBR-2 for recording the credit disbursals in respect of lendings in the rural areas under their command, but for recording the lendings in the urban areas, they are maintained only quarterly statements in LBR-U2.

The transactions are recorded daily by the officials of the credit agencies from daily vouchers and the existing books of accounts viz. Loan registers/ledgers or the Day Book. SAS are prepared in perforated registers with three sheets for each page. Each set of pages has three different colours viz. white for LBO, green for controlling authority and pink for branch. The SAS is closed every month after striking totals and submitted on a monthly basis as at the end of each month to the LBO and the respective controlling offices by seventh of the following month to which it relates. A copy of the scroll is invariably sent to the district co-ordinator/ focal point branch whose job is to follow-up it with defaulting branches for timely submission of the scroll on a monthly basis.

After the cash book/ day book is tallied, the entries relating to advances / loan accounts are segregated from other vouchers and further segregated into those of priority and non-priority sectors. Non-priority sector transactions are to be clubbed and reported as a single item for each classification i.e. Non-priority Sector (NPS), Housing and NPS others, in the scroll LBR-2 on a daily basis and not on a voucher-wise basis.

The co-operative agencies may maintain a single LBR-2 scroll covering all the credit operations of a branch at DCCB level on a branch-wise basis. Group loans disbursed through PACs tie-up arrangements, dairy societies etc. is reported as a single account. In this context, it is pertinent to mention that non-banking financial agencies like SFCs is also follow suit so far as LBR-2 is concerned. The recording in the SAS needs to be accurate in relevant columns.

Service Area Recovery and Outstanding Statement and Recovery and Outstanding Semi-urban / Urban Branches

Service area recovery and outstanding statement is popularly known as SAR. The data regarding the recovery and outstanding of loans are given in LBR-3. As per the guidelines of RBI, the LBS returns 1-2 and 5-6 have been merged and a Service area/ Branch recovery and outstanding return LBR-3 has been introduced for submission on a quarterly basis. The procedure for filling in the format is the same as prescribed for the existing LBS returns 1-2 and 5-6.

A separate format LBR-U3 by integrating LBS 1,2 and LBS 5,6 for reporting priority sector lendings - outstandings as well as DCCB position by the semi-urban / urban branches of all agencies viz. CBs, RRBs, DCCBs, PLDBs/SFCs has been devised to facilitate integration of data in the revised system. Format columns 1 to 3 are meant for reporting outstandings, sector-wise on quarterly basis, as at the end of last Friday of March, June, September and December, the columns 4 to 9 are designed for reporting recovery position, branch-wise, as at the end of last Friday of June every year. The columns 4 to 9 are to be reported in respect of loans to agriculture and allied activities and other priority sector on a sector-wise basis and not activity-wise. For the purpose of filling in LBR-3 and LBR-U3, it is necessary that all the outstanding loans are so categorised as to fit into the alphabetical sectoral codes (A-O). Though, it is a difficult task, but it is must for branches and controlling offices should extend necessary support to the branches in this regard. These returns are compiled branch-wise and made available by all branches of credit agencies to the LBO within a month from the end of quarter to which the return relates.

The LBO provides the consolidated data for BLBC, DLCC meetings etc. as hitherto and the DDM of NABARD wherever posted will provide selective analysis/report.

Returns LBR-2 and LBR-3 duly signed under branch seal by branch managers with date, in token of authentication, is submitted alongwith identification slip, to LBO. Identification slips are different for each return and are attached at first page with each LBR return.

The district co-ordinator / focal point branch managers of various banks, co-operative bank's in-charge and non-banking financial institutions at the district level and BLBC convenors are extending help to LBO in the collection of returns from the branches of credit agencies functioning under their control/in their biocks.

The data reported in the LBR returns are being computerised at the district level. The consolidation of the data, through such computerised arrangements (service area-wise, branch-wise and institution-wise) is the responsibility of the LBO. The software package for the computer programmes are provided by the NABARD.

The LBO collects all the returns and hand over them to the computer agency. Data captured by input devices are transferred on floppies (sector/activity/special programme/code-wise etc.) and made available by the LBO to the DDM of NABARD to enable in depth analysis and monitoring on sector/activity-wise basis through personal computers and for follow-up with branches wherever necessary. The printouts are made available by the LBO to the BMs controlling offices, BLBC, DLCC, Lead Bank and SLBC convenor, as required. The LBO may obtain copies of the prescribed outputs from the computer agency and provide the usual feedback for the BLBC/DLCC review meetings to enable analytical review. The analysis reports in respect of special programmes may also be obtained and submitted to BLBC/DLCC etc. by LBO.

The submission and processing of outputs have a definite time schedule. This time schedule mentioned as under are to be strictly adhered to by the LBO as well as by the computer cell also:

	Name of return	*From*	*To submission*	*Due Date/ Period for of return*
Annual	LBR-1	LBO	Computer	1st March of the preceding financial year
	LBR-U1	LBO	- do -	- do -
	Reports LBR-1, & LBR-U1	Computer Agency	LBO	15th March of the preceding financial year year
Monthly	LBR-2	LBO	Computer Agency	10 days after the month and within 3 weeks after the month's end
Quarterly	LBR-U2	LBO	Computer Agency	within 10 days of qtr. end
	LBR-3	- do -	- do -	within 5 weeks of qtr. end
	LBR-U3	- do -	- do -	- do -
	Reports			
	(a) LBR-3&U3	LBO	LBO	within 7 weeks of qtr. end
	(b) LBR-2&U2	- do -	- do -	within 3 weeks of qtr. end

The LBO procures the printout reports from computer agency as per time schedule and send it to various officials. The channel of reporting under revised monitoring and information system is given below in a schematic chart :

SL.	*Printout reports on returns*	*To*	*Time Frame*
1.	(A) LBR-1 & LBR-U1 Block-wise/Branch-wise/ Sector-wise/Activity-wise/Service-wise credit plan	a) All branches of credit agencies. b) Concerned BLBC Convenor c) Concerned BDO d) DDM,NABARD	By the end of third week of March of preceding financial year.
	(B) For DLCC purpose Agency-wise/Branch-wise/Block-wise/ Sector-wise District Credit Plan	a) All branches of credit agencies b) All district co-ordinators of credit agencies c) DDM,NABARD d) DLCC forum	By the end of third week of March of preceding financial year in DLCC meeting.

2.	(A) LBR-2&LBR-U2 for review at block level. (a) Performance Tables Block-wise/Branch-wise/Agency-wise of (i) Service area plans (ii) Semi-urban/urban area plans (iii) Govt. Sponsored programs (b) Review/Analysis Reports	a) Concerned BLBC Convenor b) DDM, NABARD	Within three weeks from the end of relevant quarter.
	(B) For review at district level (a) Performance Tables Agency-wise/branch-wise/service-wise/area-wise/sector-wise/Govt. program-wise (b) Review/Analysis Reports	BLBC forum	In BLBC meeting
3.	(A) LBR-3 & U3 for review at (a) Performance Tables Agency-wise/Branch-wise/sector-wise/block-wise. (b) Review/Analysis reports	a) Concerned BLBC Convenor b) DDM, NABARD c) Convenor SLBC d) BLBC forum	Within three weeks from the end of relevant quarter in BLBC meeting.
	(B) For review at district level (a) Performance Tables Agency-wise/branch-wise/sector-wise. (b) Selective analysis	a) All district co-ordinators b) DLCC forum DLCC forum	Within three weeks from the end of relevant quarter. In DLCC meeting. - do -

The LBO also sends the computer prints of consolidated position for the district as a whole (credit agency-wise and special programmes) to :

(i) Convenor of SLBC

(ii) DDM/Regional office of NABARD

(iii) SFC etc. and

(iv) Development agencies concerned

Regional office of NABARD consolidates the data district-wise and state-wise and send these to :

(i) RPCD, RBI (Regional Office)

(ii) National Bank - Head Office

(iii) RPCD, RBI (Central Office) and

(iv) SLBC (State Level Bankers Committee)

Thus, there remains no doubt and hitch in accepting the fact that revised monitoring and information system has become more simple, scientific and effective than earlier one. Besides it, there is a wide network of monitoring and follow-up machinery operating right from village/ block level to the highest level of RBI. In order to ensure smooth functioning of SAA and also the new information and monitoring system, the RBI has been advising the banks from time to time to give necessary importance to it. Controlling offices of banks should ensure that the branches under their control are used to submit necessary returns as per the prescribed time schedule, so that data may be available in time for reviewing the progress of the banks under different schemes. But still, there exist a lot of problems in the implementation and monitoring of SAA due to inadequate and inaccurate data alongwith the basic problem of co-ordination between different institutions.

The success and glory of SAA rests mainly in the hands of those who implement and monitor it. Therefore, without sincere sense of belongingness and deep sense of involvement and participation on the part of all financial and developmental agencies in the process of implementation, monitoring and follow-up action, success of SAA cannot be ensured in the real sense.

REFERENCES

1. Report of the working group to review the working of lead bank scheme (Chairman - U.K. Sarma, the then Chief officer, Deptt. of Banking Operations and Development, RBI), December, 1982.

2. Revised guidelines on credit planning and monitoring under Service Area Approach, March 1991, RBI.
3. "Report of the working on priority sector lending and 20 point economic programme - Role of Banks", SBI, Monthly Review, November, 1980.
4. Organisational Framework for the Implementation of Social Objectives, RBI.
5. Sarda, D.P. - Handbook on lending to priority sector (1998), Govind Prakashan, Jaipur.
6. Arumugum, P. - Lead Bank System and Service Area Approach in India (1990), UDH Publishing House, Delhi.
7. Juneja, N.K. - Service Area Approach, 1992, Manas Publication, Delhi.
8. Kumar, Ashok - New Approach in Rural Development (1994), Anmol Prakashan, New Delhi.
9. Jatana, Renu - Lead Bank Scheme (1996), Printwell, Jaipur.
10. Krishnaswami & Sheshaih - The Lead Bank Scheme (1985), Rainbow Publications, Coimbatore, Tamil Nadu.
11. Singh. G. - Rural Credit Planning, 2000, RBSA Publishers, Jaipur.

□■□

Chapter 6

Critical Appraisal of Service Area Approach in Hadoti Region

The Hadoti region is comprised of four districts, namely Baran, Bundi, Jhalawar and Kota district of the State of Rajasthan. Though, the concept of SAA was launched on 1st April, 1989 throughout the whole country with a view to improve the quality of lending, linking the credit input with the level of production, productivity and generation of income, but the period of this study was deliberately restricted from 1991-92 to 1999-2000 with a view to have the data for the same period, so that they become comparable as district Baran came into existence only on April 10, 1991. This will help in making inter-district comparison and will also help in arriving at correct conclusions.

In this chapter, the functioning and the operational aspects of SAA in Hadoti region has been analysed during the period 1991-92 to 1999-2000. The critical analysis is done to evaluate the performance of DCP under the new scheme of credit planning known as SAA. The performance of credit plans has been evaluated not only in Hadoti region, but also inter-district comparisons have been made to find out the positive and negative points in each district alongwith the difference, nature and influence of local factors. The various operational aspects related to the critical appraisal of SAA have been discussed in length and depth in this chapter under following suitable headings.

THE PRESENT STATUS OF BANKING DEVELOPMENT

In Hadoti Region

The total number of bank branches in Hadoti region is presented in table no. 6.1 This table depicts that there were 379 total branches of all banks in the region. So far the number of bank branches in individual district is concerned, the Kota district was having the highest number of branches (141) up to the end of March, 2000 in the region, followed by Jhalawar district (85), Baran district (78) and Bundi district (75) respectively.

The *table no. 6.1* also depicts the present status of banking development in different districts of the region. On the basis of the analysis of this table the following inferences can be drawn :

District Baran

The total number of branches of all banks in district Baran was 78 at the end of March, 2000. The table exhibits that the highest number of branches were of HKGB (24), which accounted for around 31% of the total branches in the district. In terms of number of branches SBBJ stood second (15) followed by CBI (9) in the district.

The total number of branches of the DCCB, PLDB, Baran Nagrik Sahkari Bank (BNSB), PNB, UCO Bank and BOR were having 8, 6, 6, 3, 2 and 2 branches respectively, while SBI, BOB and UBI were having only one branch each in the district. The total number of all types of banks which were operating in the district were 12. Among them 8 were, CBs, 2 were co-operative banks and one each was PLDB and HKGB.

Besides the number of branches as mentioned above in district Baran Sorsan, Badora, Garada, Parania, Mundiar, Mothpur and Rajpur branches of HKGB were also functioning as a 'Satellite' office of main branches. Rajasthan Finance Corporation (RFC) and Khadi and Gramodyog Vikas Board (KVIB) were also functioning in the district having only one office each.

The Lead Bank of district Baran is Central Bank of India and was at second place after the SBBJ in terms of numbers of branches amongst CBs in the district.

District Bundi

The study of table no. 6.1 manifests that at the end of March, 2000 the total number of branches of all banks in the district Bundi were 75. The highest number of branches in the district were of Bundi-Chittor Kshetriya Gramin Bank (BCKGB) (31), which accounted for around 41% of the total branches in the district. In terms of number of bank branches, the second place was of BOB (14) in the district, followed by DCCB (9), BOR (6) and SBBJ (5) respectively, while the SBI, PNB and PLDB were having 2 branches each in the district. CBI, BOI, UCO Bank and Bundi-Urban Co-operative Bank were having only one branch each in district Bundi.

Table No. 6.1

Total Number of Bank Branches in Hadoti Region

(As on March31, 2000)

S. No.	Name of the Bank	Baran Dist. (No. of Bank Branches)	Bundi Dist (No. of Bank Branches)	Jhalawar Dist (No. of Bank Branches)	Kota Dist (No. of Bank Branches)	Total of the Region (No. of Bank Branches)
1.	Central Bank of India (CBI)	09	01	18	15	43
2.	State Bank of Bikaner and Jaipur (SBBJ)	15	05	09	20	49
3.	Bank of Baroda (BOB)	01	14	-	04	19
4.	State Bank of India (SBI)	01	02	03	04	10
5.	Punjab National Bank (PNB)	03	02	05	06	16
6.	The Bank of Rajasthan Ltd. (BOR)	02	06	04	13	25
7.	United Commercial Bank of India (UCO)	02	01	-	03	06
8.	Union Bank of India (UBI)	01	-	-	02	03
9.	Bank of India (BOI)	-	01	-	06	07
10.	State Bank of Indore	-	-	-	01	01
11.	Oriental Bank of Commerce (OBC)	-	-	-	03	03
12.	Punjab and Sindh Bank	-	-	-	01	01
13.	Allahabad Bank	-	-	-	01	01

Contd....

S. No.	Name of the Bank	Baran Dist. (No. of Bank Branches)	Bundi Dist (No. of Bank Branches)	Jhalawar Dist. (No. of Bank Branches)	Kota Dist (No. of Bank Branches)	Total of the Region (No. of Bank Branches)
14.	Bank of Maharashtra	-	-	-	01	01
15.	Dena Bank	-	-	-	01	01
16.	Indian Overseas Bank	-	-	-	01	01
17.	Syndicate Bank	-	-	-	01	01
18.	Canara Bank	-	-	-	01	01
19.	State Bank of Patiyala	-	-	-	01	01
20.	State Bank of Hyderabad	-	-	-	01	01
21.	Corporation Bank	-	-	-	01	01
22.	Hadoti Kshetriya Gramin Bank (HKGB)	24	31	25	34	114
23.	Primary Land Development Bank (PLDB)	06	02	07	05	20
24.	District Central Co-operative Bank (DCCB)	08	09	14	11	42
25.	Nagrik Sahkari Bank	06	-	-	04	10
26.	Bundi Urban Co-operative Bank	-	01	-	-	01
	TOTAL	**78**	**75**	**85**	**141**	**379**

Source: DCP of 2000-2001 of Baran, Bundi, Jhalawar and Kota districts.

The total number of banks which were operating in Bundi district were 12. Among them 8 were CBs, 2 were Co-operative banks, 1 each was PLDB and RRB. RFC and KVIB were also functioning in Bundi district having only one office each in the district.

The Lead Bank of district Bundi is Bank of Baroda and it was having prime position amongst CBs in terms of number of branches in the district.

District Jhalawar

In district Jhalawar, there were 85 branches in all. Out of these total branches, the highest number of branches were of HKGB (25) followed by CBI (18), DCCB (14), SBBJ (9) and PLDB (7). The number of branches of PNB, BOR and SBI were 5, 4 and 3 respectively. The total number of banks operating in the Jhalawar district were 8 and out of them 5 were CBs, 2 Co-operative banks and 1 RRB. RFC and KVIB were also functioning and having only one office each in the district.

The Lead Bank of district Jhalawar is Central Bank of India which was having highest number of branches amongst the CBs in the district.

District Kota

There were 141 total bank branches in district Kota and out of them 87 branches were of CBs, 34 branches of HKGB and 20 branches of Co-operative banks. The total number of banks operating in the district were 25 and out of them 21 were CBs, 3 were Co-operative banks and 1 RRB.

Amongst all banks, HKGB was having highest number of branches (34) in the district which was around 24% of the total branches, followed by CBI (15), BOR (13) and KCCB (11). The total number of branches of the BOI, PNB, PLDB, SBI, BOB, Nagrik Sahkari Bank, UCO Bank, OBC and UBI were 6,6,5,4,4,4,3,3 and 2 respectively. Rest of the CBs in the district were having only one branch each as indicated in the table. RFC and KVIB were also functioning in the district and were also having one office each respectively.

The Lead Bank of district Kota is Central Bank of India and it was at second place after the SBBJ in terms of number of branches amongst CBs in the district.

The Nature/Type of Bank Branches in Hadoti Region

The type of bank branches in Hadoti region is shown in *table no. 6.2.* The study of this table reveals the following facts :

(1) There were 379 total bank branches in the region. Out of them 213 were rural branches, which was just more than half (56%) of the total branches in the region. The total number of Semi-urban branches were 94 (25%), followed by Urban branches numbering 72 (19%).

(2) There were in all 78 total branches of banks in district Bara. Out of them rural branches were 46 which accounted for around (59%) of the total bank branches. The total number of semi-urban branches were 32, which was around 41% of the total branches. The astonishing fact about the district is that it does not have any urban branch at district head quarter itself has been termed as semi-urban area as per the norms of RBI.

Table No.6.2

Nature/Type of Bank Branches in Hadoti Region

(*As on March 31, 2000*)

S. N.	Nature/Type of Bank Branches in Hadoti	BARAN	BUNDI	JHALAWAR	KOTA	Total of the Region
1.	Rural Branches	46 (59)	50 (66.67)	60 (70.59)	57 (40.42)	213 (56.20)
2.	Semi-Urban Branches	32 (41)	24 (32)	25 (29.41)	13 (9.22)	94 (24.80)
3.	Urban Branches	-	01 (1.33)	-	71 (50.36)	72 (19)
	TOTAL	78	75	85	141	379

Note : Percentage in bracket denotes percentage of total.

Source: PLP of NABARD 2000-2001 of Baran, Bundi, Jhalawar and Kota Districts

(3) Out of the total 75 bank branches in district, Bundi 50 branches were rural, which accounted for 66.66% of the total ; while the semi-urban branches were 24, which was around 32% of the total and remaining 1 branch was urban.

(4) There were 78 total branches of banks in district Jhalawar. Out of which rural branches were 60 which accounted for 70.5% of the total. The total number of semi-urban branches were 25, which was 29.41% of the total in the district. It is surprising to mention here that the district Jhalawar does not have any single urban branch.

(5) In district Kota, there were 141 total branches, out of them 57 were rural branches, which was 40.42% of the total branches. The total number of urban branches were 74 which was 50.36% of the total, followed by semi-urban branches numbering 13 (9.22%).

Thus, on the basis of above analysis, we can generalise as under :

(1) In the whole region, the highest number of branches were in rural areas followed by semi-urban and urban areas.

(2) The total number of rural branches in the region exceeded the total number of semi-urban and urban branches. This clearly snows that banks accorded more priority in opening-up branches in the rural areas than the semi-urban and urban areas in the region. This indicates that the development of rural communities has received more attention in the region over the years, which is a good sign.

(3) The highest number of rural branches in whole region is in Jhalawar district, followed by Kota, Bundi and Baran district respectively.

(4) Taking together the semi-urban and urban branches, the Kota district stood first followed by Baran district. Bundi district and Jhalawar district were having the same number of semi-urban and urban branches.

(5) The lead banks of all four districts in the region were having fairly large number of branches in view of the lead role in their respective district. While making inter-district comparison, it comes to our notice that the lead bank in district Jhalawar was having highest number of bank branches (18), followed by district Kota (15), Bundi (14) and Baran (9) respectively.

Average Number of Villages in a Service Area in Hadoti Region

The SAA is a framework in which each bank branch concentrates on a specified area for extending productive lending to the rural people. Under the SAA each bank branch has a definite 'Service Area' covering certain number of villages between 15 to 25 in a cluster and the particular bank branch is made responsible for meeting out credit needs of all villages in that specified service area. The performance of a particular branch, besides other factors, depends upon the number of villages included in a service area. Therefore, it is pertinent to know about the average number of villages served by a particular bank branch for the effective and successful implementation of SAA.

The *table no. 6.3* depicts the average number of villages in a service area in the Hadoti region. The analysis of this table reveals the following facts :

(1) The average number of villages in a service area in the whole region was 17.88 at the end of March, 2000, which was well within the national norm of 15 to 25 villages. Therefore, the average number of villages served by a service area bank branch is highly satisfactory in the region as compared to national norm.

Table No.6.3

Average Number of Villages in a Service Area in Hadoti Region

(*As on March 31, 2000*)

S. N.	Name of District	Total Number of villages (inhabited)	Total Number of Serivice Area Branches	Average Number of Villages Service Area	Range of Number of Villages in a Service Area fixed by RBI
1.	BARAN	1206	58	20.79	15-25
2.	BUNDI	860	63	13.65	15-25
3.	JHALAWAR	1448	64	22.62	15-25
4.	KOTA	848	59	14.37	15-25
Total of the Region		**4362**	**244**	**17.88**	**15-25**

Source :

- *PLP of NABARD year 2000-2001 of Baran, Bundi, Jhalawar and Kota districts.*
- *Panchayat Samiti-wise service area and village code list of Baran, Bundi, Jhalawar and Kota districts.*

2) While comparing inter-district average number of branches in a service area, it is found that the Bundi district was having the lowest average number of villages (13.65), followed by Kota district (14.37), Baran district (20.79) and Jhalawar district (22.62) respectively.

3) The average number of villages in a service area in Bundi and district Kota was below the national norm. Therefore, in terms of number of villages served by a service area branch in these two districts is ideal and highly satisfactory for the effective coverage of the service area by a branch. So far the average number of villages in Jhalawar and Baran district is concerned, they were within the national norm of 15-25 villages and hence be termed as satisfactory.

District-wise Position of Average Number of Villages in a Service Area in Hadoti Region

The comparative position of average number of villages in a service area of different districts of Hadoti region is shown in **table no. 6.4** The analysis of the table reveals the following facts :

(1) Out of total 244 service areas in the region, 85 service areas were having 15 to 25 villages under their command, which could be termed an ideal number as per the norms fixed by RBI for a service area.

(2) 112 service areas in the region were such in which the number of villages were less than 15 which was less than the norm. The percentage of such service areas was as high as 46% of the total.

(3) There were 39 service areas in the region, which were having more than 25, but upto 40 villages under their command and they accounted for 16% of the total.

(4) The number of service areas which were having more than 40 villages under their command were only 8 and they accounted for 3% of the total service areas of the region.

Table No. 6.4

District-wise Position of Average Number of Villages in a Service Area in Hadoti Region

(*As on March 31, 2000*)

S. N.	*Name of District*	*Number of Service Area*				
		Below-15 Villages	*15 to 25 Villages*	*More than 25 but upto 40 Villages*	*More than 40 Villages*	*Total Service Area*
1.	BARAN	24 (41)	14 (24)	15 (26)	05 (9)	58
2.	BUNDI	36 (27)	24 (38)	03 (5)	Nil	63
3.	JHALAWAR	19 (29)	28 (44)	14 (22)	03 (5)	64
4.	KOTA	33 (56)	19 (32)	07 (12)	Nil	59
Total of the Region		112 (46)	85 (35)	39 (16)	08 (3)	244

Note : Figures in bracket denotes percentage of total.

Source: Panchayat Samiti/Bank-wise Service Area and village code list of Baran, Bundi, Jhalawar and Kota Districts

District Baran

1) Out of total 58 service areas in the district, 41% service areas (24) were having less than 15 villages under their command, which was sizeable.

2) There were 14 service areas having 15 to 25 villages under their command, which accounted for 24% of the total. These service areas were having number of villages as per the norm, hence could be termed as ideal.

3) 15 service areas were having more than 25, but upto 40 villages under their command, which was a substantial percentage (26%) of the total. This represents dis-satisfactory position.

4) Only 5 service areas were having more than 40 villages under their command which accounted for 9% of the total representing unhappy position.

District Bundi

1) As much as 36 service areas out of total 63 in the district were having less than 15 villages under their command, which was very high and accounted for 57%.

2) The number of service areas having 15 to 25 villages under their command as per the norm were only 24 which was 38% of the total service areas in the district. This shows that a comparatively small number of service areas were having number of villages under their jurisdiction as per the norm.

3) The number of service areas having more than 25 but upto 40 villages were only 3, 5% of the total, which was comparatively a small number.

4) There was not a single service area in which the number of villages were more than 40.

District Jhalawar

1) Out of total 64 service areas, 19 were serving less than 15 villages, which was 29% of the total. This was a highly delighted situation.

2) The number of service areas having 15 to 25 villages as per the norm were as high as 28, which accounted for 44% representing a happy position.

3) There were 14 service areas having more than 25 but upto 40 villages under their command which was about 22%.This is a sign of dis-satisfactory position.

4) Only 3 service areas in the district were having more than 40 villages, which was 5% of the total number of service areas. Really, this was unmanageable number for a branch for effective credit planning point of view and a sign of unhappy position.

District Kota

1) As high as 33 service areas out of total 59 were serving less than 15 villages and the percentage of such service areas was 56 which was substantial in number, hence this represents a nice situation.
2) 32% service areas (19) were serving 15 to 25 villages as per the norm.
3) The number of service areas which were serving more than 25 but up to 40 villages were 7. The percentage of them was 12. This represents unsatisfactory situation.
4) It is heartening to note that there was no single service area under which number of villages was more than 40.

Though, the average number of villages in a service area in the whole region and as well as in all four districts of the region was satisfactory and within the range of average number of villages fixed for a service area at the national level, but it does not necessarily mean that each service area branch in the region has such a number of villages which can be termed as satisfactory or as per the norm. Infact, in this context, two extreme situations have been observed by the researcher which is evident from the *table no. 6.4*

The first extreme situation was that there were many service areas in which the number of villages covered by a branch were far-far more than the national norm. For instance in district Jhalawar, 'Gainhu Khedi' branch of SBI in Bakani Panchayat Samiti, HKGB Manohar Thana branch and SBI Akelera branch were having 55, 50 and 42 villages under their respective command areas. Similarly, in Baran district, 'Relawan' branch of HKGB, HKGB Shahabad, SBBJ Shahabad, HKGB Pali and HKGB Chabara branch were having 57, 47, 46, 45 and 43 villages respectively in their command areas. Likewise, in Kota district, HKGB branch in Ladpura block, branch of SBBJ in Sangod block were having more than 35 villages in their service areas. In Bundi district 'Basoli' branch of HKGB in Hindoli block and 'Sumerganj Mandi' branch of HKGB in Kaishoraipatan block were also having 36 and 33 villages respectively under their service areas. Infact, this indicates highly unpleasant situation.

On the contrary to it, the other extreme situation was that there were several service areas under which the number of villages were too less than the norm fixed at the national level. This can be illustrated with the help of some extreme examples such as in Baran district, Anta branch of CBI, 'Fatepur' branch and 'Bohat' branch of HKGB were having only 1, 3 and 4 villages respectively under their command areas. Similarly, in Bundi district 'Capren' branch of BOR was serving only 4 villages which was the minimum number under any service area in the district. The similar situation was also found in district Jhalawar, where the 'Sunel' branch of SBBJ was having only 4 villages under its service area which was minimum in the district. So far the Kota district is concerned, 'Kunhadi' branch of CBI and 'Kherabad' branch of HKGB was having as low as one village under their command area. This has an adverse impact on the economic viability and profitability of a branch.

Thus, on the basis of above analysis, we can infer that there was quite uneven allotment of number of villages in different service areas of all districts in the region, which was either less than or more than the prescribed norm in substantial number of service areas. The primary reason behind this unevenness was the geographical location leading to the facility of minimum distance between branch and village. The second reason was, closure of unviable bank branches resulting into the increased number of villages after the re-allotment of villages among the service areas.

Thus, on the basis of above analysis , we can generalise that :

1) A very low percentage (35%) of service areas in the region were serving the number of villages within the range of 15-25 villages prescribed national norm for a service area.
2) A very high percentage (65%) of service areas were serving either more than or less than the number of villages in the region against the prescribed norm.
3) The position of district Jhalawar was the best amongst all districts of the region in terms of number of villages served by a service area as per the national norm followed by Bundi district and Kota district respectively. The district Baran was having the lowest percentage of service areas fulfilling the national norms.
4) District Bundi was at the top in terms of percentage of service areas which were having less than 15 villages, followed by disdrict Kota. The percentage share of Bundi and Kota district was more or less the same, 57 and 56 respectively. District Baran was at the third place and the district Jhalawar was at the last place in this regard.

5) In regard to the service areas serving more than 25 and above villages, the position of the district Bundi was the least worst as it was having minimum number of such service areas followed by Kota, Jhalawar and Baran district.

Overall Performance of Credit Plans in Hadoti Region

The overall performance of credit plans in Hadoti region during 1991-92 to 1999-2000 depicted in table no. 6.5. The study of this table reveals the following facts :

1) The figures of overall target of the region reveal that there has been a consistent rise in the targets year after year and these have increased from Rs. 7030.57 lacs in 1991-92 to Rs. 33390.27 lacs in 1999-2000 showing thereby an increase of 374.93%. The average annual growth rate in target of the whole region was 41.66 % during 1991-92 to 1999-2000.
2) The factual position of overall achievement reveals a continuous increasing trend except for the year 1993-94 when a slight fall was noticed (from Rs. 8368.42 lacs in 1992-93 to Rs. 8276.78 lacs in 1993-94, of about 1.09%). The figures of achievements in 1991-92 were 6836.46 lacs which increased tremendously to the tune of Rs. 32238.89 lacs in 1999-2000 depicting thereby an increase of 371.57%. This was quite substantial and impressive. The average annual growth rate of achievements for the whole region was 41.28%, which could be termed as impressive.
3) The comparison of year-wise figures of target and achievement reveals that the achievement exceeded the target only in the year 1997-98 (103.70%), which was highest also during the period of analysis. The lowest percentage achievement was in 1993-94 (81.78%). In remaining years of the period of study, the percentage achievement was ranging between a minimum of 87.26 in 1992-93 to a maximum of 99.02 in 1998-99.

The overall performance of credit plans in different districts of the region has been analysed below :

District Baran

1) The target figures of the district show a continuous increasing trend throughout the period of study except for the year 1993-94 when there has been a short fall (from Rs. 2187.23 lacs in 1992-93 to Rs. 2149.96 lacs in 1993-94) of about 1.70%. The target figures

increased from Rs. 1409.98 lacs in 1991-92 to Rs. 7549.00 lacs in 1999-2000 registering thereby a growth of 435.40%, which sounds very high. The average annual growth rate of target figures in the district was 48.38%, which could be termed as impressive.

2) A continuous increasing trend has been noticed in the achievement of targets except for the year 1993-94 and 1999-2000. In 1993-94 a marginal fall of 0.24% was noticed whereas in 1999-2000 a substantial fall of 12.86% was noticed. The achievement which was Rs. 1383.56 lacs in 1991-92 increased to as high as Rs. 6144 lacs in 1999-2000, has shown an increase of Rs. 4760.44 lacs thereby indicating a growth of 344% over the base year. The average annual growth rate of achievement was 38.23% in the district during the course of the study.

3) By comparing the figures of target with achievement of various years, we find that the overall achievement of credit plan in the district was satisfactory as the achievement was always higher than 81%. Besides this, the achievement was higher than the targets for five years continuously from 1994-95 to 1998-99. There has also been a heartening trend of overall achievement in the district as the achievement exceeded the over all target (101%).

District Bundi

1) The figures of target in the district depict an overall rising trend as these have increased from Rs. 1682.66 lacs in 1991-92 to Rs. 6101 lacs in 1999-2000, showing thereby an improvement of 262.58%. The average annual growth rate of target during the period of whole study was 29.17%,which was satisfactory.

2) So far the achievement is concerned, the trend has been continuously increasing except for the year 1993-94, which marked a marginal decline in comparison to the previous year. The achievement figures rose from Rs. 1434.57 lacs in 1991-92 to Rs.6152.00 lacs in 1999-2000, showing thereby an increase of 329%. Thus, the average annual growth rate of achievement during the whole period of study was 36.54% over the base year,which was also satisfactory.

3) Comparing achievement with target, the overall performance is highly satisfactory as it exceeds the target (108%). Regarding the achievement of different years, the trend path is fluctuating between minimum 85.26% to maximum 125%, but the worth mentioning fact here is that the achievement exceeded the target in many years (1994-95, 1996-97, 1997-98 and 1998-99) of the study. Thus, the overall performance could be termed as satisfactory.

Table No. 6.5

Overall Performance of Credit Plans in Hadoti Region

(1991-92 to 1999-2000)

(Amount in Rs. Lacs)

Annual Credit Plan	BARAN			BUNDI			JHALAWAR			KOTA			TOTAL of the Region		
Year	*Target*	*Achieve-ment*	*Achv. in %*	*Target*	*Achieve ment*	*Achv. in %*	*Target*	*Achieve ment*	*Achv. in %*	*Target*	*Achieve ment*	*Achv. in %*	*Target*	*Achieve ment*	*Achv. in %*
1991-1992	1409.98	1383.56	98.12	1682.66	1434.57	85.26	1227.81	1185.98	96.59	2710.12	2832.38	104.51	7030.57	6836.46	97.23
1992-1993	2187.23	2057.31	94.06	1879.56	1757.14	93.50	1810.68	1645.83	90.90	3712.57	2908.13	78.33	9590.04	8368.42	87.26
1993-1994	2149.96	2052.35	95.46	1980.00	1730.00	87.00	2463.08	2037.91	82.71	3527.71	2456.52	70.00	10120.75	8276.78	81.78
1994-1995	2315.19	2403.38	103.81	2571.00	2946.00	115.00	3115.47	2430.00	78.00	4163.99	3788.97	91.00	12165.65	11568.36	89.39
1995-1996	3165.64	3713.96	117.32	3439.00	3380.00	98.00	3989.60	3234.00	81.06	5204.53	5726.39	110.00	15798.77	16054.35	97.14
1996-1997	3962.67	4319.05	108.98	3777.00	4144.00	110.00	6037.88	4358.42	72.18	6077.99	5898.13	97.00	19855.54	18719.60	94.27
1997-1998	5140.28	5824.95	113.30	4183.00	5164.00	123.00	5325.23	5313.82	99.79	7690.07	6862.58	89.00	22338.58	23165.35	103.70
1998-1999	6764.72	7051.00	104.24	4857.00	6075.00	125.00	7031.46	6192.79	88.07	9772.38	8828.91	90.34	28425.56	28147.70	99.02
1999-2000	7549.00	6144.00	81.38	6101.00	6152.00	101.00	8409.70	6168.79	73.35	11330.57	13774.10	122.00	33390.27	32238.89	92.26
TOTAL	**34644.67**	**34949.56**	**100.88**	**30470.22**	**32782.71**	**108.00**	**39410.91**	**32567.95**	**82.64**	**54189.93**	**53076.11**	**97.94**	**158715.91**	**153377.14**	**96.63**

Source: DCPs of various years of Baran, Bundi, Jhalawar and Kota Districts.

District Jhalawar

1) A continuous increasing trend has been noticed in the targets of credit plans in the district as indicated by the figures of targets. The target figures have increased from Rs. 1227.81 lacs in 1991-92 to Rs. 8409.76 lacs in 1999-2000 denoting thereby an increase of 585%. The average annual growth rate in targets was of the order of 65% during the period of study, which was highly impressive.
2) The overall achievement in the district has gone up from Rs. 1185.98 lacs in 1991-92 to Rs. 6168.79 lacs in 1999-2000 registering an improvement of about 420%. The average annual growth rate of achievement in the district has been around 47%, which could be termed impressive.
3) Inter-relating the figures of target with achievement a zig-zag trend has been observed. The percentage share of achievement was fluctuating between 72 (in 1996-97) to 99.79 (in 1997-98). The performance of credit plans in the district never reached the cent-percent level.

District Kota

1) The study of target figures of the district denotes an ever increasing trend besides the year 1993-94, where in the target declined by around 5%. The target of credit plan was Rs. 2710.12 lacs in 1991-92, which increased to Rs. 11330.57 lacs in 1999-2000, registering thereby more than three times (318%) increase. The average annual growth rate in targets of the district was about 35%,which was satisfactory on the whole.
2) An upward continuous trend has been noticed in the achievement of credit plans in the district. The achievement figures have increased from Rs.2832.38 lacs in 1991-92 to Rs. 13774.10 lacs in 1999-2000, showing a growth of around 386%. The average annual growth rate of achievement in the district has been of the order of around 43%, which could be termed impressive.

On the basis of forgoing analysis, it can be generalised that :

1) The overall performance of credit plans in the region seems to be highly satisfactory as the overall achievement was around 97%-slightly less than cent-precent.
2) There has been continuous increase in both target and achievement of the credit plans in the region and there has been

similar growth pattern in both the achievement and target in all four districts of the resion.

3) With regard to overall performance of different districts in the region the district Bundi was at the top (108%) followed by district Baran (100.88%) and district Kota (99.93%). The overall performance in district Jhalawar was lowest (82.64%) in the region.

4) The share of Kota district in the total target of credit plans in Hadoti region was highest (34.14%) which was followed by Jhalawar (24.83%) and district Baran (21.83%). The share of district Bundi was lowest (19.20%) in the region.

5) The percentage achievement of Kota district was highest (35.06%) in the region which was followed by district Baran (22.63%) and district Bundi (21.22%). The percentage achievement of district Jhalawar was lowest (21.09%) in the region.

PERFORMANCE OF SERVICE AREA CREDIT PLANS IN AGRICULTURE AND ALLIED SECTOR IN HADOTI REGION

Agriculture is the backbone of the rural economy of the Hadoti region. Agriculture and allied activities still enjoy a sizeable portion of the economy of all four districts of the region. The performance of service area credit plans in agriculture and allied sector for the period of 1991-92 to 1999-2000 in the region has been shown in table no. 6.6. This table shows the performance of agriculture and allied sector for the whole region and also for the different districts separately. The study of the table highlights the following facts :

1) A crystal clear continuously increasing path has been visible in the targets of credit plan for agriculture and allied sector in the region which is evident from this fact that the figures of targets have increased from Rs. 4937.57 lacs in the base year to Rs. 24680.30 lacs in the final year of the present study thereby registering a growth of around 340% which is around five times of the base year. The average annual growth rate in targets has been about 44%,which could be termed satisfactory.

2) The achievement of credit plan for agriculture and allied sector is more or less on the similar lines of the targets in regard to its growth rate. The growth pattern of achievement figures

indicates a continuous increase except for the year 1993-94 when there has been a marginal decline of around 0.5%. The amount disbursed to agriculture and allied sector went-up from Rs. 5296.41 lacs in 1991-92 to 22006.41 lacs in 1999-2000 representing thereby an increase of 315.50% or slightly more than four fold increase. The average annual growth rate of achievement in the whole region has been 35% during the period of study, which was satisfactory.

3) The overall achievement of credit plan for agriculture and allied sector in relation to its targets has been highly satisfactory except three years (1993-94, 1997-98 and 1999-2000) as achievement always exceeded the target; i.e. more than 100%.

4) The performance of service area credit plans for agriculture and allied sectors in different districts of the region has been analysed below on the basis of figures given in *table no. 6.6.*

District Baran

1) The absolute figures of target of the district have shown an increasing trend. The overall target of credit plans has shown a remarkable improvement of about 375% as the target increased from Rs. 1264.28 lacs in the base year to Rs. 6002.03 lacs in the final year of the study thus, depicting about five times increase. The average per annum growth rate in target was around 42%, which could be treated satisfactory.

2) A similar trend of considerable improvement in the achievement figures has been noticed in the district except for the last year of the study, where about 11% declined was noticed. The figures of overall achievement have shown a quantum jump of about 305%. These went-up to Rs. 1268.42 lacs in 1991-92 to Rs. 5128.54 lacs in 1999-2000 thereby depicting of about four fold increase. The average per annum growth rate in overall achievement has been of the order of 34%, which was satisfactory.

3) The overall percentage achievement of the credit plan in the district has been highly satisfactory as the achievement was more than 100 percent (108.29%). The performance of credit plans for various years has also been excellent except for the year 1992-93 and 1993-94 . The perfomance was more than 100% in rest of the years of the study.

Table No. 6.6

Performance of Credit Plans in Agriculture and Allied Sectors in Hadoti Region (1991-92 to 1999-2000)

(Amount in Rs. Lacs)

Annual Credit Plan	BARAN			BUNDI			JHALAWAR			KOTA			TOTAL of the Region		
Year	*Target*	*Achieve-ment*	*Achv. in %*	*Target*	*Achieve-ment*	*Achv. in %*	*Target*	*Achieve-ment*	*Achv. in %*	*Target*	*Achieve-ment*	*Achv. in %*	*Target*	*Achieve-ment*	*Achv. in %*
1991-1992	1264.28	1268.42	100.53	1227.73	1175.86	95.77	1002.77	1019.27	101.65	1442.79	1832.86	127.03	4937.57	5296.41	107.27
1992-1993	1872.16	1831.52	97.58	1433.86	1395.72	97.34	1339.18	1533.35	114.50	2340.97	2353.08	100.51	6986.17	7113.67	101.82
1993-1994	1930.06	1875.50	97.17	1533.00	1447.00	94.00	1840.69	1887.54	102.54	2189.78	1868.54	85.00	7493.53	7078.58	94.46
1994-1995	2020.72	2156.87	106.73	1998.00	2370.00	119.00	2342.20	2228.00	95.12	2423.38	2455.21	101.00	8784.30	9210.08	104.85
1995-1996	2674.46	3105.17	116.10	2626.00	2654.00	101.00	2676.13	2890.00	107.99	2952.06	3785.22	128.00	10929.25	12434.39	113.77
1996-1997	2884.27	3550.34	123.09	2860.00	3295.00	115.00	3949.46	3911.41	99.03	3299.89	3862.17	117.00	12993.62	14618.92	112.51
1997-1998	3655.29	5284.27	144.56	3208.00	3949.00	123.00	4355.61	4805.99	110.34	4222.90	4579.56	108.00	15441.80	18618.82	120.57
1998-1999	5363.56	5760.24	107.40	3735.00	4222.00	113.00	6012.86	5625.44	93.56	5976.82	4870.30	81.00	21087.54	20477.98	97.11
1999-2000	6002.03	5128.54	85.44	4415.00	4445.00	101.00	7303.23	5339.36	73.10	6960.12	7093.51	102.00	24680.30	22006.41	89.17
TOTAL	**27666.84**	**29960.87**	**108.29**	**23036.59**	**24953.58**	**108.32**	**30822.13**	**29240.36**	**94.86**	**31808.71**	**32700.75**	**102.80**	**113335.08**	**116855.26**	**103.00**

Source: DCPs of various years of Baran, Bundi, Jhalawar and Kota Districts.

District Bundi

1) It is significant to mention that there has been continuously increasing trend in the targets for agriculture and allied sector as these have risen up from Rs. 1227.73 lacs in 1991-92 to Rs. 4415.00 lacs in 1999-2000 depicting thereby an increase of about 260% i.e. more than three and half times in comparison to the base year. The average annual growth rate in target was 28.84% during the period under review, which could be termed satisfactory.
2) A similar trend of continuous growth in achievement has been noticed as there has been a phenomenal increase in the absolute figures of achievement. These have spiralled up from Rs. 1175.86 lacs in 1991-92 to Rs. 4445.00 lacs in 1999-2000 thereby denoting a growth of about 278% or around four fold increase. The average growth rate per annum was 30.89%.
3) While studying the achievement of credit plans for the agriculture and allied sector in comparison to the target we find highly satisfactory performance as the overall achievement was more than 100% and as high as 108.32%. So far the year-wise performance is concerned, the performance was more than 100% from the year 1994-95 to 1999-2000. In remaining three years of the period of study, the percentage achievement was 94 and above. Thus, signifying a grand success.

District Jhalawar

1) A remarkable progress has been noticed in the credit outlays for agriculture and allied sector in the district as the percentage growth rate during the period of study was around 628% or more than seven times. The absolute figures of target increased tremendously from Rs. 1002.77 lakhs in 1991-92 to Rs. 7303.23 lakhs in 1999-2000. The per annum average growth rate was also very high to the level of around 70%.
2) The growth path of achievement was of the same trend as that of targets there has been a continuous increase in achievemant up to 1998-99, but in the year 1999-2000 the achievement declined from Rs. 5625.44 lacs in 1998-99 to Rs. 5339.36 lacs which was about 5%, but the overall trend of achievement was more than five times in comparison to the base year. The figures of achievement went up from Rs. 1019.27 lacs in 1991-92 to Rs. 5339.36 lacs in 1999-2000 signifying a growth of about 424%. The per annum growth rate of achievement was around 47% which washighly satisfactory.

3) Comparing overall achievement against the overall targets of the district a satisfactory trend was noticed as the achievement was around 95%. The analysis of year-wise performance reveals a highly satisfactory situation for the years 1991-92, 1992-93, 1993-94, 1995-96 and 1997-98 as the achievement was more than 100% ranging between a minimum of 101.65% in 1991-92 to a maximum of 114.50% in 1992-93.

District Kota

1) The figures of target for the district reveal a continuous rising trend except for the year 1993-94 wherein there was a fall of 6.46% from the targets of preceding year. The target climbed up from Rs. 1442.79 lacs in 1991-92 to Rs. 6960.12 lacs in 1999-2000 indicating a rise of 382% or around five fold increase. The average annual growth rate in target was 42.50%.

2) A similar rising trend was noticed in the achievements except for the year 1993-94 wherein a substantial fall of about 21% was visualised as the amount went down from Rs. 2353.08 lacs in 1992-93 to Rs. 1868.54 lacs in 1993-94. The amount of overall achievement has risen from Rs. 1832.86 lacs in 1991-92 to Rs. 7093.51 lacs in 1999-2000, thereby showing an increase of about 287% or around four times more than the base year. The average annual growth rate has been around 32%, which was satisfactory.

3) The overall percentage achievement against the targets was around 106%, which could be termed highly satisfactory by all means. Out of the total nice years of the study, the performance of credit plans in seven years, was more than 100% except for the year 1993-94 (85%) and 1998-99 (81%).

The range of achievement was between 100.51% in 1992-93 to 128% in 1995-96 during all these years when the percentage achievement was more than 100%.

Thus, on the basis of above analysis, we can derive following generalisation :

1) The overall performance of credit plans in agriculture and allied sector in the region has been highly satisfactory as the overall percentage achievement was more than 100%.

2) On the whole, a continuous rising trend was clearly visible in both targets and achievements in the region. More or less similar growth trend was noticed in both targets and achievements.

3) The percentage share of district Kota and district Jhalawar in total targets of the credit plans in Hadoti region was more or less the same.

Performance of Credit Plans in Industrial Sector in Hadoti Region

Table no. 6.7 presents the performance of service area credit plans in industrial sector in Hadoti region. The analysis of the table highlights the following facts :

1) A continuous growing trend was seen in the credit plan outlays earmarked for industrial sector in the region except for the year 1992-93 and 1993-94. The credit plan outlays have increased from Rs. 1160.23 lacs in 1991-92 to Rs. 3271.30 lacs in 1999-2000 signifying a growth of 182%, which is around three times more over the base year figure. The per annum average growth rate in target outlays was of the order of 22.22%, which was satisfactory.

2) A zig-zag trend has been noticed in the achievement of targets. Inspite of the fact that there has been an overall increase in terms of absolute amount of achievement as this has gone up from Rs. 922.45 lacs in 1991-92 to Rs. 3408.47 lacs in 1999-2000, thereby, showing an improvement of about 269%, which was more than three and half times in comparison to the base year achievement. The average annual growth rate was around 30%, which could be termed as good.

3) The overall performance of the credit plans in industrial sector was 82.60% against the targets. This can not be termed satisfactory as it was less than 100%. The analysis of year-wise performance reveals highly fluctuating trend as the performance was between the order of 49.12% in 1992-93 to 104.49% in 1999-2000. Besides only in the year 1999-2000 (104.19%), the achievement has always been less than 100%. The achievement was very poor particularly in 1992-93 when it was as low as 49.12%.

4) District Kota was having lion's share in the total size of DCPs of the region. The share of Kota district was about 60% of the total size of the DCPs of the region. It was followed by Bundi district (20.79%) and Jhalawar district (9.69%). The share of Baran district was minimal in the region and it was as low as 7.45%.

Table No. 6.7

Performance of Credit Plans in Industrial Sector in Hadoti Region (1991-92 to 1999-2000)

(Amount in Rs. Lacs)

Annual Credit Plan	BARAN			BUNDI			JHALAWAR			KOTA			TOTAL of the Region		
Year	*Target*	*Achievement*	*Achv. in %*	*Target*	*Achievement*	*Achv. in %*	*Target*	*Achievement*	*Achv. in %*	*Target*	*Achievement*	*Achv. in %*	*Target*	*Achievement*	*Achv. in %*
1991-1992	67.19	25.04	37.30	255.11	164.66	64.54	119.54	86.53	72.38	718.39	646.22	89.95	1160.23	922.45	79.50
1992-1993	106.77	57.63	53.98	256.83	190.35	74.11	155.84	61.03	39.17	631.71	256.49	40.60	1151.15	565.50	49.12
1993-1994	49.00	29.12	61.07	226.00	125.00	55.00	142.14	97.10	68.31	638.92	304.29	48.00	1056.06	556.31	52.68
1994-1995	55.98	37.80	67.52	280.00	255.00	91.00	128.45	74.00	57.60	910.43	600.23	66.00	1374.86	967.03	70.34
1995-1996	121.20	103.88	85.70	400.00	305.00	76.00	190.74	162.00	84.93	1165.93	1137.41	98.00	1877.87	1708.29	90.17
1996-1997	225.88	113.46	50.23	453.00	420.00	93.00	191.59	69.87	36.46	1307.99	1035.96	79.00	2178.46	1639.29	75.25
1997-1998	265.95	76.08	28.60	402.00	389.00	171.00	294.57	240.64	81.69	1656.14	913.32	55.00	2618.66	1919.04	73.28
1998-1999	198.93	73.18	36.79	424.00	1053.00	248.00	256.00	223.20	87.19	1853.40	1355.31	73.00	2732.33	2704.06	98.97
1999-2000	206.75	77.13	37.30	925.00	811.00	88.00	209.80	311.51	148.47	1929.75	2208.83	114.46	3271.30	3408.47	104.19
TOTAL	**1297.67**	**594.73**	**45.78**	**3621.94**	**4013.01**	**110.79**	**1688.67**	**1326.70**	**78.56**	**10812.66**	**8457.76**	**78.22**	**17420.92**	**14390.47**	**82.60**

Source: DCPs of various years of Baran, Bundi, Jhalawar and Kota Districts.

The performance of Credit Plans in Industrial Sector in different districts of Hadoti Region has been analysed below :

District Baran

1) Although, the credit outlays in the district have shown an overall growing trend, but there has been substantial fluctuations year-wise. Thus, a zig-zag trend was noticed. The credit outlays have gone-up from Rs. 67.19 lacs in 1991-92 to Rs. 206.75 lacs in 1999-2000 representing an increase of about 208%. The average annual growth rate in plan outlays was slightly above 23%, which was satisfactory.
2) A similar fluctuating trend was also noticed in absolute amount of achievement, inspite of an overall increasing trend. The achievement amount which was Rs. 25.04 lacs in 1991-92 surged-up Rs. 77.13 lacs in 1999-2000, thereby denoting a rise of about 208%, which was three fold of the base year. The average annual growth rate has been slightly above 23%, which could be said as satisfactory.
3) The overall performance of credit plans for industrial sector in the district has been very poor as the overall percentage achievement was only 45.78%. Inter-linking year-wise achievement with the targets an uneven trend has been obseved fluctuating between as low as 28.60% in 1997-98 to as high as 85.70% in 1995-96. The distinguishing fact about the achievement was that the targets could not be achieved in any year of the whole period of the study.

District Bundi

1) The credit outlays of various years for industrial sector in the district have shown a zig-zag trend inspite of that there has been an overall increasing trend as the targets have increased from Rs. 255.11 lacs in 1991-92 to Rs. 925.00 lacs in 1999.2000, depicting thereby an increase of about 263%, which is three and half times more from the base year. The per annum average growth rate in target was around 29%, which could be termed as satisfactory.
2) The absolute amount of achievement have risen from Rs. 164.66 lacs in 1991-92 to Rs. 811.00 lacs in 1999-2000, thus, signifying a growth rate of 393%, which comes around five times more of the base year. The average annual growth rate during the whole period of study has been around 44%, which could be termed as highly satisfactory. 1993-94 was an exception year in which achievement declined by Rs. 65.35 lacs which was around 34% in comparison to the preceding year.

3) The overall performance of credit plans in the district has been highly satisfactory as the percentage achievement was more than 110% (110.79%). In regard to the year-wise performance of credit plans against targets, the performance in 1997-98 and 1998-99 was excellent as it was 171% and 248% respectively. In rest of the years the performance was not only uneven, but also less than 100% ranging between a minimum of 55% in 1993-94 to a high of 93% in 1996-97.

District Jhalawar

1) District Jhalawar also witnessed a fluctuating trend in the plan outlays for industrial sector, but the over all trend was increasing. It is evident from the figures that the credit outlay targets have gone up from the Rs. 119.54 lacs in 1991-92 to Rs. 209.80 lacs in 1999-2000, thus representing a growth rate of about 76%, which was just more than one and half times over the base year. The average annual growth rate in the credit plan outlays was just about 8.40%, which was not satisfactory.

2) Although, the performance of the credit plans, on the whole, has improved in terms of absolute amount as these have gone up from Rs. 86.53 lacs in 1991-92 to Rs. 311.51 lacs in 1999-2000 showing an improvement of about 260%, which was more than three and half time of the achievement in initial year. The average annual growth rate of achievement has been around 29%, which was satisfactory.

3) The overall performance of credit plans for industrial sector has been around 79% for the whole period of study, which cannot be said as satisfactory. The year-wise performance of credit plans has shown an oscillated trend inspite of this hard mentioning fact that except for the year 1999-2000 (148.47%) targets could never be achieved. The performance was not only poor in many years, but it was as low as 36.46% in 1996-97 and 39.17% in 1992-93. The range of fluctuations was too wide between 39.17% to 148.47%.

district Kota

1) A consistent growing trend has been observed in the projected credit outlays except for the year 1992-93, which witnessed a fall of around 12%. The absolute amount of target was Rs. 718.39 lacs in the initial year which went-up to Rs. 1929.75 lacs in the final year of the study, denoting a growth rate of around 168%, *i.e.* three times of the base year figure. The average annual growth rate in credit plan outlays has been 18.73%, which was so-so.

2) Although, the absolute amount of achievement witnessed an overall increasing trend, but there has been lot of fluctuations in various years of the period of study. The absolute amount varied between Rs. 256.49 lacs in 1992-93 to Rs. 2208.83 lacs in 1999-2000. The overall growth in achievement was around 242% over the base year. The absolute amount of achievement was Rs. 646.22 lacs in initial year which increased to Rs. 2208.83 lacs in final year of the study, which was more than three times in comparison to the base year. The average annual growth rate in credit outlays was 27% during the whole period of the study, which could be said satisfactory.

3) The overall performance of credit plans was less than 80% (78.80%) signifying that the targets could not be achieved. The analysis of year-wise performance of credit plans also reveals that the achievement has always been less than 90% except for 1995-96 (98%) and 1999-2000 (114.46%). The percentage achievement was as low as 40.60% in the year 1992-93.

Thus, on the basis of above analysis the following generalisation can be made :

1) The overall performance of credit plans for industrial sector in the region was satisfactory on the whole.
2) On the whole an increasing trend was noticed both in the absolute amount of targets and achievements, but the overall percentage growth in achievement was more than the percentage growth in targets.
3) Comparing the overall performance of the different districts of the region, the Bundi district remained at the top (110.79%). The performance of Jhalawar and Kota has been more or less the same around 78%. The district performance of district Baran has been very poor (45.78%) and was lowest in the region.

Performance of Credit Plans in Tertiary Sector in Hadoti Region

Table no. 6.8 depicts the performance of credit plans in tertiary sector in Hadoti region. The analysis of the table highlights the following facts :

1) Except for the year 1997-98, the projected credit plan outlays have been continuously increasing as the amount in 1991-92 was Rs. 932.77 lacs which soared-up to Rs. 5438.35 lacs

registering a growth of about 483%. Thus, the target figures have increased by around six times over the figures of initial year. The average annual growth rate in the target was of the order of 54%, which could be termed as robust growth.

2) Although, there has been a zig-zag trend in the performance of credit plans for various years of the study, but on the whole, it was on rising path. This is evident by this very fact that the achievement was Rs. 617.63 lacs in the initial year which surged up to a big total of Rs. 6824.40 lacs in the final year of the study, signifying a high growth of around 105%, which was eleven fold increase. The average per annum growth rate in credit plan outlays has been of a very high order around 112%, which was really robust growth.

3) The overall performance of credit plans for the tertiary sector in the region has been moderate as it was around 79%. An oscillating trend has been seen in the year-wise percentage achievement for the region. It was as low as 40.83% in 1993-94 and as high as 125.49% in 1999-2000. In remaining years of the study the achievement was less than 70%.

4) So far the proportionate share of different districts in the total size of the DCPs in the region for the entire period of the study, is concerned, the district Kota enjoyed the highest share of around 41.38%, followed by district Jhalawar 24.68% and district Baran 21.31%. The share of Bundi district was 13.63%, which was lowest in the region.

The performance of credit plans in tertiary sector in different districts of Hadoti region has been analysed in length and depth below :

District Baran

1) The projected credit outlays have been increasing throughout the period of study except for the year 1993-94 and 1998-99. The growth in plan outlays was tremendously high of about 1607% representing seventeen fold increase over the initial year. The absolute figures of target surged-up from a very low of Rs. 78.51 lacs in 1991-92 to a very high of Rs. 1339.98 lacs in 1999-2000. Thus, a remarkable progress has been noticed in the absolute amount of credit plan outlays.

Table No. 6.8

Performance of Credit Plans in Tertiary Sector in Hadoti Region (1991-92 to 1999-2000)

(Amount in Rs. Lacs)

Annual Credit Plan	BARAN			BUNDI			JHALAWAR			KOTA			TOTAL of the Region		
Year	*Target*	*Achieve-ment*	*Achv. in %*	*Target*	*Achieve-ment*	*Achv. in %*	*Target*	*Achieve-ment*	*Achv. in %*	*Target*	*Achieve-ment*	*Achv. in %*	*Target*	*Achieve-ment*	*Achv. in %*
1991-1992	78.51	90.10	114.76	199.82	94.05	47.06	105.50	80.18	76.00	548.94	353.30	64.36	932.77	617.63	66.21
1992-1993	208.30	168.16	80.73	188.87	171.07	90.57	315.69	51.11	16.19	739.89	298.56	43.35	1452.75	688.90	47.42
1993-1994	170.90	146.93	85.98	221.00	158.00	71.00	480.25	53.27	11.09	699.81	283.69	41.00	1571.96	641.89	40.83
1994-1995	238.49	208.71	87.51	293.00	321.00	110.00	644.82	128.00	19.85	830.18	733.53	88.00	2006.49	1391.24	69.34
1995-1996	369.98	504.91	136.46	413.00	421.00	102.00	1122.73	182.00	16.21	1086.54	803.76	74.00	2992.25	1911.67	63.89
1996-1997	852.72	655.25	76.25	464.00	429.00	92.00	1896.83	377.14	19.88	1470.11	1000.00	68.00	4683.66	2461.39	52.53
1997-1998	1219.04	464.60	38.11	573.00	526.00	92.00	675.05	267.19	39.58	1811.03	1369.70	76.00	4278.12	2627.49	61.42
1998-1999	1202.23	1216.58	101.19	698.00	800.00	115.00	762.60	344.08	45.12	1942.16	2603.30	134.00	4604.99	4963.96	107.79
1999-2000	1339.98	938.72	70.05	761.00	896.00	118.00	896.67	517.92	57.16	2440.70	4471.76	183.00	5438.35	6824.40	125.49
TOTAL	**5680.15**	**4393.96**	**77.36**	**3811.60**	**3816.12**	**100.12**	**6900.14**	**2000.89**	**29.00**	**11569.36**	**11917.60**	**103.00**	**27961.34**	**22128.51**	**79.14**

Source: DCPs of various years of Baran, Bundi, Jhalawar and Kota Districts.

2) A similar trend of tremendous growth has been observed in the actual amount of credit disbursement . The absolute amount of achievement has increased by leaps and bounds form a very low level of Rs. 90.10 lacs in the initial year to a very high of Rs. 938.72 lacs in the final year of the study. The percentage growth was of a very high order of around 942% *i.e.* about more than ten times from the base year. The average growth rate per annum was more than 100% (104.65%). The worth mentioning fact in the absolute amount of achievement is that there have been wide ranging fluctuations owing to some reason or the other.

3) The overall performance of credit plans has been around 77% signifying a moderate success in tertiary sector. So far the year-wise performance is concerned it has been fluctuating every year from a very low of 38.11% in 1997-98 to a high of 136.46% in 1995-96. Thus, a variation of around 98 points. It is also worth mentionin here that in three years of the study, the performance of credit plans has been more than 100% in the year 1991-92, 1995-96 and 1998-99.

District Bundi

1) An overall growing trend was visible clearly in the credit plan outlays for the district. The figures of target have gone-up from Rs. 199.82 lacs in the initial year to Rs. 761.00 lacs in the final year of the period of study. Thus, the growth in credit plan outlays was around 289%, which was just four times more over the base year. 1992-93 was an exceptional year in which there has been a slight fall in credit plan outlays of about 5.50%. The average per annum growth rate in achievement was about 31%, which could be termed as satisfactory.

2) A crystal clear rising trend has been visualised in the absolute amount of achievement continuously except for the year 1993-94 (a decline of about 7.6%). The amount of achievement climbed up from Rs. 94.05 lacs in the base year to a very staggering figure of Rs. 896.00 lacs in the final year of the study, depicting thereby an increase of about 853%, which was nine and half times more of the base year. The average annual growth rate has been around 95%.

3) The overall performance of credit plans in tertiary sector in the district was 100%, which could be termed as highly satisfactory. The year-wise performance of credit plans had generally been more than 90% except in 1991-92 (47.06%) and 1993-94 (74%). In the year 1994-95, 1995-96, 1998-99 and 1999-2000 the performance was highly satisfactory as it crossed the 100% mark.

District Jhalawar

1) There has been substantial variation in the credit plan outlays of various years, but the overall trend was increasing. The absolute amount in the base year was Rs. 105.50 lacs which soared-up to Rs. 896.67 lacs in 1999-2000 thereby indicating an up-surge of 750% or about eight and half times more than that of the base year amount. The amount of target was increasing up to 1996-97 and it was all time high equal to the amount of Rs. 1896.83 lacs in 1996-97, but thereafter there has been substantial decline was noticed in the next year. The per annum average growth rate in targets for the period of whole study was 83%, which could be termed as robust growth.
2) The absolute amount of achievement climbed up from Rs. 80.18 lacs in 1991-92 to Rs. 517.92 lacs in 1999-2000 depicting thereby an increase of about 546% i.e. more than six fold increase. But year-wise there has been substantial variations in the amount of achievement as it was a minimum of Rs. 51.11 lacs in 1992-93 and a maximum of Rs. 517.92 lacs in 1999-2000. The average annual growth rate of achievement was of the order of around 61%, which was excellent.
3) The overall performance of credit plans in tertiary sector in the region has been very poor to a very low level of 29%. A highly skewed trend was noticed in the year-wise performance. It was as low as 11.09% in 1993-94 to a high of 76% in 1991-92. On the whole the performance of credit plan in tertiary sector was highly dis-satisfactory.

District Kota

1) A substantial variation in the credit plan outlays was visible despite of fluctuations the overall trend was on the positive side as the figures rose-up from Rs. 548.94 lacs in 1991-92 to Rs. 2440.70 lacs in 1999-2000, which was 345% high or more than four fold increase. The per annum average growth rate was around 38%, which was good.
2) Inspite of decline in initial two years the absolute amount of achievement, on the whole, has gone from Rs. 353.30 lacs in 1991-92 to a staggering level of Rs. 4471.76 lacs in 1999-2000 depicting a phenomenal growth of about 1166%, which was more than twelve times. The average annual growth rate was also very high of about 130%, really a robust growth.

3) While analysing the overall achievement in tertiary sector of the district for the whole period under review, it was slightly above 100% (103%) which could be termed as highly satisfactory. The performance has been oscillated throughout the period of study between the range of 41% in 1993-94 to 183% in 1999-2000. The performance was exceptionally good in 1998-99 (134%) and 1999-2000 (183%).

The following generalisation can be deduced on the basis of above analysis :

1) The overall performance of credit plans in tertiary sector has been moderately successful, but the performance in Jhalawar district was extremely poor.

2) In terms of the ranking of performance Kota district was at the top (103%), followed by district Bundi and Baran district (77.36%). The district Jhalawar at the last having substantially low performance of about only 29%.

Sector-wise Percentege Share of Target in Total Credit Plan in Hadoti Retion

Sector-wise percentage share of target in total credit plan has been depicted in *table no. 6.9*. The critical analysis of the table reveals the following facts :

Agriculture and Allied Sector

The agriculture and allied sector was having lion's share of the total size of the credit plans in the region. The overall percentage share of agriculture and allied sector in the total size of credit plans was 71.43%, followed by tertiary sector (17.61%) and industrial sector (10.96%). This clearly indicates that the agriculture and allied sector was having the dominant share slightly above 2/3 of the total size of the plan of the region. This also indicates the role and importance of agriculture in the economy of the region and the credit absorption capacity in this sector. The importance of agriculture sector is also evident from the year-wise percentage share of this sector in the total size of the credit plan as this was never less than 65%. Besides this, the percentage share of this sector has also been increased marginally from 70.23% in the initial year to 73.56% in the final year of the study. Of course, there has been marginal fluctuations in the percentage share every year during the period of study.

Table No. 6.9

Sector-wise Percentage Share of Target in Total Credit Plans in Hadoti Region (1991-92 to 1999-2000)

Annual Credit Plan	BARAN			BUNDI			JHALAWAR			KOTA			TOTAL of the Region		
Year	*Agri. & Allied Sec. %*	*Industrial Sector %*	*Teritary Sector %*	*Agri. & Allied Sec. %*	*Industrial Sector %*	*Teritary Sector %*	*Agri. & Allied Sec. %*	*Industrial Sector %*	*Teritary Sector %*	*Agri. & Allied Sec. %*	*Industrial Sector %*	*Teritary Sector %*	*Agri. & Allied Sec. %*	*Industrial Sector %*	*Teritary Sector %*
1991-1992	89.67	04.77	05.56	72.96	15.16	11.88	81.67	09.73	8.60	53.20	26.50	20.30	70.23	16.50	13.27
1992-1993	85.60	04.88	09.52	76.28	13.67	10.05	73.96	08.61	17.43	63.05	17.02	19.93	72.85	12.00	15.15
1993-1994	89.77	02.28	07.95	77.43	11.41	11.16	74.73	05.77	19.50	62.08	18.07	19.85	74.04	10.43	15.53
1994-1995	87.28	02.42	10.30	77.71	10.90	11.39	75.18	04.12	20.70	58.20	21.86	19.94	72.20	11.31	16.49
1995-1996	84.48	03.83	11.69	76.36	11.63	12.01	67.07	04.79	28.14	56.72	22.40	20.88	69.18	11.88	18.94
1996-1997	72.78	05.70	21.52	75.72	12.00	12.28	65.41	03.18	31.41	54.29	21.52	24.19	65.44	10.97	23.59
1997-1998	71.11	05.17	23.72	76.70	09.60	13.70	81.79	05.53	12.68	54.91	21.54	23.55	69.13	11.72	19.15
1998-1999	79.29	02.94	17.77	76.90	08.73	14.37	85.51	03.64	10.85	61.17	18.96	19.87	74.18	09.61	16.21
1999-2000	79.51	02.74	17.75	72.37	15.16	12.47	86.84	02.50	10.66	61.43	17.03	21.54	73.56	09.74	16.70
TOTAL	**79.86**	**03.74**	**16.40**	**75.60**	**11.89**	**12.51**	**78.21**	**04.28**	**17.51**	**58.70**	**19.95**	**21.35**	**71.43**	**10.96**	**17.61**

Source: DCPs of various years of Baran, Bundi, Jhalawar and Kota Districts.

Industrial Sector

The percentage share of industrial sector in the total size of plan was not only low, but also showed an overall declining trend. It declined from 16.50% in 1991-92 to 9.74% in 1999-2000 thereby depicting a decline of about 7 points. The percentage share of industrial sector has been fluctuating every year marginally except in the beginning. The relative share of this sector is an indication of industrial backwardness of the region, but if proper policies are followed and adequate infra-structure facilities are provided, the potential of the development of this sector could not only be taped but could also be enhanced.

Tertiary Sector

The overall percentage share of tertiary sector was 17.61% of the total size of the credit plans in the region. Of course, it is not too high, but it has shown an overall increasing trend as this has gone up marginally from 13.27% in the beginning to 16.70% at the end thereby denoting an increase of 3.43 points. The figures of percentage share of this sector have fluctuated between the range of 13.27% in 1991-92 to 23.59% in 1996-97. The low percentage share of tertiary sector tells the story of unhealthy and poor growth of this sector in the region. The possibility of the development of this sector may get momentum with passage of time and improvement in the skills of the people alongwith the expansion of economic base in the region.

Thus, there has been marginal change in the percentage share of agriculture and allied sector and tertiary sector in the region, but the percentage share of industrial sector has gone down to a great extent.

The percentage share of different sectors in the credit plans in different districts of the region has been analysed below :

DISTRICT BARAN

Agriculture and Allied Sector

1) In view of the importance of the agriculture in terms of employment and income this sector occupies a prominent place in economy of the district, therefore, the highest priority has been accorded to this sector in the total size of the DCPs throughout all years of the study. The overall percentage share of agriculture and allied sector in the total size of DCPs was 79.86% for the period under review. This signifies a dominant role of agriculture and allied sector not only in the credit plans, but in the economy of the district.

2) The analysis of year-wise percentage share of agriculture and allied sector in the total size of DCP_S reveals this fact that the percentage share of this sector in different years was varying and it was the lowest in the year 1997-98 to a level of 71.11% and it was highest in 1991-92 to a tune of 89.67%.

3) The overall trend of percentage share of agriculture and allied sector has shown a South-word trend as it has declined from 89.67% in the initial year to 79.51% in the last year of the study, thus it declined by around 10 points.

Industrial Sector

1) The overall percentage share of industrial sector in the district for the whole period of the study was very low to a level of 3.74% of the total size of DCP. This signifies the industrial backwardness of the district's economy.

2) The overall percentage share has witnessed a declining trend as it went down from 4.77% in 1991-92 to 2.74% in 1999-2000, which was around 2 points less.

3) Though, the percentage share of industrial sector has fluctuated over the years with a zig-zag trend, but it was lowest in 1994-95 (2.42%) and highest in 1997-98 (5.7%).

Tertiary Sector

1) The overall percentage share of tertiary sector in the district was of the order of 16.40% for the whole period of the study.

2) A substantial up-surge has been observed in the percentage share of tertiary sector as this has gone-up from 5.56% in the initial year to as high as 17.75% in the final year of the study, which showed around three times increase or 12 points increase. This signifies that the importance of tertiary sector is growing rapidly.

3) There has not been consistency in the growth pattern of the percentage share of this sector as it was fluctuating with uneven points. The lowest share of this sector was 5.56% in the base year and it was highest to a level of 23.72% in 1997-98.

Thus, on the basis of aforementioned analysis, we can infer that the overall percentage share of agriculture in the district was highest followed by tertiary sector and industrial sector. The importance of agriculture has declined over the years while the importance of tertiary sector has increased. Although, the importance of industrial sector has gone

-up over the years, but the share of this sector is as usually insignificant in the total size of the DCPs.

DISTRICT BUNDI

Agriculture and Allied Sector

1) The overall percentage share of agriculture and allied sector in the total size of DCPs was 75.60% signifying a dominant share of this sector in the economy of the district.
2) Although the overall trend of percentage share of agriculture and allied sector has witnessed a slight fall, but that is insignificant. The percentage share of this sector in the initial year was 72.96% which declined to 72.37% in 1999-2000, a fall of about 0.6 points.
3) The year-wise percentage share increased marginally up to 1994-95 (77.71%), but after that the trend was skewed and ultimately it declined in the final year (72.37%).

Industrial Sector

1) The overall percentage share of industrial sector in the total size of DCPs was 11.89% which was not significant from the point of view of industrial development of the economy.
2) The astonishing fact about the percentage share of industrial sector in the total size of DCPs was that it didn't change. The interesting point worth mentioning here is that there has been no change in the percentage share of industrial sector during the period of study as it was exactly the same (15.16%) in the base year as well as in the final year.
3) So far the year-wise percentage share is concerned, there has been marginal fluctuations every year, but it was the lowest in 1998-99 (8.73%) and highest in 1991-92 and 1999-2000 (15.16%).

Tertiary Sector

1) The overall percentage share of tertiary sector in the total size of the DCPs was 12.51% which was comparatively low. This also symbolises a comparatively less importance of this sector in the economy of the district.
2) Though, there has been an overall increase in the percentage share of tertiary sector, but it is marginal and insignificant as this has increased slightly from 11.88% in the base year to 12.47% in the final year of the study.

3) Regarding the year-wise percentage share a marginal up and down movement has been witnessed. The lowest percentage share was 10.05% in 1992-93 and it was highest in 1998-99 to a tune of 14.34%.

On the basis of above analysis we can generalise that :

1) Though, there has been almost negligible change in the percentage share of agriculture over the years, it was still enjoying a lion's share in the economy of the district, followed by tertiary sector and industrial sector.

2) The place of industrial sector in the economy of the district has remained as it is as there was no change in its percentage share. Although, the percentage share of tertiary sector has increased marginally over the years, but it is not significant.

DISTRICT JHALAWAR

Agriculture and Allied Sector

1) The overall percentage share of agriculture and allied sector in the total size of DCPs was 78.21% for the whole period of the study. It signifies that the agriculture has prominent role in the economy of the district. On the pattern of Baran and Bundi districts this primary sector has lion's share in the total size of the DCPs of this district too.

2) The percentage share of agriculture and allied sector has went up marginal from 81.67% in 1991-92 to 86.84% in 1999-2000, thereby showing an improvement of roughly around 5 points.

3) The year-wise percentage share has shown a wide ranging fluctuation in different years and the difference between minimum and maximum percentage was more than 21 points. This was minimum 65.41% in 1996-97 and was highest 86.84% in 1999-2000.

Industrial Sector

1) The overall percentage share of Jhalawar district was only 4.28% in the total size of DCP_S. It signifies a very poor and pitiable position of this sector in the economy of the district.

2) The percentage share of industrial sector has gone down substantially during the period of analysis. It was 9.37% in 1991-92 which slashed down only to 2.50% in 1999-2000,a decline of slightly more than seven points. This is an indication of declining industrial activities in the economy of the district which is a cause of concern for the policy planners.

3) The year-wise percentage achievement has been oscillated ranging between a minimum of 2.5% in the final year to a maximum of 9.72% in 1991-92.

Tertiary Sector

1) The overall percentage share of tertiary sector was 17.51%, which was moderate comparatively, but not so significant.
2) The percentage share of this sector has marginally improved from 8.60% in 1991-92 to 10.66% in 1999-2000, showing an upward trend of only around 2 points.
3) A wide ranging fluctuations have been noticed in the percentage share of this sector in various years and this variation was as high as 22.81 points. It was a minimal of 8.60 percent in the base year; while it was 31.41% in 1996-97.

On the basis of above analysis the following can be generalised :

1) Agriculture and allied sector still not only occupies a dominant share in the economy of the district, but its percentage share has also gone-up.
2) The industrial sector has only negligible share in the total size of DCPs, signifying that this sector is totally unimportant sector.
3) The role of tertiary sector has slightly increased and it has become more important than the industrial sector.
4) The comparative position of industrial and tertiary sector in the district has changed as tertiary sector now occupies second place and the industrial sector occupies the third place.

DISTRICT KOTA

Agriculture and Allied Sector

1) The overall percentage share of agriculture and allied sector in the total size of DCPs in the district was 58.70%. Although, it is significant in terms of relative share, but it is far less than the share of this sector in comparison to three other districts of the region. Although agriculture occupies an important place in the economy of the district, but the other sectors have also shown their presence felt.
2) A North-word trend was visible in the percentage share of agriculture and allied sector as the percentage share has gone-up from 53.20% in 1991-92 to 61.43% in 1999-2000 thus, an improvement of over 8 points.

3) A zig-zag trend was found in the year-wise percentage share of this sector. The percentage share was varied from a low of 53.20% in 1991-92 to a high of 61.43% in 1999-2000.

Industrial Sector

1) The overall percentage share of industrial sector in the total size of DCP_S was 19.95% indicates that the district has some industrial base.
2) A perceptible change has been seen in the percentage share of industrial sector during the period of study. It has shown a South-word trend of about 9.5 points. The percentage share in the base year was 26.5% which went down to 17.03% in the final year of the study.
3) The figures of percentage share of this sector has oscillated every year. The lowest percentage share was 17.02% in 1992-93 and it was highest 26.50% in 1991-92.

Tertiary Sector

1) The overall share of tertiary sector in the total size of credit plans was 21.35% which is significant. It signifies a comparative importance of this sector in the district's economy.
2) There has been marginal improvement in the percentage share of this sector during the whole period of study as it increased slightly (1.24 points) from 20.30% in 1991-92 to 21.54%in 1999-2000. Thus, showing an improvement of 1.24 points. It is an indication of this fact that the role of this sector has remained more or less the same during the period of study.
3) The figures of year-wise percentage share have fluctuated marginally except for the year 1996-97 when there was an increase of 3.89 points from the base year.

Thus, on the basis of above analysis, we can infer the following :

1) The agriculture and allied sector has comparatively a large percentage share and remained at the top, followed by tertiary sector and industrial sector.
2) Both industrial and tertiary sector have important place in the district's economy.
3) Although, the comparative position of industrial and tertiary sector has changed, but there has not been much difference in their comparative position. The tertiary sector has come at second place from the third in the beginning and industrial sector has shifted from its second position to the third position.

4) The declining role of industrial sector indicates sluggishness in industrial activities in the district and slightly increasing share of tertiary sector indicates its growing role in the economy.

Thus, on the basis of foregoing analysis the following generalisation can be deduced :

1) The agriculture and allied sector has taken a lion's share not only in the total size of credit plans of the region as a whole, but also in the DCPs of all four districts of the region. The share of this sector has always been more than the half size of the total credit plan.
2) In terms of percentage share of agriculture and allied sector in the total size of DCPs the highest share was of Baran district followed by Jhalawar and district Bundi. The lowest percentage share was in Kota district.
3) The percentage share of tertiary sector has not only increased during the period of analysis, but it has also become more than the percentage share of industrial sector.
4) The percentage share of industrial sector has not only gone down significantly ,but it has also become less than the tertiary sector.
5) The position of agriculture and allied sectors has slightly improved in terms of percentage share and it remained at the top, but the position of industrial and tertiary sector has changed during the period of analysis. The tertiary sector which was at last place in the initial period of the study and it's position has changed from third to the second position from 1992-93.
6) The percentage share of industrial sector in the total size of DCPs was highest in Kota district (19.95%), followed by Bundi district (11.89%) and Jhalawar district (4.28%). The percentage share of Baran district was not only very small, but also lowest in the region.
7) Kota district was having the highest percentage share in tertiary sector of the region (21.35%) which was followed by Jhalawar district (17.51) and Baran district (16.40%). The percentage share of Bundi district was the lowest (12.51%)

FINANCIAL INSTITUTIONS-WISE PERFORMANCE OF CREDIT PLANS IN HADOTI REGION

Table no. 6.10 depicts the targets and achievements of financial institutions in Hadoti region. In other words, this table shows institution-wise performance of targets and achievements during 1991-92 to 1999-2000. The institution-wise analysis has been classified in to four major categories of Commercial Banks, Regional Rural Banks, Co-operative Banks and other financial institutions. The other financial institutions include Rajasthan Financial Co-operation (RFC) and Khadi Village Industry Board (KVIB). The analysis of the table reveals the following facts :

Targets and Achievements of Commercial Banks

1) The absolute amount of overall targets of CBs for the whole region has jumped up from Rs. 3688.09 lacs in 1991-92 to Rs. 12655.17 lacs in 1999-2000 showing an increase of around 243% or more than three times from the initial year. The average annual growth rate was of the order of 27%. The year-wise analysis of the figures of targets reveals a continuous upward trend except for the year 1993-94 when the target declined marginally by about 48.16 lacs from the preceding year.

2) The absolute amount of achievement has also shown an upward trend except for the year 1992-93 and 1993-94. The decline in achievement was significant (14.12%) particularly in 1993-94. The amount of achievement has gone up from Rs. 3420.22 lacs in 1991-92 to a very high of Rs. 14591.29 lacs in 1999-2000 thereby registering a growth of about 327%, which was more than four times. The average annual growth rate of achievement was around 36%.

3) The overall of achievement against the targets has been around 102% for the whole region, which could be termed highly satisfactory. The year-wise percentage achievement has been oscillated and has shown a zig-zag trend. The percentage achievement varied between the lowest of 66.68% in 1993-94 to the highest of 123.20% in 1998-99. The percentage achievement has been more than 100% in 1997-98 (110.53%), 1998-99 (123.20%) and 1999-2000 (115.30%) but contrary to it, it was exceptionally poor in 1992-93 (76.79%) and in 1993-94 (66.68%).

Table No. 6.10

Target and Achievement of Financial Institutions in Hadoti Region (1991-92 to 1999-2000)

(Amount in Rs. Lacs)

BARAN DISTRICT												
Annual Credit Plan	**Commercial Banks**			**Regional Rural Banks**			**Co-operative Banks**			**Other Financial Institutions (RFC and KVIB)**		
Year	*Target*	*Achievement*	*Achv. in %*	*Target*	*Achievement*	*Achv. in %*	*Target*	*Achievement*	*Achv. in %*	*Target*	*Achievement*	*Achv. in %*
1991-1992	608.45	723.16	118.85	91.03	63.67	69.94	672.90	589.82	87.65	37.60	6.91	18.37
1992-1993	791.82	838.37	105.38	93.67	81.76	87.28	1295.24	1135.89	87.70	06.50	1.29	19.83
1993-1994	822.44	715.49	87.00	96.73	96.48	99.00	1230.79	1236.84	100.00	-	3.54	-
1994-1995	900.07	986.48	110.00	175.52	154.00	88.00	1239.60	1262.82	102.00	-	-	-
1995-1996	1204.86	1402.12	116.37	222.93	198.51	89.04	1737.55	2113.33	121.60	-	-	-
1996-1997	1392.61	1603.03	115.10	301.36	134.38	44.59	2213.72	2574.19	116.26	55.00	7.62	15.26
1997-1998	1768.87	2251.10	127.70	260.16	381.69	146.70	3002.05	3125.18	104.10	109.20	66.89	61.30
1998-1999	2262.00	3172.00	140.00	335.00	300.00	89.00	4073.00	3566.00	88.00	95.00	13.00	14.00
1999-2000	2394.00	2212.00	92.00	450.00	427.00	95.00	4632.00	3486.00	75.00	73.00	19.00	27.00
TOTAL	**12145.12**	**13903.75**	**114.48**	**2026.40**	**1837.49**	**90.68**	**20096.85**	**19099.07**	**95.00**	**376.30**	**118.25**	**31.42**

Contd. on page no. 195

Table No. 6.10 Continued....

(Amount in Rs. Lacs)

BUNDI DISTRICT												
Annual Credit Plan	**Commercial Banks**			**Regional Rural Banks**			**Co-operative Banks**			**Other Financial Institutions (RFC and KVIB)**		
Year	*Target*	*Achieve-ment*	*Achv. in %*	*Target*	*Achieve-ment*	*Achv. in %*	*Target*	*Achieve-ment*	*Achv. in %*	*Target*	*Achieve-ment*	*Achv. in %*
1991-1992	1118.40	1067.41	87.59	155.60	48.56	31.21	323.50	270.26	83.54	85.12	48.34	56.79
1992-1993	1209.00	1030.30	85.00	272.00	178.00	65.00	352.00	497.00	141.19	46.60	52.52	112.70
1993-1994	1208.00	761.00	63.00	298.00	181.00	61.00	403.00	766.00	190.01	71.00	22.00	30.98
1994-1995	1343.00	1344.00	100.00	518.00	519.00	100.00	633.00	1063.00	167.93	77.00	20.00	25.97
1995-1996	1557.00	1420.00	91.00	969.00	527.00	54.00	880.00	1420.00	161.34	33.00	13.00	39.39
1996-1997	1964.00	1748.00	89.00	829.00	424.00	51.00	947.00	1918.00	202.53	37.00	54.00	146.00
1997-1998	2048.00	2584.00	126.00	565.00	613.00	108.00	1512.00	1930.00	127.64	58.00	37.00	64.00
1998-1999	2404.00	3314.00	138.00	628.00	1080.00	172.00	1725.00	1612.00	93.45	100.00	69.00	69.00
1999-2000	3258.00	3469.00	106.47	803.00	935.00	117.00	1940.00	1665.00	85.82	100.00	83.00	83.00
TOTAL	**16109.40**	**16739.41**	**103.91**	**5037.60**	**4505.56**	**89.44**	**8715.50**	**11141.26**	**127.82**	**607.72**	**398.86**	**65.63**

Contd. on page no. 196

Table No. 6.10 Continued....

(Amount in Rs. Lacs)

JHALAWAR DISTRICT												
Annual Credit Plan	**Commercial Banks**			**Regional Rural Banks**			**Co-operative Banks**			**Other Financial Institutions (RFC and KVIB)**		
Year	*Target*	*Achieve-ment*	*Achv. in %*	*Target*	*Achieve-ment*	*Achv. in %*	*Target*	*Achieve-ment*	*Achv. in %*	*Target*	*Achieve-ment*	*Achv. in %*
1991-1992	487.27	376.36	77.24	99.80	66.93	71.98	551.25	681.15	123.56	89.49	61.54	68.77
1992-1993	522.55	334.93	64.09	121.67	58.40	48.00	1138.96	1201.42	105.48	27.50	51.18	186.11
1993-1994	569.84	373.20	65.49	185.31	96.79	52.23	1641.72	1510.91	92.03	66.21	57.01	86.10
1994-1995	483.55	377.17	78.00	204.46	104.57	51.14	2361.60	1902.96	80.58	65.86	45.30	68.78
1995-1996	696.90	565.67	81.17	215.65	126.20	58.52	2987.00	2478.93	82.99	90.05	63.20	70.18
1996-1997	799.79	741.82	92.75	293.69	132.56	45.14	4857.60	3419.76	70.39	86.80	64.58	74.40
1997-1998	940.83	956.15	101.63	269.40	197.09	73.16	4025.00	4036.74	100.29	90.00	123.84	137.60
1998-1999	1173.06	1158.86	98.79	337.50	314.70	93.24	5377.20	4604.65	85.63	143.70	114.51	88.08
1999-2000	1604.40	1170.08	72.93	400.00	394.93	96.23	6305.30	4430.94	70.27	100.00	172.92	172.92
TOTAL	**7278.19**	**6054.24**	**83.18**	**2127.48**	**1492.17**	**70.14**	**29245.63**	**24267.46**	**82.98**	**759.61**	**754.08**	**99.27**

Contd. on page no. 197

Table No. 6.10 Continued....

(Amount in Rs. Lacs)

KOTA DISTRICT												
Annual Credit Plan	**Commercial Banks**			**Regional Rural Banks**			**Co-operative Banks**			**Other Financial Institutions (RFC and KVIB)**		
Year	*Target*	*Achievement*	*Achv. in %*	*Target*	*Achievement*	*Achv. in %*	*Target*	*Achievement*	*Achv. in %*	*Target*	*Achievement*	*Achv. in %*
1991-1992	1473.97	1253.29	85.00	109.67	65.22	59.00	954.03	1107.30	116.00	172.45	406.57	236
1992-1993	1822.39	1133.77	62.00	108.05	69.49	64.00	1782.13	1704.87	95.66	-	-	-
1993-1994	1697.32	1016.09	60.00	99.82	177.18	177.50	1730.57	1263.25	74.15	-	-	-
1994-1995	1974.63	1898.19	96.00	363.35	337.00	93.00	1814.86	1553.78	85.61	11.15	-	-
1995-1996	2664.87	2216.96	83.00	414.46	370.05	89.00	1916.50	2985.15	155.70	208.70	154.23	74.00
1996-1997	3052.15	2552.44	83.62	637.04	378.93	60.00	2294.80	2904.05	126.55	94.00	62.71	67.00
1997-1998	3406.17	3232.52	95.00	519.00	757.24	146.00	3639.90	2768.47	76.00	125.00	104.35	83.00
1998-1999	4435.37	5013.68	113.00	675.53	984.21	145.69	4466.80	2649.00	59.30	194.68	182.02	93.50
1999-2000	5398.77	7740.21	143.37	800.00	1025.61	128.00	5061.80	4676.64	115.14	70.00	331.64	473.77
TOTAL	**25925.64**	**26057.15**	**100.51**	**3726.92**	**4164.93**	**111.75**	**23661.39**	**21609.46**	**93.92**	**875.98**	**1241.52**	**141.73**

Contd. on page no. 198

Table No. 6.10 Continued....

(Amount in Rs. Lacs)

TOTAL OF THE REGION

Annual Credit Plan	Commercial Banks			Regional Rural Banks			Co-operative Banks			Other Financial Institutions (RFC and KVIB)		
Year	*Target*	*Achieve-ment*	*Achv. in %*	*Target*	*Achieve-ment*	*Achv. in %*	*Target*	*Achieve-ment*	*Achv. in %*	*Target*	*Achieve-ment*	*Achv. in %*
1991-1992	3688.09	3420.22	92.74	456.10	243.88	53.47	2501.68	2648.53	105.87	384.66	523.36	136.06
1992-1993	4345.76	3337.07	76.79	595.39	387.65	65.11	4568.33	4539.18	99.36	80.60	104.99	130.26
1993-1994	4297.60	2865.78	66.68	679.86	551.45	81.11	5006.08	4777.00	95.42	137.21	82.55	60.16
1994-1995	4701.25	4605.84	97.97	1261.33	1114.47	88.36	6049.06	5782.56	95.59	154.01	65.30	42.40
1995-1996	6123.63	5604.75	91.53	1822.04	1221.76	67.05	7521.05	8997.41	119.63	331.75	230.43	69.46
1996-1997	7208.55	6645.29	92.19	2061.09	1069.87	51.91	10313.12	10816.00	104.88	272.80	188.91	69.25
1997-1998	8163.87	9023.77	110.53	1613.56	1749.02	108.39	12178.95	11860.39	97.38	382.20	332.08	86.89
1998-1999	10274.43	12658.54	123.20	1976.53	2678.91	135.54	15642.00	12431.54	79.47	537.38	378.53	70.44
1999-2000	12655.17	14591.29	115.30	2453.00	2782.54	113.43	17939.10	14258.58	79.48	343.00	606.56	176.84
TOTAL	**61458.35**	**62752.55**	**102.10**	**12918.40**	**11999.60**	**92.89**	**81719.37**	**76111.19**	**93.14**	**2619.61**	**2513.71**	**95.96**

Source: DCPs of various years of Baran, Bundi, Jhalawar and Kota Districts.

Targets and Achievements of Regional Rural Banks

1) There has been significant increase in the absolute amount of targets of RRBs except for the year 1997-98 as these have gone-up from Rs. 456.10 lacs in the base year to Rs. 2453.00 lacs in the final year of the study, thereby indicating a growth of about 438%, which was around five and half times more from the base year. The per annum growth rate of target was around 49% for the whole region, which was excellent.

2) The absolute amount of achievement has shown a North-ward trend except for the year 1996-97, when it declined by about 14.20%. The amount of achievement was Rs. 243.88 lacs in absolute terms in the initial year which surged-up to a staggering amount of Rs. 2782.54 lacs in the final year of the study, thereby showing exceptionally a very high growth rate of 1041%, which was more than eleven times from the base year. The average annual growth rate for the whole region was about 116%, which could be termed as robust growth.

3) The overall percentage achievement for the region was 92.89%, which could be termed as satisfactory. The year-wise percentage achievement of RRB_S, has been fluctuating continuously and it remained between 51.91% to 88.30% during 1991-92 to 1996-97. But thereafter the percentage achievement has always been more than 100% and it was highest in 1998-99, (135.54%)

Targets and Achievements of Co-operative Banks

1) Remarkable growth of about 617% has been observed in the absolute amount of targets of co-operative banks in the region. The absolute amount of targets have increased tremendously from Rs. 2501.68 lacs in the initial year to a staggering figure of Rs. 17939.10 lacs in the final year of the study. This amounts to more than seven fold increase. The average annual growth rate of targets was about 69%, which was excellent.

2) The year-wise absolute amount of achievement has witnessed a continuous and significant improvement during the period of analysis. This has gone-up from Rs. 2648.53 lacs in the base year to Rs. 14258.58 lacs in the final year of the study, depicting thereby an upsurge of about 438% i.e. more than five times increase. The average per annum growth rate in achievements was of the order of about 49% for the whole region.

3) The overall percentage achievement of co-operative banks in the region was around 93% during the whole period of study, which can be termed as satisfactory. The percentage achievement has been fluctuating continuously, but on the whole it was satisfactory as it was always more than 95% except for two years 1998-99 and 1999-2000, when it was almost the same around 79%. The performance in terms of percentage achievement has been exceptionally good in 1991-92 (105.87%), 1995-96 (119.63%) and 1996-97 (104.88%) as it remained more than 100%.

Targets and Achievements of Other Financial Institutions

1) The absolute amount of targets of other financial institutions has shown an overall declining trend as this has declined by Rs. 41.66 lacs (10.83%). These figures were fluctuating heavily during the period of analysis between a minimum of Rs. 80.60 lacs in 1992-93 to a maximum of Rs. 537.38 lacs in 1998-99.
2) The overall absolute amount of achievement has oscillated substantially during the period of analysis and has shown a slight improvement of about 14%. The figures have gone-up from Rs. 523.36 lacs in the base year to Rs. 606.56 lacs in the final year of the study.
3) The overall percentage achievement for the whole region was 95.96%, which could be termed as satisfactory. The year-wise percentage achievement has also been highly fluctuating on the pattern of absolute figures of achievement. The range of fluctuations has been between a minimum of 42.40% in 1994-95 to a maximum of 176.84% in 1999-2000.

The performance of various financial institutions in DCPs of different districts of the region has been analysed below :

DISTRICT BARAN

Targets and Achievements of Commercial Banks

1) There has been a consistent upward trend in the absolute amount of targets as these have gone-up from Rs. 608.45 lacs in the initial year to a high of Rs. 2394 lacs in the final year of the study, denoting thereby a growth of about 294%; i.e. around four times more from the base year. The average annual growth of in the targets was 32.61%.
2) Though, there has been an overall increasing trend in the absolute amount of achievements as these have increased from Rs.723.16 lacs in 1991-92 to Rs. 2212 lacs in 1999-2000, denoting thereby an increase

of about 206% or about three times more from the base year, but the achievement figures declined in 1993-94 (14.66%) and also in 1999-2000 (33.26%). The average annual growth rate in achievement was of the order of 22.88%, which was satisfactory.

3) The overall performance of CBs in the district has been highly satisfactory as it was 114.48%.The year-wise analysis of percentage achievement, has been more than 100% except only in two years; i.e. 1993-94 (87%) and 1999-2000 (92%). The percentage achievement has been exceptionally good in 1998-99 when it was highest (140%).

Targets and Achievements of Regional Rural Banks

1) The absolute figures of targets have registered a growth rate of about 394% in the whole period of analysis as these have surged-up from Rs. 91.03 lacs in 1991-92 to Rs. 450 lacs in 1999-2000 which was about five fold increase. The average per annum growth rate in targets of RRBs in the district was 43.81, which was good.
2) Except for the year 1996-97 and 1998-99 the absolute amount of achievement has increased and have also shown an overall increasing trend. The absolute figures of achievement have climbed up from Rs. 63.67 lacs in the beginning to Rs. 427 lacs at the end of the period of study, denoting thereby a high growth rate of 571% or around seven fold increase. The average annual growth rate in achievements was 63.40%, which was excellent.
3) The overall percentage achievement of RRBs in the district has remained 90.68%, which is moderately good. The percentage achievement has been fluctuating substantially during the period of analysis. The range of fluctuations has been between a very low of 44.59% in 1996-97 to a very high of 146.70% in 1997-98, a gap of more than 100 points. In rest of the years the performance has been satisfactory except in 1991-92 when it was 69.94%.

Targets and Achievements of Co-operative Banks

1) The absolute amount of targets was Rs. 672.90 lacs in 1991-92 which went-up to Rs. 4632 lacs in 1999-2000 indicating a growth of about 588% or seven times more than the base year. There has been continuous increasing trend in targets throughout the period of study except for the year 1993-94 (declined by Rs. 64.45 lacs or around 5% compared to the preceding year). The average annual growth rate in targets was 65.37% for the whole period of the study.

2) There has been an upward trend in the absolute amount of achievement as this has spiralled from Rs. 589.82 lacs in initial year to Rs. 3486 lacs in the final year of the study depicting thereby an increase of about 491% (six fold increase). The average annual growth rate in achievement was 54.56% during the period of analysis, which was excellent.

3) The overall performance of co-operative banks in the district has remained 95% during the period of study, which could be said satisfactory. The year-wise percentage performance reveals that this has been exceptionally good in 1993-94 (100%), 1994-95 (102%), 1995-96 (121.60%), 1996-97 (116.26%) and in 1997-98 (104.10%). In rest of the years of the study, the performance was satisfactory as it was not less than 75%.

Targets and Achievements of Other Financial Institutions

1) An uneven growth pattern was observed in the absolute amount of targets due to substantial fluctuations. In 1992-93 it declined by a very high percentage of 82.93%. The absolute amount of target was only Rs. 6.50 lacs in 1992-93 which was lowest and Rs. 109.20 lacs in 1997-98 when it was highest. Thus, the range of fluctuations was more than 100 points. The striking fact about the targets was that no allocation was made to other financial institutions in the credit plans continuously for three years (from 1993-94 to 1995-96). The overall trend, inspite of all odds, has been increasing as the targets went-up from Rs. 37.60 lacs in the initial year to Rs. 73 lacs in the final year of the study, which was just double or about 93%. The average annual growth rate in target was only 10.31%, which was highly dis-satisfactory.

2) The absolute figures of achievement have oscillated, but even then these have increased from Rs. 6.91 lacs in the base year to Rs. 19 lacs in the final year of the study, registering a growth of about 186%. Besides this, the strange fact was that the achievement was Rs. 3.54 lacs in 1993-94 against target. The average per annum growth rate in achievement was dismal as it was only 20.70%.

3) The overall performance of other financial institutions in the district has been very poor of the order of only 31.42%.

4) So far the percentage achievement of other financial institutions is concerned, this has been very poor throughout the whole period of the study except 1997-98 (61%) as this was always less than 27% and has been as low as 15.20% in 1996-97.

BUNDI DISTRICT

Targets and Achievements of Commercial Banks

1) There has been overall up-surge in the absolute amount of targets as these have spiralled-up from Rs. 1118.40 lacs in the base year to Rs. 3258 lacs in the final year of the study, denoting an improvement of about 191% or around three fold increase. The average annual growth rate in targets was of the order of 22%.
2) Inspite of decline in absolute amount of achievement initially in 1992-93 (8.10%) and in 1993-94 (26.14%), there has been an upward trend. The absolute amount of achievement was Rs. 1067.41 lacs in 1991-92 which climbed up to Rs. 3469 lacs in 1999-2000 showing an increase of about 225% or more than three fold increase. The average annual growth rate in achievement was 25%, which could be termed as satisfactory.
3) The overall performance of CBs was highly satisfactory as it crossed the 100% mark (104%). The achievement has shown a zig-zag trend as this was fluctuating between a low of 63% in 1993-94 to a high of 138% in 1998-99. In four years (1994-95, 1997-98, 1998-99 and 1999-2000) of the period of study the performance has been highly satisfactory as it was more than 100%. In rest of the years the performance could be termed satisfactory as it was generally more than 85%.

Targets and Achievements of Regional Rural Banks

1) Upto 1995-96, the target figures have shown an upward trend, but thereafter they declined continuously for three years and ultimately it increased. The overall trend was North-ward as the absolute amount of targets went-up from Rs. 155.60 lacs in the base year to Rs. 803 lacs in the final year of the study which marked a growth of 416% i.e. about five fold increase. The average per annum growth rate during the period of study has remained 46%.
2) There has been exceptionally a remarkable growth in the absolute amount of achievement as it was as high as 1825% which was about nineteen times more than that of the base year. The absolute figures jumped-up from a very low level of Rs. 48.56 lacs in 1991-92 to a very high of Rs. 935 lacs in 1999-2000. The as average per annum growth rate in achievement of RRBs was as high as of 203%, which could be termed as excellent.

3) The overall performance of RRBs has been 89.44% throughout the whole period of study. The achievement has been uneven and fluctuated severely between a very low of 31.21% in 1991-92 to a very high of 172% in 1998-99, a difference of around 40 points. The achievement in 1994-95 (100%), 1997-98 (108%), 1998-99 (172%) and 1999-2000 (117%) was highly satisfactory, but in other years of the study it was not up to the mark.

Targets and Achievements of Co-operative Banks

1) There has been consistent growth in the absolute amount of targets. These increased continuously in all years and spiralled-up from Rs. 323.50 lacs in 1991-92 to Rs. 1940 lacs in 1999-2000 which was an up surge of about 500% or six fold more than that of the base year. The average annual growth rate in targets was 55.52%, which was highly satisfactory by all means.
2) The absolute amount of achievement has increased continuously till 1997-98 and it declined thereafter, but the overall trend has been towards the positive side as the figures of absolute achievement went-up from Rs. 270.26 lacs in the initial year to Rs. 1665 lacs in the last year of the study, signifying a growth of 516% or about six fold increase. The average per annum growth rate was 57%, which was really good.
3) The overall achievement of co-operative banks in the district was 127.82%, which could be termed as highly satisfactory. Exceptionally high fluctuations have been noticed in the performance of co-operative banks as these ranged between a low of 83.54% in 1991-92 to a very high of 202.53% in 1996-97-a wide gap of 119 points. The performance. Co-operative banks has been excellent in all years, as it was more than 127% except the 1991-92, 1998-99 and 1999-2000. In these three years, the performance has remained satisfactory, as it was more than 83%.

Targets and Achievements of Other Financial Institutions

1) Inspite of overall increase in the absolute amount of targets there has been a zig-zag trend year-wise. The figures of targets have ultimately increased marginally from Rs. 85.12 lacs in 1991-92 to Rs. 100 lacs in 1999-2000-a meagre growth of about 17.50%. The average annual growth rate in targets was exceptionally very small of about 1.94%, which was very bad.

2) The absolute amount of achievement has shown an overall marginal growth only of about 71.70%. The figures of achievement has increased from Rs. 48.34 lacs in 1991-92 to Rs. 83 lacs in 1999-2000. The average annual growth rate in achievement was very low of around 8%.

3) The overall achievement of other financial institution was only 65.63% which could not be termed satisfactory. Regarding the year-wise achievement the trend has been quite uneven ranging between as low a 25.97% in 1994-95 to as high as 146% in 1996-97. Except for two years 1992-93 (112.70%), 1996-97 (146%), the percentage achievement was not satisfactory.

DISTRICT JHALAWAR

Targets and Achievements of Commercial Banks

1) The absolute amount of targets of CBs in the district has been increasing throughout the period of study except for 1994-95 and the rate of growth was about 229% i.e. more than three times increase. The absolute figures went-up from Rs. 487.27 lacs 1991-92 to Rs. 1604.40 lacs in 1999-2000. The average annual growth rate in targets was of the order of 25.45%, which was satisfactory.

2) The absolute amount of achievement which was Rs. 376.36 lacs in 1991-92 increased to Rs. 1170.08 lacs in 1999-2000 denoting thereby a growth of 211% or more than three times increase than that of base year. The average annual growth rate was 23.43%.

3) The overall achievement of CBs was 83.18% for the whole period of study, which could be termed satisfactory. The achievement has oscillated every year sometimes more and sometimes less. It was minimum in 1992-93 (64.09%) and maximum in 1997-98 (101.63%). In remaining years performance achievement was never less than 65% and not more than 99%.

Targets and Achievements of Regional Rural Banks

1) There has been continuous and consistent growth in absolute amount of targets except for the year 1997-98 when the amount declined by 8.27%. The target figures went-up from Rs. 99.80 lacs in 1991-92 to Rs. 400 lacs in 1999-2000, registering a growth of about 301% or four fold increase. The average annual growth rate of targets was 23.43% which was comparatively low.

2) A similar trend as that of targets in absolute amount of achievement was observed. The figures of achievement have gone-up by 490% (six fold increase) as these have spiralled-up from Rs. 66.93 lacs in the initial year to Rs. 394.93 lacs in the final year of the study. The average annual growth rate of achievement was 54.45%, which was excellent.

3) The overall trend of achievement for the whole period of study was 70.14%. The surprising fact about the year-wise achievement of RRBs was that the targets could not be achieved even in a single year of the period under analysis. The achievement has varied between the band of 45.14% to 96.23%.

Targets and Achievements of Co-operative Banks

1) A remarkable high growth rate in targets of 1044% was seen during the whole period of study. The absolute amount of targets have risen from Rs. 551.25 lacs in 1991-92 to a very staggering level of Rs. 6305.30 lacs in 1999-2000. The average per annum growth rate in targets was 116%, which was excellent and robust.

2) The absolute amount of achievement has increased continuously till 1998-99, but it declined in the last year of the study by about 3.80%. The overall trend in absolute amount of achievement was increasing as the figures of achievement increased from Rs. 681.15 lacs in the initial year to Rs. 4430.94 lacs in the final year of the study, depicting thereby a growth of 550.51% or about six and half times increase over the base year. The average annual growth rate was fairly good to a high of 61%.

3) The overall achievement of co-operative banks for the whole period of study was of the order of 82.41%. Except for the year 1991-92 (123.56%), 1992-93 (105.48%) and 1997-98 (100.29%) the achievement in rest of the years of the period of study has remained less than 93%, but it was never less than 70%.

Targets and Achievements of Other Financial Institutions

1) The overall growth rate in absolute amount of targets has been very low of about 11.74%, which was poor comparatively. The absolute amount of targets surged-up from Rs. 89.49 lacs in 1991-92 to Rs. 100.00 lacs in 1999-2000 with uneven fluctuations every year marginal as well as substantial. The average annual growth rate in targets was negligible to a very low level of only 1.30%.

2) There has been a zig-zag trend in the absolute amount of achievement as these figures have oscillated every year, but there has been an overall upward trend as the absolute amount which was Rs. 61.54 lacs in 1991-92 increased to Rs. 172.92 lacs in 1999-2000, demonstrating a growth of about 181% or three fold increase. The average per annum growth rate was 20.11%.

3) The overall percentage achievement of other financial institutions has remained slightly less than 100% (99.27%) which could be termed as fairly good. Comparing year-wise achievement with targets we find an uneven trend as the achievement has varied between a low of 68.77% in 1991-92 to a high of 186.11% in 1992-93. Besides, 1992-93 the performance has also been exceptionally good in 1997-98 (137.60%) and in 1999-2000 (172.92%). In rest of the years the performance was more than 68%.

DISTRICT KOTA

Targets and Achievements of Commercial Banks

1) There has been a continuous upward trend in the absolute amount of the targets except for 1993-94 when the amount declined by 6.86% over the preceding year. The absolute figures of targets have shown a growth of about 266% (more than three and half times increase) as these have gone up from Rs. 1473.97 lacs in the initial year to Rs. 5398.77 lacs in 1999-2000. The average annual growth rate in targets of CBs has been of the order of 29.58%.

2) The growth rate in absolute amount of achievement was much higher than the growth rate in targets. It was around 518%. The absolute figures of achievement went up from Rs. 1253.29 lacs in the base year to Rs. 7740.21 lacs in the final year. In 1992-93 and 1993-94, the amount of achievement went down by 9.54% and 10.38% respectively. The average annual growth rate of achievement was as high as 57.51%, which was fairly good.

3) The overall achievement of CBs for the whole period of study was more than cent-percent (100.51%), which can be said highly satisfactory. Except for 1998-99 and 1999-2000, the achievement has always been less than 96%. The achievement in above said two years was 113% and 143.37% respectively. The trend of achievement was uneven as it was fluctuating every year. The minimum level of achievement was 60% in 1993-94.

Targets and Achievements of Regional Rural Banks

1) The absolute amount of targets has shown an overall growth pattern as this amount has gone-up from Rs. 109.67 lacs in the initial year to Rs. 800 lacs in the final year of the study, registering a growth of 629% or a growth of more than seven times. Of course, the trend of growth has been uneven.
2) A staggering growth rate has been registered in absolute amount of achievement of about 1473% i.e. sixteen times more than that of base year. This is reflected by the changes in the absolute amount of achievement as these increased from a low level of Rs. 65.22 lacs in the base year to a very high amount of Rs. 1025.61 lacs in the final year of the study. The average annual growth rate in achievements was as high as 163.61%, which signifies an excellent performance of RRBs in the district.
3) The overall performance of RRBs in district Kota has been excellent as this was more than 111% (111.75%). The year-wise achievement has been fluctuating every year and this was exceptionally good in 1993-94 (177%), 1997-98 (146%), 1998-99 (145.69%) and 1999-2000 (128%). In remaining years this was ranging between 59% in 1991-92 to 93% in 1994-95.

Targets and Achievements of Co-operative Banks

1) The absolute figures of targets have increased except in the year 1992-93 as it is evident from this fact that these increased from Rs. 954.03 lacs in the initial year to Rs. 5061.80 lacs in the final year of the study, depicting thereby an increase of 431% i.e. more than five fold increase. The average annual growth rate of co-operative banks in the district was fairly good of the order of 47.84%.
2) There has been a zig-zag trend in the absolute amount of achievement. Inspite of that, they have shown an overall increasing trend as they have gone-up from Rs. 1107.30 lacs in 1991-92 to Rs. 4676.64 lacs in 1999-2000, registering a growth of about 323% (more than four fold increase). The average annual growth rate of achievement was 35.82% – a satisfactory performance.
3) The overall performance of co-operative banks in the district was 93.92% which could be said satisfactory. A lot of variations have been observed in the year-wise percentage achievement ranging between a minimum of 59.30% in 1998-99 to a high of 155.70% in 1995-96, a difference of about 96 points. The performance has been extremely well in 1991-92 (116%), 1995-96 (155.70%), 1996-97 (126.55%) and in 1999-2000 (115.14%).

Targets and Achievements of Other Financial Institutions

1) A downward disgusting trend has been observed in the absolute amount of targets which have fallen from Rs. 172.45 lacs in 1991-92 to a very low of Rs. 70 lacs in 1999-2000, a fall of about 59.40%. The trend in target figures has also been uneven and no provision for credit was made for 1991-92 and 1992-93.
2) A similar declining trend has also been found in the absolute amount of achievement as these have gone down from Rs. 406.57 lacs in the beginning to Rs. 331.64 lacs at the end of the period of study a decline of about 18.42%.
3) The overall achievement of other financial institutions has been extremely of high order equal to 141.73%. Regarding the year-wise achievement there has been exceptionally good performance specially in 1991-92 (236%) and in 1999-2000 (473.77%) and in rest of the years the performance varied between a low of 67% in 1996-97 to a high of 93.50% in 1998-99.

Thus, on the basis of above analysis the following generalisation can be deduced :

1) The absolute amount of overall targets of co-operative banks in the whole region have exceeded the combined targets of CBs, RRBs and other financial institutions.
2) The absolute amount of overall achievements of co-operative banks have exceeded the combined targets of CBs and RRBs in the whole region. Thus, the overall performance of co-operative banks has been commendable.
3) In terms of overall achievement the commercial banks remained at the top and their performance was more than 100%, followed by co-operative banks, and RRBs. The performance of other financial institutions, though was higher than co-operative banks and RRBs, but in view of their insignificant share in the total size of credit plan it has got no significance.
4) In terms of absolute amount of targets of CBs in the region, the district Kota remained at the top, followed by district Bundi, district Baran,and district Jhalawar.
5) In terms of absolute amount of targets of RRBs, the prime position was of district Bundi in the region, followed by district Kota, district Jhalawar and district Baran.
6) Regarding the ranking in terms of absolute amount of targets district Jhalawar was at the top in the region, followed by Kota district, Baran district and Bundi district as respectively.

7) The district Kota was at the top in the region in regard to the absolute amount of targets of other financial institutions, followed by Jhalawar, Bundi and Baran districts.

8) So far the performance of CBs in terms of absolute achievement is concerned, the position of the Kota district was the best in the region followed by Bundi district, Baran district and Jhalawar district.

9) The performance of RRBs in terms of absolute amount of achievement, Jhalawar district was at the top in the region which was followed by Kota district, Baran district and Bundi district.

10) In terms of absolute amount of co-operative banks in the region, district Jhalawar enjoyed the supremacy. The second place was of Kota district followed by Baran district and Bundi district.

11) Kota district remained at the top in the region in terms of absolute amount of achievement of other financial institutions, followed by Jhalawar, Bundi and Baran districts.

PERCENTAGE SHARE OF TARGET OF FINANCIAL INSTITUTIONS IN TOTAL CREDIT PLAN IN HADOTI REGION

The percentage share of target of financial institutions in total size of credit plans in Hadoti region has been shown in *table no. 6.11*. The study of this table depicts the following facts :

1) The overall share of CBs in the total size of the credit plans in the region has declined from 52.46% in the base year to 37.90% in the final year of the study, thus, a fall of 14.56 points. The overall share of CBs in the total size of credit plans of the region was 38.72%, which was significant.

2) The share of RRBs in the total size of credit plans has increased marginally in the last year of the period of study in comparison to the base year, thus, the increase was of the order of 0.86 points. The overall share of RRBs in total size of credit plans was 8.14% in the region, which was not so significant.

3) The overall trend of comparative share of co-operative banks in the total size of credit plans has shown an increasing trend. The share has gone up from 35.58% in 1991-92 to 53.72% 1999-2000, depicting thereby an up surge of about 18 points which was significant. The overall share of co-operative banks in total credit plan was 51.49% in the region, which was highly significant.

Table No. 6.11

Percentage Share of Target of Financial Institutions in Total Credit Plan in Hadoti Region (1991-92 to 1999-2000)

Annual Credit Plan	BARAN				BUNDI				JHALAWAR				KOTA				TOTAL of the Region			
Year	Comm. Banks	Reg. Rural Banks (HKGB)	Co-op. Banks	Other Inst. (RFC & KVIB)	Comm Banks	Reg. Rural Banks (HKGB & BCKGB)	Co-op. Banks	Other Inst. (RFC & KVIB)	Comm. Banks	Reg. Rural Banks (HKGB)	Co-op. Banks	Other Inst. (RFC & KVIB)	Comm. Banks	Reg. Rural Banks (HKGB)	Co-op. Banks	Other Inst. (RFC & KVIB)	Comm. Banks	Reg. Rural Banks (HKGB)	Co-op. Banks	Other Inst. (RFC & KVIB)
1991-1992	43.15	06.46	47.72	02.67	66.47	09.25	19.22	05.06	39.69	08.12	44.90	07.29	54.39	04.05	35.20	06.36	52.46	06.49	35.58	05.47
1992-1993	36.20	04.28	59.22	00.30	64.32	14.47	18.73	02.48	28.86	06.72	62.90	01.52	49.09	02.91	48.00	-	45.31	06.21	47.64	00.84
1993-1994	38.25	04.50	57.25	-	61.01	15.05	20.35	03.59	23.13	07.52	66.65	02.70	48.11	02.83	49.06	-	42.46	06.72	49.46	01.36
1994-1995	38.88	07.58	53.54	-	52.24	20.14	24.62	03.00	15.52	06.56	75.81	02.11	47.42	08.73	43.58	00.27	38.64	10.37	49.72	01.27
1995-1996	38.06	07.04	54.90	-	45.27	28.18	25.59	00.96	17.47	05.40	74.87	02.26	51.20	07.96	36.83	04.01	38.76	11.54	47.60	02.10
1996-1997	35.15	07.60	55.86	01.39	52.00	21.95	25.07	00.98	13.25	04.86	80.45	01.44	50.22	10.48	37.75	01.55	36.30	10.38	51.95	01.37
1997-1998	34.42	05.06	58.40	02.12	48.96	13.50	36.15	01.39	17.67	05.06	75.59	01.69	44.29	06.75	47.33	01.63	36.55	07.22	54.52	01.71
1998-1999	33.44	04.95	60.21	01.40	49.50	12.92	35.52	02.06	16.68	04.80	76.48	02.04	45.39	06.91	45.71	01.99	36.14	06.95	55.03	01.89
1999-2000	31.71	04.96	61.36	00.97	53.40	13.16	31.80	01.64	19.07	04.76	74.98	01.19	47.65	07.06	44.67	00.62	37.90	07.35	53.72	01.03
TOTAL	**35.06**	**05.85**	**58.01**	**01.08**	**52.87**	**16.53**	**28.61**	**01.99**	**18.47**	**05.40**	**74.20**	**01.93**	**47.84**	**06.88**	**43.66**	**01.62**	**38.72**	**08.14**	**51.49**	**01.65**

Source: DCPs of various years of Baran, Bundi, Jhalawar and Kota Districts.

4) The percentage share of other financial institutions in total size of credit plans in the region was comparatively negligible and it has shown an overall declining trend from 5.47% in the base year to a very low of 1.03% in the final year of the study, thus, depicting a fall of 4.44 points. The overall percentage share of other financial institutions in total credit plan was negligible (1.61%).

The above analysis of percentage share of targets of different financial institutions in the total credit plan reveals that the comparative position of different financial institutions have changed. The percentage share of CBs was highest in the base year followed by co-operative banks, RRBs and other financial institutions, but in the last year of the study, co-operative banks stood first, followed by CBs, RRBs, and other financial institutions.

Analysis of percentage share of target of different financial institutions in total credit plan of different districts of the region has been given below:

District Baran

1) The share of CBs in total credit plan of the district has declined from 43.15% in initial year to 31.71% in the final year of the study-a fall of about 11.44 points, which was significant. The overall share of CBs in total credit plan was about 35%, which was sigificant.
2) The share of RRBs in total credit plan has also declined marginally from 6.46% in the base year to 5.96% in the final year i.e. a decline of 0.5 points. The overall share of RRBs in total credit plan was comparatively small of about 5.85%.
3) Contrary to the trend of CBs and RRBs, the share of co-operative banks in the district has increased substantially from 47.72% in 1991-92 to 61.36% in 1999-2000; i.e. an increase of about 14 points. The overall of co-operative banks was slightly more than 58% (58.01%), which was highly sigificant.
4) The share of other financial institutions though negligible, but has declined from 2.67% in the base year to only 0.97% in the final year. The overall share of other financial institutions was only 1.08%, which is insignificant.

District Bundi

1) The share of CBs has been significant sizeable, but on the whole it was declining. It was 66.47% in 1991-92 which decclined to 53.40% in 1999-2000, a decline of about 13 points. The overall share of

CBs in the total credit plan of the district has been more than half (52.87%), which was significant.

2) The share of RRBs in total credit plan has shown an upward trend which is evident from this fact that the share of these banks has gone-up from 9.25% in base year to 13.16% in the final year *i.e.* a surge of around 4 points. The overall share of these banks was of the order of 16.53%.

3) There has been an upward trend in the relative share of co-operative banks in total credit plan as this has gone-up from 19.92% in 1991-92 to 31.80% in 1999-2000, a jump of about 12 points, which was substantial. The overall share of co-operative banks in total credit plans was 28.61%.

4) Though the relative share of other financial institutions in total credit plans has been negligible throughout the whole period of study and also has shown an overall declining trend from 5.06% in 1991-92 to 1.64% in 1999-2000. The overall share of these institutions in total size of credit plans was around 2% (1.99%), which was insignificant.

District Jhalawar

1) The relative share of CBs in total credit plan has declined substantially from 39.69% in 1991-92 to 19.07% in 1999-2000, which was more than 20 points. The overall share of CBs in total credit plan was 18.47%.

2) Similar to CBs the relative share of RRBs in total credit plan has also gone down from 8.12% in 1991-92 to 4.76% in 1999-2000, *i.e.* of around 3 points. The overall share of RRB in total size of credit plans was 5.40%, which was comparatively very low.

3) Inspite of a zig-zag trend, the relative share of co-operative banks has gone-up significantly by around 30 points from 44.90% in initial year to 74.98% in the final year of the study. The overall share of co-operative bank was very high of order of 74.20%.

4) The relative share of other financial institutions has declined substantially from 7.29% in 1991-92 to 1.19% in 1999-2000, *i.e.* slightly more than 6 points. The overall share of these institutions was only 1.39%, which was negligible.

District Kota

1) Though the relative share of CBs in total credit plan has been significant and has always been more than 44%, it has shown a

declining trend. The share has slashed from 54.39% in 1991-92 to 47.65% in 1999-2000, which was about 6.70 points less. The overall share of CBs in total credit plan was 47.84%, which was significant.

2) There has been a growing trend in the achievement of RRBs as their share has moved from 4.05% in 1991-92 to 7.06% in 1999-2000, depicting a growth of about 2 points. The overall share of RRBs was 6.88%.

3) The relative share of co-operative banks has been sufficiently large in total size of credit plan and also showed an increasing trend. The share of this category of banks has risen from 35.20% in the base year to 44.67% in the final year of the study i.e. around 9 points. The overall share of co-operative banks in total credit plans was 43.66%, which was slightly less than the share of CBs.

4) Regarding the other financial institutions, the relative share slashed from 6.36% in the initial year to a very low of 0.62% in the final year of the study, which was more than 5 points. The overall share of these institutions was only 1.62%, which is insignificant.

Thus, on the basis of above analysis we can generalise :

1) The relative share of co-operative banks in the region was highest and it was more than 50%. This has also shown an upward trend which signifies their increasing role in the credit plans and also in the development of the region's economy. Although, the share of CBs was also very high and they were second to co-operative banks, but a substantial declining trend was clearly visible which highlights that their comparative importance is diminishing gradually. Though, the relative share of RRBs has increased marginally in total credit plan, but their share was not significant. The percentage share of other financial institutions was not only insignificant, but negligible too.

2) District Bundi ranked first in regard to the percentage share of CBs in total size of credit plan and its share was slightly by above 50%. The position of Kota district was second in this regard and its share was also too high and was slightly less than the district Bundi. The percentage share of CBs in Baran district was one third of the total followed by Jhalawar district wherein the share was comparatively small.

3) Regarding the percentage share of RRBs in total size of the credit plans district Bundi was at the top and also having substantially higher percentage share than the other districts of

the region. The district Kota stood second in this regard followed by Baran and Jhalawar district respectively whose share were more or less the same and comparatively small.

4) The share of Co-ooerative banks in district Jhalawar was around three fourth and topped the region. District Baran was second in rank and the share of co-operative banks was more than 50%, followed by district Kota and district Bundi.

5) Comparing the percentage share of other financial institutions in different districts, the district Bundi remained at the top, followed by district Jhalawar, district Kota and district Baran. In all these districts the share of these institutions was less than 2% of the total size of credit plans.

TOTAL DEPOSITS AND THEIR GROWTH RATE IN HADOTI REGION

Table no. 6.12 depicts the position of total deposits of CBs in the Hadoti region along with their growth rate. The study of the table reveals the following facts :

The total deposits of CBs in the region were Rs. 46452.73 lacs in 1991-92 which increased to Rs. 178906.43 lacs in 1999-2000, thereby showing a growth of about 285% which could be considered significant. The total deposits have increased continuously throughout the period of study.

The growth rate of deposits in the region has fluctuated between the minimum range of 13% in 1993-94 to the maximum range of 21.73% in 1995-96. In view of stiff competition with other financial institutions operating in the region, the growth rate could be termed as satisfactory. The compound average annual growth rate (CAGR) in deposits of the region was around 16% during the period of study.

The Position of total deposits and their growth rate in different districts of Hadoti region has been analysed below :

District Baran

There has been continuous and consistent growth in total deposits as these have increased from Rs. 5573.25 lacs in 1991-92 to Rs. 20214 lacs in 1999-2000, thereby indicating an overall growth of about 263%.

The year-wise percentage growth in deposits has shown a continuous fluctuating trend. The percentage growth rate was only 9.24% in 1998-99 while contrary to it the highest growth rate was 26.54% in 1994-95, which could be termed highly stisfactory.

Table No. 6.12

Total Deposits and Their Growth Rate in Hadoti Region and in the State of Rajasthan (1991-92 to 1999-2000)

YEAR	BARAN		BUNDI		JHALAWAR		KOTA		TOTAL OF THE REGION		STATE OF RAJASTHAN	
	Total Deposits (Rs. in lacs)	Growth Rate %	Total Deposits (Rs. in lacs)	Growth Rate %	Total Deposits (Rs. in lacs)	Growth Rate %	Total Deposits (Rs. in lacs)	Growth Rate %	Total Deposits (Rs. in lacs)	Growth Rate %	Total Deposits (Rs. in crores)	Growth Rate %
1991-1992	5573.25	-	6825.36	19.01	5124.26	13.51	28929.86	01.23	46452.73	19.64	5891.20	–
1992-1993	6559.36	17.69	8145.00	19.33	6242.64	21.82	34972.65	20.88	55919.65	20.38	7128.60	20.90
1993-1994	7231.00	10.24	8400.00	3.13	8109.81	29.91	39456.04	12.81	63196.85	13.01	8075.70	13.30
1994-1995	9150.00	26.54	10561.00	25.72	10081.00	24.31	45604.73	13.48	75396.73	19.30	10305.24	20.20
1995-1996	10161.00	11.04	11635.00	10.17	11538.00	14.45	58443.61	21.96	91777.61	21.73	12045.43	16.89
1996-1997	12679.00	24.78	13517.00	16.18	15215.00	28.78	67428.09	13.32	108839.09	18.59	14186.00	17.77
1997-1998	14456.00	14.01	17217.00	27.37	17467.07	14.80	80711.26	16.45	129851.33	19.31	16961.00	19.56
1998-1999	15792.00	9.24	21715.00	26.13	21201.00	21.38	92451.08	14.54	151159.08	14.10	20357.00	20.02
1999-2000	20214.00	28.00	25476.00	17.31	22714.74	7.14	110501.69	19.52	178906.43	18.37	23373.00	14.81
TOTAL	**101815.61**		**123491.36**		**117693.52**	**176.10**	**558499.01**		**901499.50**		**118323.17**	–

Source: • *DCPs of various years of Baran, Bundi, Jhalawar and Kota Districts.*
• *Agenda papers of various meetings of SLBC, Jaipur (64th Meeting to 75th Meeting of SLBC)*

The compound average annual growth rate in deposits in district Baran was 15.5% during the period of study.

District Bundi

The absolute figures of deposits have shown a continuous increasing trend. These have gone up from Rs. 6825.36 lacs in the initial year of the study to Rs. 25476 lacs in the final year of the study, thereby depicting a growth of about 273%.

Severe fluctuations have been noticed in the pattern of year-wise percentage growth rate in deposits. The percentage growth rate in deposits was as low as 3.13% in 1993-94 to as high as 27.37% in 1997-98. The compound average annual growth rate in total deposits for the whole period of study was 15.8%.

District Jhalawar

The absolute figures of total deposits exhibit a continuous and consistent growth as these have spiralled-up from Rs. 5124.26 lacs in 1991-92 to Rs. 22714.74 lacs in 1999-2000, revealing an impressive growth of around 343%.

Regarding the year-wise percentage growth rate in deposits, a zig-zag trend has been observed. In the last year of the period of study, the growth rate was very poor (7.14%) and it was 29.91% in 1993-94, which was highest. The compound average annual growth rate in deposits was fairly good (18%).

District Kota

There has been a consistent growth in the total deposits as these have increased from Rs. 28929.86 lacs in the beginning to Rs. 110501.69 lacs at the end of the period of study, reflecting a growth of about 282%.

The year-wise percentage growth pattern of deposits has been highly fluctuating and it was as low as 1.23% in 1991-92 to as high as 20.88% in 1992-93. The compound average annual growth rate during the whole period of study was slightly above 16%, which was satisfactory.

1) The analysis of the percentage share of different districts in the total deposits of the region, reveals that the Kota district has dominant share, which was as high as 61.95% and it was much more than the combined share of remaining three districts in the region. The share of district Bundi was 13.07%, followed by district Jhalawar (13.06%) and district Baran (11.29%).

2) In terms of compound average annual growth rate, the district Jhalawar remained at the top (18%). The district Kota was at second place (16.1%), followed by district Bundi (15.8%) and district Baran (15.5%).

Thus, on the basis of above analysis, we can generalise that :

1) The district Kota was having lion's share in the total deposits in the region and its share was exceeding the combined share of all remaining three districts in the region.

2) District Jhalawar has shown the highest compound average annual growth rate, followed by district Kota. The compound average annual growth rate was more or less the same in Bundi and Baran district. The compound average annual growth rate in the region as well as in all four districts of the region, on the whole, remained satisfactory on the whole.

3) Comparing the percentage growth rate of total deposits in Hadoti region during 1991-92 to 1999-2000 with the State of Rajasthan the growth rate in the region slightly lowe than the Rajasthan. The growth rate in total deposits of the region was 285.14% in comparison to 296.76% of the Rajasthan. The all India growth rate of total deposits was slightly higher than the deposits of the region. All India growth rate of deposits for the whole period of study was 288.10% in comparison to 285.14% of the region. Thus, the all India growth rate was higher by 3 points. On the basis of this comparison we can generalise that the growth rate pattern of deposits of the region, Rajasthan and India has been more or less on the same pattern.

TOTAL ADVANCES AND THEIR GROWTH RATE IN HADOTI REGION

Table no. 6.13 shows the total advances and their growth rate in Hadoti region. The study of the table highlights the following facts :

The absolute amount of total advances in the region have shown a consistent growth trend as these have increased from Rs. 40134.72 lacs in the initial year to Rs. 95642.89 lacs in the final year of the study, signifying an improvement of 138% i.e. more than two times.

Analysis of year-wise percentage growth rate of advances reveals a zig-zag trend within the range of 9.49% in 1996-97 to 18.50% in 1991-92. The compound average annual growth rate in total advances was 10.1%, which was not satisfactory.

Table No. 6.13

Total Advances and Their Growth Rate in Hadoti Region and in the State of Rajasthan (1991-92 to 1999-2000)

YEAR	BARAN		BUNDI		JHALAWAR		KOTA		TOTAL OF THE REGION		STATE OF RAJASTHAN	
	Total Advance (Rs. in lacs)	Growth Rate %	Total Advance (Rs. in lacs)	Growth Rate %	Total Advance (Rs. in lacs)	Growth Rate %	Total Advance (Rs. in lacs)	Growth Rate %	Total Advance (Rs. in lacs)	Growth Rate %	Total Advance (Rs. in crores)	Growth Rate %
1991-1992	4652.02	-	5981.68	16.68	4224.76	15.40	25274.26	00.76	40134.72	18.50	3280.00	-
1992-1993	5786.10	24.37	6988.49	16.82	4882.21	15.56	28157.24	11.41	45814.04	14.15	3901.80	18.9
1993-1994	6561.00	13.39	7288.00	04.29	5738.35	17.54	31389.50	11.48	50976.85	11.27	4081.80	4.6
1994-1995	7507.00	14.41	8509.00	16.75	6834.00	19.09	33747.69	07.51	56597.69	11.03	4646.59	13.8
1995-1996	8376.00	11.57	8901.00	04.61	7756.00	13.49	37359.70	10.70	62392.70	10.24	5442.76	17.13
1996-1997	8788.00	04.92	9106.00	02.30	10181.00	31.27	40237.56	07.70	68312.56	09.49	6522.00	19.83
1997-1998	9622.00	09.49	9884.00	08.54	15402.00	51.28	41145.97	02.58	76053.97	11.33	7891.00	20.99
1998-1999	10345.00	07.51	12266.00	24.09	15618.00	01.40	48272.30	17.31	86501.30	13.74	8678.00	9.97
1999-2000	11373.00	09.94	13949.00	13.72	18570.00	18.90	51750.89	07.23	95642.89	10.57	10513.00	21.15
TOTAL	**73010.12**	–	**82873.17**	–	**89206.32**		**337335.11**	–	**582426.72**	–	**54956.95**	–

Source: • *DCPs of various years of Baran, Bundi, Jhalawar and Kota Districts.*

• *Agenda papers of various meetings of SLBC, Jaipur (64th Meeting to 75th Meeting of SLBC)*

The position of total advances and their growth rate in different districts of Hadoti region has been analysed below :

District Baran

A constant and continuous improvement in total advances in the district has been noticed. The total advances have increased from Rs. 4652.02 lacs in 1991-92 to Rs. 11373 lacs in 1999-2000, thereby indicating a growth of around 144%.

A zig-zag trend has been observed in the growth rate of advances. The growth rate was lowest 4.92% in 1996-97 and it was highest in 1992-93 (24.37%). The compound average annual growth rate in advances was 10.4% during the whole period of the study, which was moderate.

District Bundi

The absolute amount of advances in the district has depicted a constant and continuous increase during the whole period of the study. Total advances have increased from Rs. 5981.68 lacs in the beginning to Rs. 13949 lacs at the end of the study, thereby representing a growth of about 133%.

A severe and continuous fluctuations have been observed in the figures of percentage growth rate pattern of advances. The growth rate was low as 2.30% in 1996-97 to as high as 24.09% in 1998-99, a difference of about 22 points. The compound annual average growth rate of advances in Bundi district was slightly less than 10% (9.80%), which could not be termed as satisfactory.

District Jhalawar

The total advances have shown an overall impressive growth rate of about 340% during the whole period of the study as these have increased from Rs. 4224.76 lacs in 1991-92 to Rs. 18570 lacs in 1999-2000, thus depicting a continuous and consistent growth trend.

The analysis of year-wise percentage growth rate of advances reveals a fluctuating trend from a very low percentage of only 1.40% in 1998-99 to a high of 31.27% in 1996-97, a substantial difference of about 30 points. The compound average annual growth rate of advances was 17.9%in the district, which was satisfactory.

District Kota

The analysis of the total advances in the district highlights a continuous increase as these have gone-up from Rs. 25274.26 lacs in the initial year to Rs. 51750.89 lacs in the final year of the study thereby depicting an improvement of around 105%, which is slightly more than the double.

A zig-zag trend was visible in the percentage growth rate of advances. This was lowest only to 00.76% in 1991-92 to the highest of 17.31% in 1998-99, a difference of about more than 15 points. The compound average annual growth rate of total advances was comparatively low at about 8.2%, which was dis-satisfactory.

Analysis of inter-district comparison of percentage share of different districts in the total advances of the region reveals that the district Kota was at the top and enjoying more than 50% share (57.92%) of the total advances of the region, which was more than the combined share (42.08%) of remaining three districts of the region. The district Jhalawar stood at second place (15.32%), followed by Bundi district (14.23%) and Baran district (12.53%).

In terms of compound average annual growth rate district Jhalawar remained at the top (17.9%). The district Baran stood at second place (10.4%) which was followed by district Bundi (9.8%) and district Kota (8.2%).

On the basis of above analysis we can infer the following :

1) District Kota was having lion's share in the total advances of the region which accounted for more than the combined share of remaining all districts in the region.
2) The compound average annual growth rate of advances was highest in Jhalawar district, while this growth rate was poor in Bundi and Kota districts as it was not even in double digits. The overall compound average annual growth rate in the region could not be termed as satisfactory and in different districts the same position was noticed except in district Jhalawar.
3) Comparing the percentage growth rate in total advances of CBs in the Hadoti region during 1991-92 to 1999-2000 with the State of Rajasthan and India.

We find comparatively a dismal picture of the growth rate in advances in the region. The growth rate in total advances in the region was only 138% during the whole period of study in comparison to 220.52% and 207.97% in state of Rajasthan and in India respectively. Thus, we find a glaring difference in growth rate pattern and also reach to this conclusion that the growth rate in total advances in the region has not been on the lines of the State of Rajasthan and India.

CREDIT DEPOSIT RATIO IN HADOTI REGION

CDR is the proportion of the credit disbursed in the particular region to the total deposits collected from the same region. It is a measure to know the extent to which a region is benefited from bank credit out of its own resources collected through deposits. As per the recommendations of the Ghosh Committee (1985) banks were advised to adhere to the norm of 60% for rural and semi-urban branches by each individual bank.

Table no. 6.14 spotlights the position of CDR in Hadoti region. The study of this table elucidates the following facts :

1) There has been an overall declining trend in the CDR in the region as it has declined from 86.79% in 1991-92 to 53.46% in 1999-2000, thus, a decline of about 33% which was significant and cause of concern to the policy planners and executors.
2) It is a matter of delight that in most of the years of the period of study, the CDR has been higher than the norm prescribed, besides that, in last three years of the study (1997-98 to 1999-2000), wherein this was slightly less than the norm prescribed.
3) The overall CDR of the region for the whole period of study was 64.61%, which was slightly higher than the prescribed norm.

The present position of CD ratio and its growth rate in different districts of the region is being analysed below :

District Baran

1) The CDR in the district has shown an overall declining trend, inspite of year-wise zig-zag trend as this has declined from 83.47% in the beginning to 56.26% in the final year of the study. Thus, it has declined by about 27 points, which was significant and also a cause of concern.
2) Except for the year 1999-2000, the CDR in all years of the study has been more than the prescribed norm of 60%.
3) The overall CDR in the district has been 71.71% for the whole period of the study, which was much higher than the prescribed norm.

District Bundi

1) A continuous declining trend has been noticed in the CDR as it declined from a very high of 87.60% in the base year to a low of 54.75% in the final year of the study, thus a decline of around 33% which was substantial and cause of anxiety.

Table No. 6.14

Credit Deposit Ratio in Hadoti Region and in the State of Rajasthan (1991-92 to 1999-2000)

YEAR	BARAN		BUNDI		JHALAWAR		KOTA		TOTAL OF THE REGION		STATE OF RAJASTHAN	
	Norms %	*Achieve-ment %*	*Norms %*	*Achieve-ment %*	*Norms %*	*Achieve-ment %*	*Norms %*	*Achieve-ment %*	*Norms %*	*Achieve-ment %*	*Norms %*	*Achieve-ment %*
1991-1992	60	83.47	60	87.60	60	82.43	60	87.00	60	86.79	60	55.60
1992-1993	60	88.21	60	85.80	60	78.21	60	80.51	60	81.93	60	54.70
1993-1994	60	90.73	60	86.76	60	70.76	60	79.56	60	80.66	60	50.50
1994-1995	60	82.04	60	80.57	60	67.80	60	74.00	60	75.07	60	47.88
1995-1996	60	82.43	60	76.50	60	67.22	60	63.92	60	67.98	60	48.11
1996-1997	60	69.31	60	67.37	60	66.91	60	59.67	60	62.76	60	48.80
1997-1998	60	66.56	60	57.41	60	88.18	60	50.98	60	58.57	60	49.80
1998-1999	60	65.51	60	56.46	60	73.67	60	52.21	60	57.22	60	45.50
1999-2000	60	56.26	60	54.75	60	81.75	60	46.83	60	53.46	60	48.00
TOTAL	**60**	**71.71**	**60**	**67.11**	**60**	**75.79**	**60**	**60.40**	**60**	**64.61**	**60**	**45.00**

Source:
- *DCPs of various years of Baran, Bundi, Jhalawar and Kota Districts.*
- *SLBC meeting agenda of various years (BOB, Jaipur)*

2) The CDR in all years of the study has been substantially higher than the norm prescribed except for the last three years of the period of study wherein this was slightly lower than the norm.

3) The overall CDR for the whole period of study was higher (67.11%) than the prescribed norm.

District Jhalawar

1) A zig-zag trend has been observed in CDR for various years, but on the whole it has declined marginally from 82.43% in 1991-92 to 81.75% in 1999-2000.

2) It is a matter of delight to mention here that the CDR in all years of study has been higher than the norm prescribed and in three years it was more than 80%.

3) The overall CDR has been 75.79%, which was significantly higher than the norms prescribed. This situation was highly satisfactory.

District Kota

1) There has been continuous decline in CDR except for 1998-99, thus signifying an overall declining trend. The CDR which was as high as 87% in 1991-92 declined to a very low level of 46.83% in 1999-2000. Thus, a decline of around 40%, which was not only too high but also a cause of great concern to the policy planners and executors.

2) The prescribed norm of CDR could only be achieved in first five years of the period of study, but thereafter it could not be achieved in last four years of the period of study. The performance of banks in attaining the CDR norm has been very poor particularly in last three years of the period study. This tendency clearly indicates that there may be a lack of adequate bankable projects, therefore limited absorptive capacity for bank credit in district Kota. Thus, it is a cause of concern for policy planners.

3) Inspite of poor performance in last four years, the pleasant fact is that the overall CDR for the whole period of the study 60.40% was equal to the norm prescribed .

On the basis of above analysis, we can generalise the following :

1) The overall achievement of CDR for the whole region has been satisfactory as it was slightly higher than national norm.

2) All districts of the region could achieve the prescribed norm of CDR.

3) In terms of ranking of performance of CDR, district Jhalawar was the first place. District Baran stood second in this regard, followed by Bundi and Kota districts.

4) Comparing the latest position of CDR in Hadoti region with the State of Rajasthan in 1999-2000, we find that the achievement of the region is better than the State of Rajasthan. The CDR in Hadoti region was 53.46% at the end of March, 2000 in comparison to 48% for the State of Rajasthan, but the CDR in region was slightly less than the all India CDR. The all India CDR was 56%, which was higher than 2.54 points than that of the region.

DISTRICT-WISE PERFORMANCE OF COMMERCIAL BANKS IN FINANCING TO PRIORITY SECTOR IN HADOTI REGION

The main objective of the nationalisation of bank was socialisation of credit which could be achieved only by providing minimum quantum of funds to the priority sectors at liberal terms and condition by replacing the concept of credit worthiness by the concept of purpose worthiness. Therefore, the Ghosh Committee recommended the norm of 40% to this sector of the total credit extended by the banks.

Table no. 6.15 depicts the district-wise performance of CBs in financing to priority sector in Hadoti region. The study of the table reveals the following facts :

District Baran

1) It is delighted to mention here that the percentage achievement of CBs in financing to priority sector in all years of the period of study has been significantly higher (around double) than the prescribed norm of 40%. The achievement has always been more than 78% and it was as high as 85.57% in 1993.

2) Though a slight zig-zag trend was observed in the figures of percentage achievement, but the overall trend has shown a slight declining trend as the achievement declined from 84.69% at the end of March 1992 to 78.95% at the end of March, 2000.

District Bundi

1) The percentage achievement in financing to priority sector has always been substantially higher (more than double) throughout the period of study.

Table No. 6.15

District-wise Performance of Commercial Banks in Financing to Priority Sector in Hadoti Region

(1991-92 to 1999-2000)

(Achievement in %)

Name of the District	*Norm (% of Total (Advances)*	*March 1992 Achv. (% of Total Advances)*	*March 1993 Achv. (% of Total Advances)*	*March 1994 Achv. (% of Total Advances)*	*March 1995 Achv. (% of Total Advances)*	*March 1996 Achv. (% of Total Advances)*	*March 1997 Achv. (% of Total Advances)*	*March 1998 Achv. (% of Total Advances)*	*March 1999 Achv. (% of Total Advances)*	*March 2000 Achv. (% of Total Advances)*
Baran	40	84.69	85.57	79.91	78.93	78.65	83.45	82.75	82.76	78.95
Bundi	40	85.60	84.90	87.93	87.30	90.29	88.00	88.00	84.00	85.00
Jhalawar	40	82.20	69.22	72.47	75.59	70.19	67.99	72.26	81.96	79.03
Kota	40	38.00	36.00	40.00	39.00	36.00	36.00	38.00	39.77	40.12

Source: DCPs of various years of Baran, Bundi, Jhalawar and Kota districts.

2) Inspite of slight zig-zag trend in the percentage achievement the overall trend has slightly declined from 85.60% in base year to 85% in the final year of the study.

District Jhalawar

1) The percentage achievement has always been much higher than the norm prescribed as it was always more than 67% and it was as high as 82.20% in the initial year.

2) There has been substantial fluctuations in the percentage achievement during the course of study, but the overall trend has been declining. The achievement which was 82.20% at the end of March, 1992 which declined to 79.03% at the end of March, 2000, a fall of around 3 points.

District Kota

1) Contrary to other districts of the region, the percentage achievement has always been less than the prescribed norm except at the end of March, 1994 and March, 2000.

2) Though, the figures of percentage achievement have shown an overall marginally increasing trend as this has gone-up from 38% at the end of March, 1992 to 40.12% at the end of March, 2000. Thus, an increase of around 2 points.

On the basis of above, we can infer the following :

1) The overall performance of CBs in financing to priority sector in Hadoti region has been highly satisfactory as it exceeded the prescribed norm.

2) Except the Kota district, the performance in remaining all three districts of the region has been excellent.

3) District Bundi stood first in the performance, followed by Baran and Jhalawar districts. District Kota remained at bottom in the rank and its performance was not satisfactory.

4) Comparing the performance of CBs in financing to priority sector in the region with the State of Rajasthan and India in the year 1999-2000, we find that the performance of CBs in financing to priority sector in the Hadoti region was better than the performance of these banks in the State of Rajasthan and in India. The performance of CBs in Hadoti region was 58.77%; while the performance in the State of Rajasthan and also in

India was 51.20% and 43.6% respectively. Thus, it is clearly evident that in the Hadoti region, the CBs have performed well in financing to priority sector in comparison to the state of Rajasthan and India.

DISTRICT-WISE PERFORMANCE OF COMMERCIAL BANK IN FINANCING TO DIRECT AGRICULTURE IN HADOTI REGION

Table no. 6.16 depicts district-wise performance of CBs in financing to direct agriculture in region. The analysis of the table reveals the following facts :

District Baran

It is heartening to mention that the percentage achievement of CBs in direct agriculture financing has always been much higher than the prescribed norm. The achievement has always been more than 61%. It was as high as 70.57% at the end of March, 1993. Thus, the performance of CBs in direct agriculture financing could be termed as excellent.

District Bundi

The performance of CBs has been excellent throughout the whole period of study, as it was always significantly higher than the prescribed norm and it has been always three times more than the prescribed norm. It was between the minimum range of 58.27% to a maximum range of 68%.

District Jhalawar

The performance of CBs has been highly satisfactory throughout the period of study, as it was not only always higher than the prescribed norms, but also not less than 51% in any year of the whole period of study and it was as high as 69.79% at the end of March, 1999.

District Kota

The performance of CBs in direct agriculture financing was not satisfactory on the whole as the percentage achievement was less than the prescribed norm in six years of the period of the study; while in two years it was around the set norm. The exceptional good year was 1992 when the achievement was as high as 46.84%. Besides the poor performance, the another disturbing fact was that the overall trend has shown a substantially decline as the achievement declined from 46.84% at the end of March 1992 to a very low level of 16.13% at the end of March, 2000.

Table No. 6.16

District-wise Performance of Commercial Banks in Financing to Direct Agriculture in Hadoti Region

(1991-92 to 1999-2000)

(Achievement in %)

Name of the District	*Norm (% of Total (Advances)*	*March 1992 Achv. (% of Total Advances)*	*March 1993 Achv. (% of Total Advances)*	*March 1994 Achv. (% of Total Advances)*	*March 1995 Achv. (% of Total Advances)*	*March 1996 Achv. (% of Total Advances)*	*March 1997 Achv. (% of Total Advances)*	*March 1998 Achv. (% of Total Advances)*	*March 1999 Achv. (% of Total Advances)*	*March 2000 Achv. (% of Total Advances)*
Baran	18	63.94	70.57	66.13	65.73	63.79	67.89	69.00	69.00	61.52
Bundi	18	63.65	61.64	65.00	65.00	68.00	65.00	62.00	64.00	58.27
Jhalawar	18	61.15	54.02	52.92	57.99	53.35	51.39	61.40	69.79	66.08
Kota	18	46.84	17.00	19.00	18.00	16.00	15.00	16.00	16.52	16.13

Source: DCPs of various years of Baran, Bundi, Jhalawar and Kota district.

On the basis of above analysis, we can generalise the following :

1) Except the Kota district in the region, the performance of CBs in direct agriculture financing has been excellent. The performance of CBs in Kota district was not only dis-satisfactory, but also has shown a declining trend.

2) In terms of ranking of the performance of CBs, district Baran stood first, district Bundi remained at the second place followed by district Jhalawar and district Kota.

3) While making comparison of the performance of CBs in financing to direct agriculture in Hadoti region with the performance of these institutions in the State of Rajasthan and in India during the year 1999-2000 we find that the performance of CBs in Hadoti region was much better than the performance of these banks in the whole State of Rajasthan and in India. The performance of CBs in 1999-2000 was 37.38% in Hadoti region; while this was only 20.70% in the Rajasthan and 15.80% in India. Thus, it was higher by about 16 points than the Rajasthan and about 21 points than India and it was also more than double to the stipulated norm of 18%.

DISTRICT-WISE PERFORMANCE OF COMMERCIAL BANKS IN FINANCING TO WEAKERS SECTIONS OF SOCEITY IN HADOTI REGION

The Krishnaswami Working Group on Priority Sector Lending (1972) introduced the concept of financing to weaker sections in order to make the priority sector lending to be more meaningful. Further Ghosh Working Group (1982) widened this concept and now small and marginal farmers, lendless labourers, share croppers, artisans, the beneficiaries of Govt. sponsored schemes for poverty alleviation such as SGSY, PMRY, SJSRY etc. and the beneficiaries of SC/ST are incorporated in the list of weaker sections of the society. It is vital to mention here that the Narasimhan Committee on Financial Sector Reform (1991) has also advocated the need for financing the weaker sections of society. Thus, the CBs are advised to finance 10% of the total advances or 25% of priority sector advances to the weaker sections of the society. In the light of the above mentioned facts, it is pertinent to analyse the performance of CBs in regard to the financing to this sector. District-wise performance of CBs in financing to weaker sections of the society is presented in **table no. 6.17**. The study of the table depicts the following facts :

Table No. 6.17

District-wise Performance of Commercial Banks in Financing to Weaker Sections of Society in Hadoti Region

(1991-92 to 1999-2000)

(Achievement in %)

Name of the District	*Norm (% of Total (Advances)*	*March 1992 Achv. (% of Total Advances)*	*March 1993 Achv. (% of Total Advances)*	*March 1994 Achv. (% of Total Advances)*	*March 1995 Achv. (% of Total Advances)*	*March 1996 Achv. (% of Total Advances)*	*March 1997 Achv. (% of Total Advances)*	*March 1998 Achv. (% of Total Advances)*	*March 1999 Achv. (% of Total Advances)*	*March 2000 Achv. (% of Total Advances)*
Baran	10	45.61	40.35	39.51	37.71	37.72	35.70	37.07	32.91	37.36
Bundi	10	38.10	42.02	42.06	48.58	46.94	45.00	46.00	63.00	59.00
Jhalawar	10	27.05	29.46	25.83	19.59	26.82	23.22	13.15	18.56	19.21
Kota	10	9.84	9.60	10.93	9.60	9.20	9.91	9.50	12.24	12.00

Source: DCPs of various years of Baran, Bundi, Jhalawar and Kota districts.

District Baran

The performance of CBs in financing to weaker sections of society has been excellent in the district as it was always higher than the prescribed norm of 10% and it was never less than three times more of the prescribed norm. The performance of CBs fluctuated between a low of 32.91% tc a high of 45.61% during the period of analysis. The disturbing trend in this regard was that the overall trend has declined, which was evident from the performance of base year (45.61%) to the performance of the final year of the study (37.36%).

District Bundi

It is worth mentioning with pleasure that the percentage achievement of CBs in financing to weaker sections of society has been excellent as the percentage achievement has been always higher than the prescribed norm and this was as high as 63% at the end of March, 1999 and was never less than 38%. The percentage achievement of March 2000 (59%) has shown an overall increasing trend, compared to the percentage achievement of the base year (38.10%).

District Jhalawar

Although, the performance of CBs in the district has always been higher than the prescribed norm, but it was comparatively not so good as it was in case of Baran and Bundi districts. The lowest performance was 13.15% in 1998 and it was highest 29.46% in 1993. Apart from it, the overall trend of performance has also witnessed a declining trend. The performance which was 27.07% in the base year declined to 19.21% in the final year of the study.

District Kota

The performance of CBs in the district has not been satisfactory as it was below the prescribed norm of 10% and infact, it is a cause of concern for policy planners. In all years of the period of the study the performance was below except in 1994, 1999 and 2000 when it was marginally higher than the prescribed norm. The only point of satisfaction is that the performance has been much better in last two years of the study in comparison to the base year.

We can deduce the following conclusion from the above analysis :

1) The performance of CBS in Baran, Bundi and Jhalawar districts has been highly satisfactory as the achievements have always exceeded the prescribed norm, but the performance in Kota district was not satisfactory.

2) Inter-district analysis of performance reveals this fact that district Bundi was at the top place. District Baran remained at second place in this regard, followed by district Jhalawar and district Kota.

3) Making comparison of the performance of CBs in financing to weaker section of the society in the Hadoti region for the year 1999-2000 with the performance of these banks in the Rajasthan and in India we find that the performance of CBs in Hadoti region was substantially higher than the performance of these banks in Rajasthan and in India. The performance of CBs in Hadoti region in 1999-2000 was 23.03%; while their performance in Rajasthan and in India was only 11.80% and 4.77% respectively.

Thus, the performance of CBS in the region was approximately double than the performance in Rajasthan and it was more than four times than the all India performance. It brings out this fact that there has been a good tendency towards financing to the weaker sections of the society in the Hadoti region which is in tune with the object of SAA.

DISTRICT-WISE PERFORMANCE OF COMMRECIAL BANKS IN FINANCING UNDER DIFFERENTIAL RATE OF INTEREST IN HADOTI REGION

DRI scheme is introduced on the recommendations of R. K. Hazari Committee (1972). This scheme is one of the important tool for utilising the latent talent and enterpreneurial skills which go waste due to lack of credit. The purpose is to uplift the poorest among the poor by providing them opportunity to pursue some productive endeavours. The beneficiaries of the DRI scheme are provided bank credit at the concessional rate of interest of 4%. According to norm prescribed by the Ghosh Committee, CBs are required to extend atleast 1% of their total advances under this scheme.

The district-wise performance of CBs in financing under DRI scheme in Hadoti region is exhibited in **table no. 6.18.** The analysis of this table brings out the following facts :

Table No. 6.18

District-wise Performance of Commercial Banks in Financing under DRI in Hadoti Region

(1991-92 to 1999-2000)

(Achievement in %)

Name of the District	*Norm (% of Total (Advances)*	*March 1992 Achv. (% of Total Advances)*	*March 1993 Achv. (% of Total Advances)*	*March 1994 Achv. (% of Total Advances)*	*March 1995 Achv. (% of Total Advances)*	*March 1996 Achv. (% of Total Advances)*	*March 1997 Achv. (% of Total Advances)*	*March 1998 Achv. (% of Total Advances)*	*March 1999 Achv. (% of Total Advances)*	*March 2000 Achv. (% of Total Advances)*
Baran	1.00	0.68	0.63	0.88	0.50	0.32	0.33	0.31	0.30	0.69
Bundi	1.00	0.60	0.50	0.40	0.30	0.25	0.20	0.12	0.04	0.02
Jhalawar	1.00	0.46	0.58	0.54	0.43	0.59	0.22	0.40	0.20	0.10
Kota	1.00	0.26	0.20	2.00	1.00	0.10	0.10	0.10	0.06	0.03

Source: DCPs of various years of Baran, Bundi, Jhalawar and Kota districts.

District Baran

CBs never achieved the set norm under DRI scheme as their performance has always been less than the set norm. The performance has shown a zig-zag trend as it oscillated between a low of 0.3% to a high of 0.88% during the period of the study. This shows the poor performance of CBs, which is cause of anxiety and concern for the policy planners and executors.

District Bundi

The same story has been repeated in Bundi district on the lines of district Baran. The performance was even more poor than the district Baran. The set norm could never be achieved and itthe performance ranged between a very low of 0.02% in 2000 to a high of 0.6% in 1992. Besides the poor performance, the most disturbing fact is, that the performance has shown a continuous declining trend and went down to a very low level of 0.02% which is negligible in terms of achievement.

District Jhalawar

Inspite of zig-zag trend in various years, the performance has not been satisfactory as it didn't reach the level of prescribed norm. The performance fluctuated between a minimum of 0.10% to a maximum of 0.59% during the period of analysis.

District Kota

The performance of CBs has always been lower than the prescribed norm of 1% except two years in 1994 and 1995 wherein it was 2% and 1% respectively. The performance fluctuated between the range of 0.03% to 2%. In most of the years it was much below the set norm.

On the basis of above analysis, we can generalise the following :

1) The performance of CBs in financing under DRI scheme in all districts of the region has been unsatisfactory as they could not achieve the norm set for them. It is out of tune with the main objective of social banking. Therefore, it is a cause of concern for policy planners and executors.

2) Regarding the comparative position of districts, the performance of Baran district was much better than other districts of the region.

3) Though, the performance of CBs in Hadoti region was not satisfactory in relation to the prescribed norm, but it was just double than the performance of CBs in Rajasthan. The performance of CBs in financing under DRI scheme was 0.10% in the region; while it was only 0.05% in Rajasthan. Thus, it is a point of satisfaction in this regard in the region.

REFERENCES

1. DCPsof various years of district Baran.
2. DCPs of various years of district Bundi.
3. DCPs of various years of district Jhalawar.
4. DCPs of various years of district Kota.
5. Meeting Agenda of various years, SLBC, BOB, Jaipur, (64th Meeting to 75th Meeting of SLBC).
6. IBA Bulletin, Special Issue 2000-01 (March,2001)

■ □ ■

Chapter 7

An Empirical Examination of Service Area Approach in Hadoti Region

In preceding chapter of this book, we have critically analysed and evaluated the various operational aspects of SAA in detail in Hadoti region. The analysis focussed on the quantitative achievements of credit plans in relation to their targets. Though, this analysis provides a broad understanding of the performance of credit plans formulated under SAA only in terms of quantitative targets and achievements, but for having further insight into the different operational aspects, there is a need for a qualitative assessment of credit plans. Therefore, the primary focus of this chapter is on knowing and ascertaining the views of bankers and the beneficiaries on various operational aspects of SAA. Untill and unless we do not attempt to know the views of bankers and beneficiaries, the assessment of SAA will neither be correct nor complete.

The author has attempted to collect data from the bankers and beneficiaries through field survey as earnestly as possible, but even then, there may be some mistakes, which should be kept inview; while analysing the inferences and findings of the survey. In the absence of any fool proof method, the researcher has tried to substantiate the data and information obtained from the field survey by interrogating both the bankers and beneficiaries personally. Thus, a pious effort has been made to collect the correct and fruitful data/information.

Two separate sets of questionnaires were constructed for the bankers and beneficiaries. The questionnaire for BMs was used to gather information regarding the allocation and survey of villages, village and branch credit planning ,staff problems, functioning and monitoring of SAA, profitability and recovery position of branch, co-ordination with government officials and other problems related to the realistic formulation, proper implementation and effective monitoring of credit plans. The questionnaire for beneficiaries was used to gather information regarding the knowledge of different credit schemes, problems in obtaining and repayment of loans, the behaviour and working style of bankers, impact of credit on the level of income, level of living standard etc. But there was one common question asked from the bankers and beneficiaries both regarding their opinion about the overall assessment of SAA and its continuation in future. To enhance the authenticity of the data/information collected through questionnaires, the author also held verbal discussions with beneficiaries and different concerned banks and Government officials. For instance, discussions were held with LBOs of all four districts of the region, DDM of NABARD of Kota and Jhalawar districts, BDOs of different panchayat samities, BMs of different banks operating in the region, officer in-charge of DRDA in all four districts in the region and other concerned officials. This all together was done with the main purpose of getting feed back from the field functionaries in the region. Before analysing the feed back received in the form of data/information/ comments/opinions, it will not be out of place to mention that there may be some element of inaccuracy, unreliability and incompleteness in the data thus obtained. Therefore, the findings of this study will obviously have some limitations.

Feed Back Received from the Bankers

First of all, the feed back received from the bankers is being discussed below. The feed back received from the bankers was based on sample of 40% of service area bank branches in each district of the region, which was drawn randomly. On the basis of random sampling, the author selected 23 branches from Baran district, 25 branches from Bundi district, 26 branches from Jhalawar district and 24 branches from Kota district. Thus, in all 98 service area bank branches were selected from the whole region for the investigation purpose out of total 244 service area bank branches. The analysis of data/information received from the BMs through the written questionnaires is being presented below in summarized form and point-wise as a gist :

Table No. 7.1

Response of Bankers Regarding Completion of Village Survey in Stipulated Time

District		Yes	No	No Reply	Total
Baran	N	22	-	1	23
	%	95.65%	-	4.35	100%
Bundi	N	25	-	-	25
	%	100%	-	-	100%
Jhalawar	N	24	-	2	26
	%	92.31%	-	7.69	100%
Kota	N	24	-	-	24
	%	100%	-	-	100%
Total of the	N	95	-	3	98
Region	%	96.94%	-	3.06	100%

Table No. 7.2

Response of Bankers Regarding the Updating of Village Profile Annually

District		Yes	No	No Reply	Total
Baran	N	6	15	2	23
	%	26.09	65.22	8.69	100
Bundi	N	4	17	4	25
	%	16	68	16	100
Jhalawar	N	3	19	4	26
	%	11.54	73.08	15.38	100
Kota	N	5	14	5	24
	%	20.83	58.34	20.83	100
Total of the	N	18	65	15	98
Region	%	18.36	66.33	15.31	100

Table no. 7.1 depicts the response of respondent bankers regarding completion of village survey of the allocated villages in stipulated time period. Out of total 98 respondents interrogated, 96.94% respondents have said that they completed the village survey in stipulated time period. Not a single respondent said that the survey was not completed within the stipulated time period. Although 3 respondents didn't give their response in this regard.

Table no. 7.2 shows the response of bankers regarding the updating of village profile annually. Updating of village profile every year is a sine-qua-non for good quality of credit planning, but analysis of this table highlights this striking fact that 66.33% BMs of the region didn't undertake the exercise of updating the village profile every year. Only 18.36% BMs in the region updated the village profile annually. 15.31% bankers didn't respond in this regard.

Table no. 7.3 denotes the problem faced by bankers during the survey work. As high as 80.25% of BMs out of total 81 respondents said that there was shortage of technical staff. 12.35% BMs responded by telling that there was shortage of officers; while only 7.41% BMs mentioned that there was shortage of clerical staff in the branch. 56.12% (55) respondents observed that there was a problem of inadequate data without which formulation of realistic credit plan was a herculian task. 18.37% (18) respondents in the region observed that there was a problem of language for them in establishing effective and meaningful communication link with the beneficiaries. 27.55% (27) bankers of the region complained about the scattered villages which were beyond their reach and having difficulty in serving and supervising them properly. Besides, that 37.76% (37) bankers also mentioned the lack of proper transport facilities in the service areas. The another important problem was illiteracy. As much as high 41.84% (41) respondents in the region were of the opinion that illiteracy was a big problem for banks in effective and successful functioning of SAA.

Table No. 7.4 exhibits the level of co-operation of Govt. Officials/ Departments in survey work. The problem of co-operation was big in the sense that only 9.18% (9) respondents have opined that the level of co-operation of Govt. Officials/ Departments was highly co-operative. On the contrary to it, as high as 46.94% (46) respondents in the region have observed that the Government officials were indifferent; while 36.74% (36) bankers have reported that the co-operation was modest. Only 7.14% BMs told that the attitude of Govt. Officials/departments in survey work was not co-operative. Thus, it is evident that more than 50% respondents in Hadoti region were of the opinion that the attitude of Govt. officials/ departments in survey work was either indifferent or non-co-operative. Thus, it emerges as a big issue.

Table No. 7.3

Problems Faced by Bankers During Survey Work

District		Shortage of Staff				Inadequage Date	Problem of Language	Problem of Scattered Villages	Lack of Transport Facilities	Illiteracy
		Tech.	*Officer*	*Clerk*	*Total*					
Baran	N	12	4	3	19	13	5	10	11	9
	%	63.15	21.05	15.80	82.60	56.52	21.74	43.44	47.82	39.13
Bundi	N	17	3	1	21	13	4	3	10	11
	%	80.96	14.28	4.76	84	52	16	12	40	44
Jhalawar	N	20	1	1	22	15	6	11	11	12
	%	90.91	4.54	4.55	84.61	57.69	23.08	42.31	42.31	46.15
Kota	N	16	2	1	19	14	3	3	5	9
	%	84.21	10.53	526	79.16	58.33	12.50	12.50	20.83	37.5
Total of the Region	N	65	10	6	81	55	18	27	37	41
	%	80.25	12.35	7.41	82.65	56.12	18.37	27.55	37.76	41.84

Table No. 7.4

Level of Co-operation of Government Officials/ Departments in Survey Work

District		Highly Co-operative	Modest	Indifferent	Non-Co operative	Total
Baran	N	2	7	11	3	23
	%	8.70	30.43	47.83	13.04	100
Bundi	N	4	9	10	2	25
	%	16	36	40	8	100
Jhalawar	N	2	10	13	1	26
	%	7.69	38.46	50	3.85	100
Kota	N	1	10	12	1	24
	%	4.17	41.66	50	4.17	100
Total of the	N	9	36	46	7	98
Region	%	9.18	36.74	46.94	7.14	100

Table No. 7.5

Response of Bankers Regarding Getting Information/ Data from Govt. Departments in Time

District		**Yes**	**No**	**Total**
Baran	N	10	13	23
	%	43.48	56.52	100
Bundi	N	15	10	25
	%	60	40	100
Jhalawar	N	10	16	26
	%	38.46	61.54	100
Kota	N	13	11	24
	%	54.17	45.83	100
Total of the	N	48	50	98
Region	%	48.98	51.02	100

Table no. 7.5 manifests the response of bankers regarding getting information/data from government departments in time. Only 48.98% (48) respondents in the region have confirmed that they received the necessary information in time; while 51.02% (50) bankers said that they didn't received the information from government departments in time.

Thus, it seems to be another big problem because timely updating of village profile and accordingly the whole process of credit planning is affected adversely in the absence of timely information/data.

Table No. 7.6

Response of Bankers Regarding the Accuracy and Reliability of Data/Information from Govt. Departments

District		*Yes*	*No*	*No Reply*	*Total*	*If yes, then to what extent?*			
						Signifi -cant	*Margi- nal*	*No Reply*	*Total*
Baran	N	18	4	1	23	6	8	4	18
	%	78.26	17.39	4.35	100	33.33	44.45	22.22	100
Bundi	N	20	3	2	25	4	8	8	20
	%	80	12	8	100	20	40	40	100
Jhalawar	N	23	3	-	26	9	11	3	23
	%	86.46	11.54	-	100	39.13	47.83	13.04	100
Kota	N	20	2	2	24	5	13	2	20
	%	83.34	8.33	8.33	100	25	65	10	100
Total of the	N	81	12	5	98	24	40	17	81
Region	%	82.65	12.25	5.10	100	29.63	49.38	20.99	100

Table no. 7.6 highlights the response of bankers regarding the accuracy and reliability of data/information from Govt. departments. The response of bankers in this regard was highly positive. As much as 82.65% (81) respondent in the region have confirmed that the data supplied to them were accurate and reliable, while contrary to it, only 12.15% (12) respondents expressed their opinion that the data were neither accurate nor reliable. Only 5.10% respondents didn't reply. Regarding the degree of accuracy and reliability of data only 29.63% respondents reported that these were significantly accurate and reliable, while 49.38% respondents reported that these were marginally accurate and reliable. 20.99% bankers didn't express their opinion in this regard.

Table No. 7.7

Response of Bankers Regarding the Proper Dovetailing of DCP with DDP

District		Yes	No	No Reply	Total
Baran	N	19	12	2	23
	%	39.13	52.17	8.17	100
Bundi	N	10	13	2	25
	%	40	52	8	100
Jhalawar	N	13	11	2	26
	%	50	42.31	7.69	100
Kota	N	10	13	1	24
	%	41.67	54.17	4.16	100
Total of the Region	N	42	49	7	98
	%	42.86	50	7.14	100

Table no. 7.7 depicts the opinion of bankers regarding the proper dovetailing of DCP and DDP. As the DCP is based on DDP, therefore, credit planning should be synthesised with development planning for getting favourable impact on development. 50% respondents in the region reported that there was lack of proper dovetailing of DCP with DDP and therefore, according to them, it was a big problem. Out of total 98 respondents, 42.86% were of the opinion that the dovetailing of DCP with DDP was done properly; while 7.14% respondents didn't show their response in this regard.

Response of bankers regarding the consideration of different aspects of VCPs at its formulation stage is presented in *table no. 7.8*. The analysis of this table highlights the following facts :

1) 100% respondent bankers said that they consider economic viability and technical feasibility of an activity before inclusion in VCP.

2) 88.78% BMs kept the nature of scheme in mind before incorporating it in VCP. It means that majority of BMs consider this fact that whether the scheme is existing/ incomplete or altogether a new. Only a small percentage of BMs (11.22%) didn't consider the nature of scheme.

Table No. 7.8

Response of Bankers Regarding the Consideration of Different Aspects of VCP at Formulation Stage

District		Economic Viability & Technical Feasibility of Activity		Nature of Scheme : existing/ incomplete new		Targets of the Govt. sponsored Schemes		Activity-wise Credit Require-ment		Bahaviour and Attitudes of Benefici-aries regarding the end use and Repayment of Loan		Credit Worthi-ness of Benefici-aries		Resources Available with Banks		Basic Infra-structure Facilities	
		Yes	*No*	*Yes*	*No*	*Yes*	*No*	*Yes*	*No*	*Yes*	*No*	*Yes*	*No*	*Yes*	*No*	*Yes*	*No*
Baran	N	23	-	21	2	23	-	19	4	22	1	22	1	20	3	21	2
	%	100	-	91.30	8.70	100	-	82.61	17.39	95.65	4.35	95.65	4.35	86.96	13.04	91.30	8.70
Bundi	N	25	-	20	5	24	1	20	5	24	1	25	-	24	1	23	2
	%	100	-	80	20	96	4	80	20	96	4	100	-	96	4	92	8
Jhalawar	N	26	-	24	2	26	-	23	3	26	-	26	-	24	2	25	1
	%	100	-	92.31	7.69	100	-	88.46	11.54	100	-	100	-	92.31	7.69	96.15	3.85
Kota	N	24	-	22	2	23	1	22	2	24	-	24	-	20	4	22	2
	%	100	-	91.67	8.33	95.83	4.17	91.67	8.33	100	-	100	-	83.33	16.67	91.67	8.33
Total of	N	98	-	87	11	96	2	84	14	96	2	97	1	88	10	91	7
the Region	%	100	-	88.78	11.22	97.96	2.04	85.71	14.29	97.96	2.04	98.98	1.02	89.80	10.20	92.86	7.14

3) Regarding the consideration of Govt. sponsored schemes, 97.96% bankers who have responded observed that they consider targets before finalising the VCP. A very small percentage (2.04%) of BMs reported that they do not consider the targets of Govt. sponsored schemes.

4) 85.71% respondent BMs in the region have confirmed that they always consider activity-wise credit requirements at the formulation stage of VCP; while 14.29% bankers didn't subscribe to this view.

5) As much as high 97.96% BMs in the region have confirmed that they consider the behaviour and attitudes of beneficiaries regarding the end use and repayment of credit. Only 2.02% respondents reported that they do not attach importance to this aspect.

(6) 98.89% respondent BMs were of the opinion that they consider the credit worthiness of the beneficiaries before sanctioning loans to them; while only a very small percentage of bankers (1.02%) have shown no inclination towards this aspect.

7) 89.80% respondent BMs were of the view that they consider the available resources with the bank at the time of formulating credit plans; while 10.20% BMs reported that they didn't consider this aspect.

8) Regarding the basic infra-structural facilities 92.86% respondents reported that it is one of the important consideration at the time of formulating credit plans; while only 7.14% BMs expressed there opinion that they didn't consider this aspect.

Table No. 7.9

Response of Bankers Regarding the Basic Working Facilities

District		*Adequate*	*Inadequate*	*Total*
Baran	N	11	12	23
	%	47.83	52.17	100
Bundi	N	13	12	25
	%	52	48	100
Jhalawar	N	11	15	26
	%	42.31	57.69	100
Kota	N	9	15	24
	%	37.50	62.50	100
Total of the Region	N	44	54	98
	%	44.90	55.10	100

Table no. 7.9 presents the response of bankers regarding the basic working facilities. 44.90% respondents expressed their views that adequate working facilities were available to them, but a large number of bankers (55.10%) were of the opinion that the working facilities were inadequate, which affected their efficiency adversely. Thus, the majority of bankers reported the lack of necessary working facilities in their branches.

Table No. 7.10

Response of Bankers Regarding the Ingredients of Ideal Selection Criteria of Beneficiaries

District		*Viability and Feasibility of Project/ Activity*	*Borrower's Need Based*	*Past Experience about the track record of Beneficiaries*	*Repayment Capacity*
Baran	N	21	18	11	13
	%	91.30	78.26	47.83	56.52
Bundi	N	23	15	14	18
	%	92	60	56	72
Jhalawar	N	25	17	11	14
	%	96.15	68	44	53.85
Kota	N	24	14	13	20
	%	100	58.33	54.17	83.33
Total of the Region	N	93	64	49	65
	%	94.90	65.31	50	66.32

Table no. 7.10 reveals the response of bankers regarding the ingredients of ideal criteria for selecting the beneficiaries. 94.90% respondents reported that one of the major criteria should be economic viability and technical feasibility of the project/ activity. As high as 65.31% bankers favoured the borrower's need-based criteria. 50% respondents gave weightage to the past track record of the beneficiaries; while 62.32% accorded priority to repayment capacity of the borrower. Thus, in terms of ranking, top priority was accorded to economic viability and technical feasibility of project as an ingredients of ideal criteria for selecting the beneficiaries. The second priority was accorded to repayment capacity of the borrowers, followed by need based and past track record of the beneficiaries.

Table No. 7.11

Response of Bankers Regarding the Appropriateness of Selection Criteria of Beneficiaries

District		*Proper*	*Improper*	*No Reply*	*Total*
Baran	N	08	15	-	23
	%	34.78	65.22	-	100
Bundi	N	06	19	-	100
	%	24	76	-	100
Jhalawar	N	06	20	-	26
	%	23.08	73.92	-	100
Kota	N	03	21	-	24
	%	12.50	87.50	-	100
Total of the	N	23	65	-	98
Region	%	23.47	66.33	-	100

Table no. 7.11 exhibits the response of bankers regarding the appropriateness of selection criteria of beneficiaries, which is being used presently. Only 23.47% respondents were happy and expressed their opinion favourably in support of the present criteria; while 66.33% BMs showed their anguish about the present criteria of selecting beneficiaries and reported that the selection criteria is not proper.

Table No. 7.12

Role of Bankers in Identification of Beneficiaries Under Government Sponsored Schemes

District		*Yes*	*No*	*No Reply*	*Total*
Baran	N	7	12	4	23
	%	30.43	52.17	17.40	100
Bundi	N	10	15	-	25
	%	40	60	-	100
Jhalawar	N	8	18	-	26
	%	30.77	69.23	-	100
Kota	N	5	17	2	24
	%	20.83	70.83	8.34	100
Total of the	N	30	62	6	98
Region	%	30.62	63.26	6.12	100

Table no. 7.12 manifests the role of bankers in identification of beneficiaries under Govt. sponsored schemes. Majority of the bankers

(63.26%) in the region have criticised the present system on the ground that; they didn't have any say in identifying the beneficiaries while 30.62% respondents reported that there was some role of banks in identifying the beneficiaries; 6.12%, BMs didn't respond in this regard.

Table no. 7.13 depicts the response of bankers regarding the political interference in the selection of beneficiaries. 52.04% respondent bankers of the region confirmed the political interference. They have reported that owing to political interference and pressure of local leaders some non-deserving persons are also included in the list of beneficiaries. Only 20.41% respondents denied political interference, but a large percentage of bankers (27.55%) did not disclose their mind in this regard.

Table No. 7.13

Response of Bankers Regarding the Political Interference in the Selection of Beneficiaries

District		*Yes*	*No*	*No Reply*	*Total*
Baran	N	11	5	7	23
	%	47.83	21.74	30.43	100
Bundi	N	14	6	5	25
	%	56	24	20	100
Jhalawar	N	13	6	7	26
	%	50	23.08	26.92	100
Kota	N	13	3	8	24
	%	54.17	12.50	33.33	100
Total of the	N	51	20	27	98
Region	%	52.04	20.41	27.55	100

Table no. 7.14 reveals the response of bankers regarding the holding of public meetings for giving information about loan schemes and to create awareness among the beneficiaries. 100% BMs have reported that they conducted the public meetings for creating awareness about loan schemes and also for improving the recovery climate among the villagers. 80.61% respondents conducted public meetings twice a year; while 13.27% thrice a year. About 5.10% BMs held public meetings four times and only 1.02% BMs conducted public meeting five times in a year.

Table No. 7.14

Response of Bankers Regarding Holding of Public Meetings

District		Yes	No	Total	If Yes, then how many times in a year?						
					1	*2*	*3*	*4*	*5*	*More than 5*	*Total*
Baran	N	23	-	23	-	20	2	1	-	-	23
	%	100	-	100	-	86.96	8.69	4.35	-	-	100
Bundi	N	25	-	25	-	22	2	1	-	-	25
	%	100	-	100	-	88	8	4	-	-	100
Jhalawar	N	26	-	26	-	20	5	1	-	-	26
	%	100	-	100	-	76.92	19.23	3.85	-	-	100
Kota	N	24	-	24	-	17	4	2	1	-	24
	%	100	-	100	-	70.83	16.67	8.33	4.17	-	100
Total of the Region	N	98	-	98	-	79	13	5	1	-	98
	%	100	-	100	-	80.61	13.27	5.10	1.02	-	100

Response of Bankers Regarding the Level of Attendance in BLBC Meetings

District		*Upto 25%*	*26% to 50%*	*51% to 75%*	*76% to 99%*	*100%*	*Total*
Baran	N	-	2	12	9	-	23
	%	-	8.70	52.17	39.13	-	100
Bundi	N	-	1	13	11	-	25
	%	-	4	52	44	-	100
Jhalawar	N	-	1	8	17	-	26
	%	-	3.85	30.77	65.38	-	100
Kota	N	-	-	9	15	-	24
	%	-	-	37.50	62.50	-	100
Total of the Region	N	-	4	42	52	-	98
	%	-	4.08	42.86	53.06	-	100

Table no. 7.15 manifests the response of bankers regarding the level of attendance in BLBC meetings. 53.06% BMs reported that the level of attendance in BLBC meetings used to be between the range of 76 to 99%; while 42.86% BMs observed that the level of attendance has been between the range of 51 to 75%. Only 4.08% BMs mentioned that the level of attendance was between the range of 26 to 50%.

Table No. 7.16

Response of Bankers Regarding the Action Taken on Non-Participation in BLBC Meetings

District		*Disciplinary Action*	*Any Other Action*	*No Action is taken*	*Total*
Baran	N	1	4	18	23
	%	4.35	17.39	78.26	100
Bundi	N	6	3	16	25
	%	24	12	64	100
Jhalawar	N	4	1	21	26
	%	15.38	3.85	80.77	100
Kota	N	5	-	19	24
	%	20.83	-	79.17	100
Total of the Region	N	16	8	64	98
	%	16.33	8.16	65.31	100

Table no. 7.16 highlights the response of bankers regarding the action taken on non-participation in BLBC meetings. As high as 65.31% respondent BMs reported that no action was taken on non-participation in meetings. Only 16.33% respondents mentioned that some disciplinary action was taken in case of non-participation. A small percentage of BMs (8.16%) reported that some other action (warning, verbal reminder) was taken against them.

Table No. 7.17

Response of Bankers Regarding the Time of Intimation of Agenda for BLBC Meeting

District		*1 to 5 days before*	*6 to 10 days before*	*11 to 15 days before*	*More than 15 days before*	*Total*
Baran	N	3	2	15	3	23
	%	13.04	8.70	65.22	13.04	100
Bundi	N	4	7	13	1	25
	%	16	28	52	4	100
Jhalawar	N	1	9	15	1	26
	%	3.85	34.61	57.69	3.85	100
Kota	N	1	5	18	-	24
	%	4.17	20.83	75	-	100
Total of the Region	N	9	23	41	5	98
	%	9.19	23.47	41.84	5.10	100

Table no. 7.17 spells out the response of bankers regarding the intimation of agenda for BLBC meetings. According to well established practice, the intimation of agenda for BLBC meetings should reach to BMs at least before 15 days of the actual date of meeting. 9.19% bankers intimated that they received the intimation of agenda only 1 to 5 days before and 23.47% reported that they got the intimation of agenda 6 to 10 days before the meeting.

A large percentage of respondent (41.84%) reported that they got the intimation of agenda before 11 to 15 days of the meeting. A very small proportion of 5.10% respondents received the agenda more than 15 days before. Thus, it shows that most of the BMs did not get timely intimation of agenda for the BLBC meetings in the absence of which they could not prepared properly for the meeting.

Table No. 7.18

Response of Bankers Regarding the Various Points for Discussions During the BLBC Meeting

District		Conceptual Problems		Operational Problems in Formulation and Implementation		Review of the Progress of the Govt. Sponsored Schemes		Segement-wise Loan		Review of Progress of Physical Resources and Infra-structure Management		Problems of Overdue and Recovery		Court Cases for Recovery under RODA Act		Allotment of Villages of the Newly Opened Branches	
		Yes	*No*	*Yes*	*No*	*Yes*	*No*	*Yes*	*No*	*Yes*	*No*	*Yes*	*No*	*Yes*	*No*	*Yes*	*No*
Baran	N	18	5	20	3	20	3	21	2	18	5	23	-	19	4	8	15
	%	78.26	21.74	86.96	13.04	86.96	13.04	91.30	8.70	78.26	21.74	100	-	82.61	17.39	34.78	65.22
Bundi	N	14	11	22	3	24	1	23	2	15	10	24	1	21	4	6	19
	%	56	44	88	12	96	4	92	8	60	40	96	4	84	6	24	76
Jhalawar	N	17	9	21	5	26	-	25	1	19	7	26	-	20	6	5	21
	%	65.38	31.62	80.77	19.23	100	-	96.15	3.85	73.08	26.92	100	-	76.92	23.08	19.23	80.77
Kota	N	18	6	22	2	24	-	24	-	20	4	24	-	22	2	9	15
	%	75	25	91.67	8.33	100	-	100	-	83.33	16.67	100	37.50	91.67	8.33	37.50	62.50
Total of the Region	N	67	31	85	13	94	4	93	5	72	26	97	1	82	16	28	70
	%	68.37	31.63	86.73	13.27	95.92	4.08	94.90	5.10	73.47	26.53	98.98	1.02	83.67	16.33	28.57	71.43

The study of *table no. 7.18* enables us to know the response of bankers regarding the various points for discussions during the BLBC meetings. The analysis of the table reveals the following facts :

1) 68.37% respondents were of the opinion that the various conceptual problems in formulation and implementation of credit plans were discussed during the BLBC meetings; while 31.63% respondent BMs reported that such problems were not discussed.
2) 86.73% BMs reported that various operational problems pertaining to formulation and implementation of credit plans are discussed in the meeting; while only 13.27% BMs observed that such problems are not discussed.
3) 95.92% respondent BMs reported that review of the progress of the Govt. sponsored schemes are discussed in the BLBC meetings; while 4.08% BMs mentioned that such discussions did not take place during the BLBC meetings.
4) Regarding the segment-wise allocation and review of loans, 94.90%. BMs opined that thorough discussions take place; while 5.10% respondents reported that such discussions did not take place during the BLBC meetings.
5) 73.43% respondents reported that in BLBC meeting a complete review of progress of physical resources and infra-structure management was done; while a very large percentage (26.53%) of respondents reported that no such review took place.
6) One of the important points on which focussed attention was given in the meeting is the problem of overdues and recovery. As high as 98.98% respondents reported that serious discussions took place on the problem of overdues and recovery; while only 1.02% respondents observed that no discussions took place on this problem.
7) 83.67% respondents commented that BLBC discussed the court cases for recovery under RODA, but 16.33% respondent BMs intimated that this issue didn't come-up for discussion.
8) 28.57% respondent BMs mentioned this fact that discussions take place on the issue of allotment of villages to the newly opened branches in BLBC meetings, but a very high percentage of BMs (71.43%) mentioned that this issue didn't figure for discussion.

The response of bankers regarding the number of training programmes attended by them after launching the SAA has been presented in *table no. 7.19*. Majority of the respondent BMs reported this glaring fact that they did not receive any sort of training during their full tenure. The percentage of such BMs who did not receive any training was 60.20%. Only 34.70% respondent BMs reported that they attended only one training programme and that is also of not much use. A very small fraction of respondent BMs (5.10%) reported that they attended training programmes twice. None of the respondent reported about more than 2 times training. The interesting fact in this regard is that the training given is of general nature. It was not specifically meant for conceptual and operational part of SAA.

Table No. 7.19

Response of Bankers Regarding the Number of Training Programmes Attended by them after Launching the SAA

District		*0*	*1*	*2*	*3*	*4*	*5*	*More than 5*	*Total*
Baran	N	14	8	1	-	-	-	-	23
	%	60.87	34.78	4.35	-	-	-	-	100
Bundi	N	15	9	1	-	-	-	-	25
	%	60.00	36.00	4.00	-	-	-	-	100
Jhalawar	N	18	7	1	-	-	-	-	26
	%	69.23	26.92	3.85	-	-	-	-	100
Kota	N	12	10	2	-	-	-	-	24
	%	50	41.67	8.33	-	-	-	-	100
Total of the Region	N	59	34	5	-	-	-	-	98
	%	60.20	34.70	5.10	-	-	-	-	100

Table No. 7.20

Response of Bankers Regarding the Adherence of Action Calendar of Credit Plans

District		*Yes*	*No*	*No Reply*	*Total*
Baran	N	19	4	-	23
	%	82.61	17.39	-	100
Bundi	N	21	4	-	25
	%	84	16	-	100
Jhalawar	N	23	2	1	26
	%	88.46	7.69	3.85	100
Kota	N	20	2	2	24
	%	83.34	8.33	8.33	100
Total of the Region	N	83	12	3	98
	%	84.70	12.24	3.06	100

Table no. 7.20 depicts the response of bankers regarding the adherence to action calendar of credit plans. 84.70% respondents confirmed that they had adhered to the action calendar regarding the different stages of credit plans; while 12.24% respondents reported that they did not adhere to the action calendar. 3.06% respondents did not disclose their mind on this particular issue.

Table No. 7.21

Response of Bankers Regarding the Effectiveness of Monitoring System

District		*Yes*	*No*	*Total*
Baran	N	16	7	23
	%	69.57	30.43	100
Bundi	N	19	6	25
	%	76	24	100
Jhalawar	N	18	8	26
	%	69.23	30.77	100
Kota	N	15	9	24
	%	62.50	37.50	100
Total of the	N	68	30	98
Region	%	69.39	30.61	100

Table No. 7.22

Response of Bankers Regarding Impact of SAA on Increase in Production/ Productivity/ Income Level of Beneficiaries

District		Yes	No	Total	If yes, then to what extent?		
					Substantial	*Marginal*	*Total*
Baran	N	20	3	23	8	12	20
	%	86.96	13.04	100	40	60	100
Bundi	N	21	4	25	10	11	21
	%	84	16	100	47.62	52.38	100
Jhalawar	N	19	7	26	9	10	19
	%	73.08	26.92	100	47.37	52.63	100
Kota	N	21	3	24	7	14	21
	%	87.50	12.50	100	33.33	66.67	100
Total of the	N	71	17	98	24	47	71
Region	%	72.45	17.35	100	33.80	66.20	100

Table no. 7.21 presents the response of bankers regarding the effectiveness of monitoring system of credit plans. According to the response received, the majority were of the opinion that the system of monitoring was effective. 69.39% respondents were satisfied with the effectiveness of the present monitoring system; while 30.61% respondents mentioned that the system of monitoring of credit plans was not effective.

Table no. 7.22 exhibits the point of view of bankers regarding the impact of SAA on increase in production, productivity and level of income of beneficiaries. Though, 72.45% respondents BMs were of the opinion that there has been some improvement in production, productivity and level of income but nobody reported the exact percentage of increase. Contrary to this, 17.35% respondent BMs reported that there has been no increase in production, productivity and level of income. The researcher has also confronted with such exceptional cases where the economic position of beneficiaries has worsened. 66.20% respondents out of total 71 have reported that the increase in level of income has been marginal; while 33.80% BMs reported that substantial improvement has taken place in the production, productivity and level of income of beneficiaries after launching of SAA.

Table No. 7.23

Response of Bankers Regarding the Adverse Impact of SAA on Profitability of Bank Branches

District		***Yes***	***No***	***Total***	***If yes, then to what extent?***		
					Significantly	*Marginally*	*Total*
Baran	N	23	-	23	16	7	23
	%	100	-	100	69.57	30.43	100
Bundi	N	24	1	25	18	6	24
	%	96	4	100	75	25	100
Jhalawar	N	25	1	26	21	4	25
	%	96.15	3.85	100	84	16	100
Kota	N	24	-	24	15	9	24
	%	100	-	100	62.50	37.50	100
Total of the Region	N	96	2	98	70	26	96
	%	97.96	2.04	100	72.92	27.08	100

Table no. 7.23 highlights the response of bankers regarding the adverse impact of SAA on profitability of bank branches. As high as 97.96% respondent BMs reported that there has been an adverse impact on the profitability of bank branches after launching of SAA; while only 2.04%

respondent BMs mentioned that there was no adverse impact on profitability. Out of 96 respondents 70 (72.92%) respondent BMs have mentioned that there has been significant adverse impact on the profitability; while remaining 26 (27.08%) respondent BMs of the region have reported that the adverse impact on the profitability of bank branches was marginal.

Table No. 7.24

Response of Bankers Regarding the Adverse Impact of SAA on the Recovery Position of Bank Branches

District		Yes	No	No Reply	Total	If yes, then to what extent?		
						Substantial	Marginal	Total
Baran	N	15	6	2	23	2	13	15
	%	65.22	26.09	8.69	100	13.33	86.67	100
Bundi	N	19	5	1	25	5	14	19
	%	76	20	4	100	26.32	73.68	100
Jhalawar	N	17	5	4	26	3	14	17
	%	65.38	19.23	15.39	100	17.65	82.35	100
Kota	N	16	7	1	24	3	13	16
	%	66.67	29.17	4.16	100	18.75	81.25	100
Total of the Region	N	67	23	8	98	13	54	67
	%	68.37	23.47	8.16	100	19.40	80.60	100

Table no. 7.24 exhibits the response of bankers regarding the adverse impact of SAA on the recovery position of bank branches. 68.37% respondent BMs reported that there has been an adverse impact on the recovery position of bank branches; while only 23.47% respondents did not subscribe to this point of view. 8.16% respondents did not reply to this question. Those who reported that the recovery position has worsened due to the SAA, out of them only 19.40% mentioned that the impact has been substantial; while 80.60% mentioned that the impact was only marginal.

Table no. 7.25 manifests the response of bankers regarding the successful functioning of SAA. Only 28.57% respondent BMs reported that SAA has been successful; while 64.29% reported that its success was moderate. Only 7.14% respondents mentioned that SAA has been a failure. The interesting point, which is worth mentioning here, is that no body has reported about the extreme success or extreme failure of this scheme. Thus, on the basis of above analysis, we can infer that the SAA on the whole, has been successful.

Table No. 7.25

Response of Bankers Regarding the Successful Functioning of SAA

District		*Extremely Successful*	*Successful*	*Average Successful*	*Failure*	*Extreme Failure*	*Total*
Baran	N	-	5	16	2	-	23
	%	-	21.74	69.56	8.70	-	100
Bundi	N	-	9	15	1	-	25
	%	-	36	60	4	-	100
Jhalawar	N	-	6	19	1	-	26
	%	-	23.07	73.08	3.85	-	100
Kota	N	-	8	13	3	-	24
	%	-	33.33	54.17	12.50	-	100
Total of the Region	N	-	28	63	7	-	98
	%	-	28.57	64.29	7.14	-	100

Feed Back Received From Beneficiaries

As stated earlier that a separate set of questionnaire has been prepared for the beneficiaries to know their point of view in regard to the various aspects of functioning of SAA. The total size of the sample was 400 for the whole Hadoti region, selecting 100 beneficiaries from each district to accord equal weightage to all four districts of the region. The analysis of the observations/ suggestions/ opinions of the beneficiaries is presented below in summarised form :

Table No. 7.26

Literacy Level of Beneficiaries in Hadoti Region

District	*Illit.*	*Lit.*	*Pri.*	*Middle*	*Sec.*	*Hr. Sec./ Sen.Sec.*	*Grad.*	*Post-Grad.*	*Tech. Edu.*	*Total*
Baran	31	25	24	8	4	6	1	-	1	100
Bundi	35	17	28	5	7	4	2	-	2	100
Jhalawar	33	26	25	9	3	2	1	-	1	100
Kota	15	10	20	15	13	14	7	2	4	100
Total of	114	78	97	37	27	26	11	2	8	400
the Region	28.5%	19.5%	24.25%	9.25%	6.75%	6.50%	2.75%	0.5%	2%	100%

Table no. 7.26 displays the literacy level of beneficiaries in Hadoti region. With the help of it, it will be easier to ascertain the level of knowledge of the participant beneficiaries as the fate of any scheme, to a great extent, depends on the level of education and knowledge. The analysis of the table discloses the following facts :

1) 28.50% respondents were illiterate in the region. They were even unable to put their initials.
2) Only 19.50% respondent beneficiaries were literate meaning thereby that they were able to put their signature and were also able to read only few words.
3) 24.25% respondents were having qualification upto Primary level and infact, they were more or less of the literate category.
4) Only 9.25% respondents were qualified upto the 8th standard.
5) The percentage of respondents who were qualified upto Secondary level was only 6.75%.
6) Only 6.50% respondents were qualified upto the higher secondary/senior secondary standard.
7) The number of respondents qualified upto graduation level were only 11 out of total 400 respondents in the region, which were only 2.75% of the total.
8) There were only 2 respondents out of total 400 in the region who were qualified upto Post Graduate level, (only 0.50%).
9) Only 2% respondents were having technical education.

On the basis of the above mentioned facts, we can infer the following:

1) More than 1/4 respondents beneficiaries were illiterate.
2) The percentage of literate and qualified upto Primary level was very high to a level of 43.37%. This segment of respondents was more or less of illiterate category for all practical purposes except putting initials.
3) The percentage of qualified respondents upto the secondary and above was only 18.50% which could be termed as educated– a very low percentage comparatively.

This shows that the level of knowledge/education of beneficiaries in the process of credit planning was poor on the whole.

Table No. 7.27

Sources of Income of Beneficiaries

District	*Agriculture*	*Small & Cottage Industry*	*Business*	*Private/ Govt. Service*	*Other Works*	*Total*
Baran	74	5	19	-	2	100
Bundi	70	11	17	1	1	100
Jhalawar	73	4	20	-	3	100
Kota	57	24	16	1	2	100
Total of the	274	44	72	2	8	400
Region	68.5%	11%	18%	0.50%	2%	100%

With the help of the study of *table no. 7.27*, we can know the sources of income of beneficiaries. The analysis of table reveals the job profile/ occupational pattern of the beneficiaries. The source of income of 68.50% respondents was agriculture; while the source of 11% respondents was small and cottage industry. 18% respondent's source of income was business; while only 0.50% respondents were dependent for their income on private/ government service. Only 2% respondents were working in other sectors. Thus, agriculture was the main source of income of the majority of the people, followed by business and small and cottage industry.

Table No. 7.28

Response of Beneficiaries Regarding the Source of Acquaintance of Loan Schemes

District	*Newspaper Radio/TV (Media)*	*Bank Staff*	*B.D.O*	*Sarpanch /Panch*	*Relative/ Benefici-aries*	*Other*	*SHGS*	*Loan Leader*	*Total*
Baran	5	42	17	12	8	2	3	11	100
Bundi	9	44	12	15	7	-	4	9	100
Jhalawar	7	40	13	16	11	-	3	10	100
Kota	12	47	11	12	5	1	6	6	100
Total of	33	173	53	55	31	3	16	36	400
the Region	8.25%	43.25%	13.25%	13.75%	7.75%	0.75%	4.00%	9%	100%

Table no. 7.28 depicts the response of beneficiaries regarding the source of acquaintance of loan scheme. The analysis of table highlights the following facts :

1) 43.25% respondent beneficiaries reported that they got information of loan schemes from the bank staff.
2) 13.75% respondents mentioned that they received information from the Sarpanch/ Panch of the Gram panchayat concerned.
3) 13.25% respondents received information from the B.D.O. a nd his office staff.
4) 8.25% respondents received the information of different bankable schemes from the print media and electronic media. The role of print and electronic media was comparatively less significant in this regard because of the low level of income and education in the region.
5) 7.75% respondents have come across the various loan schemes from the relatives and friends.
6) 4% respondents could come to know the various schemes from the SHGs.
7) A very small percentage (0.75%) of respondents got the information from other beneficiaries of the schemes.

On the basis of above analysis, it can be said that the main sources of information of different loan schemes were bank staff, B.D.O. and his staff, Sarpanch/ Panch.

Table No. 7.29

Problems Faced by Beneficiaries at the Time of Applying for Loan

District	*Not getting application forms*	*Completion of application form*	*Security/ Guarantee*	*Total*
Baran	15	83	32	100
Bundi	12	76	20	100
Jhalawar	10	86	25	100
Kota	5	78	12	100
Total of the	42	323	89	400
Region	10.50%	80.75%	22.25%	100%

Table no. 7.29 reveals the various problems faced by the beneficiaries at the time of applying for loan. The most important problem, which have been reported by most of the respondents was of filling loan application forms in complete and correct manner. 80.75% respondent beneficiaries in the region faced the problem of how to correctly fill-up the loan application form because of illiteracy and low level of education as stated earlier in this chapter and also due to non-coperative attitude of bank officials.

The second important problem in this regard was security and the Guarantee of loans. The beneficiaries faced this problem mainly because of poverty due to which they were unable to provide collateral security and also due to too much insistence on credit worthiness of loan to some extent, rather than the purpose worthiness, besides the other reason.

The third problem which was reported by 10.50% respondents was regarding not getting loan application forms timely because of difficult accessibility of the branches to the beneficiaries.

Table No. 7.30

Time Taken by Banks in Sanctioning of Loans

District	*1 to 15 Days*	*16 days to 1 month*	*More than 1month & upto 2 months*	*More than 2 months upto 3 months*	*More than 3 months*	*Total*
Baran	1	26	48	10	15	100
Bundi	-	28	46	9	17	100
Jhalawar	-	34	43	10	13	100
Kota	4	38	36	11	11	100
Total of the	5	126	173	40	56	400
Region	1.25%	31.50%	43.25%	10%	14%	100%

Table no. 7.30 depicts the duration of time taken by banks at the time of sanctioning of loans. 31.50% respondent beneficiaries reported that banks took 16 days to one month time in sanctioning their loan; while only 1.25% respondents got their loan sanctioned within 15 days. Thus, 32.75% respondents got their loan sanctioned within a month time contrary to this, as high as 43.25% respondents mentioned that banks sanctioned their loans within the duration of more than 1 month and within 2 months; while 10% respondents reported that banks took unnecessary more time from more than 2 months and upto 3 months in sanctioning of loan. 14% respondents complained that their loan was sanctioned in more than 3 months time period. Thus, the above analysis reveals that 67.25% respondent beneficiaries in the region got their loan sanctioned in more than one month time.

The analysis of table no. 7.31 reveals the sufficiency of amount of sanctioned loan by the banks to the beneficiaries in the region. 67.58% respondent beneficiaries reported that the amount of loan sanctioned to them was sufficient for their requirement for which they obtained the loan; while 29.75% respondents mentioned that the amount of loan sanctioned to them was not sufficient. Only 2.75% respondents gave no reply.

Thus, the above analysis reveals this fact that the slightly less than 1/3 respondents didn't get the sufficient amount of loan, which caused the problem to them in completing their ventures.

Table No. 7.31

Response of Beneficiaries Regarding Sufficiency of Amount of Sanctioned Loan by the Banks

District	Yes	No	No Reply	Total
Baran	67	26	7	100
Bundi	62	38	-	100
Jhalawar	69	28	3	100
Kota	72	27	1	100
Total of the	270	119	11	400
Region	67.58%	29.75%	2.75%	100%

Table No. 7.32

Response of Beneficiaries Regarding Other Sources of Loan

District	*Friends/ Relatives*	*Money Lenders*	*Co-operative Societies*	*SHGs*	*Other Banks*	*No arran-gement made*	*Total*
Baran	7	13	-	-	3	3	26
Bundi	10	21	1	1	4	1	38
Jhalawar	7	11	5	-	2	3	28
Kota	10	12	2	2	1	-	27
Total of the	34	57	8	3	10	7	119
Region	28.57%	47.90%	6.72%	3.36%	8.40%	5.88%	100%

Table no. 7.32 provides the factual position of the other sources of loan which beneficiaries obtained because the loan sanctioned by banks to them was not sufficient for the purpose for which they took loan. The highest number of respondents obtained loan from money lenders as it was more convenient for them. As much as 47.90% respondent beneficiaries took loan from money lenders. This shows that the hold of money lenders in the rural economy of the region is still significant inspite of so much spread of institutional credit. 28.57% respondents met their remaining loan requirement from their friends and relatives. Again the reason was easy and convenient accessibility besides being soft terms and conditions of loan. The role of co-operative societies in fulfilling the credit gaps was only of 6.72% magnitude; while 3.36% respondents mentioned that they fulfill their requirement from taking loan from SHGs. 8.40% respondents reported that they borrowed funds from other banks operating in the concerned service area, but 5.88% respondents said that they couldn't arrange loan due to some reason or the other.

Table No. 7.33

Problems Faced by Beneficiaries at the Time of Sanctioning of Loan

District	*Bribe*	*Recommendation*	*Time Lag*	*Complicated Procedure/ Unnecessary Formalities*	*Misbehaviour/Indifferent attitude of Bankers*	*no Problem*	*Total*
Baran	12	9	46	25	-	8	100
Bundi	15	8	45	22	-	10	100
Jhalawar	14	11	43	23	1	8	100
Kota	20	7	35	29	-	9	100
Total of the	61	35	169	99	1	35	400
Region	15.25%	8.75%	42.25%	24.75%	0.25%	8.75%	100%

Table no. 7.33 throws light on the problems faced by beneficiaries at the time of sanctioning of loan. After analysing their response in this regard, the most important problem was of time lag. Banks took more time unnecessarily in sanctioning loan without any genuine reasons. 42.25% respondents in the region reported delay in sanctioning of loan. The second important problem was complicated procedures/unnecessary formalities required to be completed. 24.75% respondents mentioned this problem. The third important problem was bribe as 15.25% respondents reported that without giving bribe, it was very difficult to get loan sanctioned. This shows that the root of corruption was started creeping into the banking system, which is a dangerous sign. 18.87% respondents accepted the role of recommendation and reported that without recommendation getting loan is very difficult. The astonishing fact in this regard was that only the 0.25% respondents complained about the misbehaviour and indifferent attitude of bankers only. 8.75% respondents reported that they didn't face any problem in getting loan sanctioned.

Table No. 7.34

Response of Beneficiaries Regarding End Use of Credit

District	*Yes*	*No*	*No Reply*	*Total*
Baran	59	24	17	100
Bundi	68	21	11	100
Jhalawar	54	21	20	100
Kota	69	26	15	100
Total of the	250	16	63	400
Region	62.50%	21.75%	15.75%	100%

Analysis of *table no. 7.34* presents the picture of response of beneficiaries regarding the end use of credit. 62.50% respondents reported that they have utilised the credit for the purpose for which it was sanctioned to them; while 21.75% respondents reported that they didn't use the credit for the purpose it was sanctioned to them. 15.75% respondents gave no reply.

Table No. 7.35

Action Taken by Banks for Recovery of Loans

District	*Verbal Reminder*	*Written Reminder*	*Legal Notice*	*Cases Filed*	*Social Pressure*
Baran	48	46	42	32	30
Bundi	55	60	45	38	19
Jhalawar	43	58	33	28	15
Kota	40	52	50	21	10
Total of the	186	216	170	119	74
Region	46.50%	54%	42.50%	29.75%	18.50%

Table no. 7.35 depicts the action taken by banks for recovery of loans. The highest number of respondents reported that banks sent to them written reminders. This fact was reported by 54% respondent beneficiaries. 46.50% respondents reported that the bankers reminded them verbally regarding the repayment of loan. The another important action was sending legal notices by banks to the beneficiaries– 42.50% respondents reported that they got legal notice from the banks. Not only this, 29.75% respondents reported that banks filed court cases against them. Only 18.50% respondent beneficiaries accepted that social pressure has been exerted by the banks through the influential persons of the community. It seems that the role of social pressure is diminishing day by day, which is a result of weak social relations.

Table No. 7.36

Various Methods of Repayment of Loan

District	*By Incre-mental income*	*By Sell Out of income*	*By taking another loan*	*By earning income from other Business*	*By Insurance company*	*Total*
Baran	67	2	31	-	-	100
Bundi	72	1	26	-	1	100
Jhalawar	69	-	31	-	-	100
Kota	76	2	20	1	1	100
Total of	284	5	108	1	2	400
the Region	71%	1.25%	27%	0.25%	0.50%	100%

Table no. 7.36 explains the various methods of repayment of loan by the beneficiaries. 71% respondent beneficiaries reported that they paid their loan out of incremental income, which they generated through the proper end use of credit, but 27% respondents reported that they repaid their loan by taking another loan. This was either due to insufficiency of loan amount or due to mis-utilisation of sanctioned loan. The other methods of repayment were sell of property or by income from other sources, compensation received from the insurance company etc.

Table No. 7.37

Problems Faced by Beneficiaries During the Production Process

District	*Lack of Infra-structural Facilities*	*Problem of Raw-material*	*Lack of Marketing Facitlities*	*Lack of Technical Facilities*	*No Reply*
Baran	40	10	20	22	12
Bundi	15	12	10	17	-
Jhalawar	32	14	37	34	-
Kota	10	12	15	12	18
Total of the	97	48	82	85	30
Region	24.25%	12%	20.50%	21.25%	7.5%

Table no. 7.37 denotes various problems faced by beneficiaries during the production process. The most important problem which respondent reported was lack of infra-structural facilities in the service area. 24.25% beneficiaries faced this problem. The second important problem was lack of technical facilities, which was reported by 21.25% respondents. Lack of marketing facilities was another big problem, which was reported by 20.50% respondents. The problem of raw material was reported by only 12% respondents; while 7.5% respondents did not disclose their mind on this issue.

Table No. 7.38

Response of Beneficiaries Regarding Repayment of Loan in Time

District	*Yes*	*No*	*No Reply*	*Total*
Baran	65	31	4	100
Bundi	72	26	2	100
Jhalawar	74	25	1	100
Kota	68	30	2	100
Total of the	279	112	09	400
Region	69.75%	28%	2.25%	100%

With the help of analysis of *table no. 7.38*, we come to know the response of beneficiaries regarding repayment of loan in time. As high as 69.79% respondents reported that they paid their loan in time. The percentage of beneficiaries, which couldn't pay their loan in time was 28%. Remaining 2.25% respondents did not reply in this regard.

Table No. 7.39

Reasons for Timely Repayment of Loans

District		*Sufficient Income*	*Fear of Legal Action*	*Social Status*	*Timely Reminder by Bank*	*Obtaining Credit in Future*	*Self Satis-faction*	*Total*
Baran	N	44	2	11	3	5	-	65
	%	67.70	3.08	16.92	4.61	7.69	-	100
Bundi	N	31	8	20	6	7	-	72
	%	43.06	11.11	27.78	8.33	9.72	-	100
Jhalawar	N	39	13	8	5	9	-	74
	%	52.70	17.57	10.81	6.76	12.16	-	100
Kota	N	43	5	13	2	4	1	68
	%	63.23	7.35	19.12	2.94	5.89	1.47	100
Total of the	N	157	28	52	16	25	1	279
Region	%	56.27	10.03	18.64	5.73	8.97	0.36	100

Table no. 7.39 throws light on the reasons for timely repayment of loans as mentioned by respondent beneficiaries. As high as 56.27% respondents reported that they could be able to repay their loan timely because of generation of sufficient income due to proper utilisation of loan amount. 18.64% respondents repaid their loan because they were conscious of their social status. 8.97% respondents repaid their dues timely because they wanted to avail credit facility in future; while 0.36% respondents repaid their dues only for their self satisfaction. The role of banks in sending timely reminder to the beneficiaries in this regard was accepted only by 5.73% respondents. Only 10.03% respondents reported that they paid their dues timely because of the fear of legal action. Thus, a very small fraction of beneficiaries were afraid of legal action, which dampened the recovery process and adversely affected the recovery climate.

Table No. 7.40

Reasons for Non-Payment of Loans

District		*Inadequate Income*	*Consumed in other Uses*	*No Fear of Legal Action*	*Possibility of Loan Waiver*	*Total*
Baran	N	11	8	4	8	31
	%	35.48	25.81	12.90	25.81	100
Bundi	N	10	6	4	6	26
	%	38.46	23.08	15.39	23.07	100
Jhalawar	N	7	5	4	9	25
	%	28	20	16	36	100
Kota	N	8	6	6	10	30
	%	26.67	20	20	33.33	100
Total of the Region	N	36	25	18	33	112
	%	32.14	23.32	16.08	29.46	100

Table no. 7.40 exhibits the reasons for non-repayment of loans reported by the beneficiaries. The analysis of the table reveals the following facts :

1) The most important reason for non-repayment of loans was inadequate income, which didn't allow the borrower to pay the dues timely. 32.14% respondents mentioned this reason and there were several reasons for generation of inadequate income including the improper end use of credit and poor monitoring system.

2) 29.46% respondents reported that they didn't repay the loan deliberately as they were expecting the possibility of loan wavier in future on the past pattern. Infact, it was more a psycho-problem than the genuine one.

3) 23.32% respondents reported that they have used the amount of loan in some other uses rather than the uses for which it was obtained. This reflects not only on the behaviour of the beneficiaries as well as on the working of bankers.

4) 16.08% respondents mentioned that they were not afraid of legal action, hence, they didn't pay the loan. This shows the flaws in our legal systems.

Table No. 7.41

Number of Visits of Bankers with Beneficiaries During a Year

District	*Not a Single time*	*1 time*	*2 times*	*3 times*	*4 times*	*More than 4 times*	*Total*
Baran	-	16	81	3	-	-	100
Bundi	-	7	89	4	-	-	100
Jhalawar	-	14	82	4	-	-	100
Kota	-	8	85	7	-	-	100
Total of the	-	45	337	18	-	-	400
Region	-	11.25	84.25	4.50	-	-	100

Table no. 7.41 reveals the number of visits by bankers with beneficiaries during a year. 84.25% respondents reported that the bankers visited their village and met them twice; while 1.25% respondents mentioned that there was only a single visit in a year. Only 4.50% respondents reported that the bankers visited three times in a year. None of the respondent reported about the four times visits and also no visit at all in a year.

Table no. 7.42 reveals the response of beneficiaries regarding the interest taken by bankers in their village level activities. Only 5.25% respondents accepted this fact that bankers took keen interest in their village activities; while 49.50% respondents reported that bankers took only normal interest. But as high as 45.25% respondents mentioned that bankers took least interest or no interest in their village activities, which shows the indifferenceness of the bankers in village activities of beneficiaries. Thus, the non-involvement of banker with the beneficiaries is one of the important reasons for the failure of SAA.

Table No. 7.42

Response of Beneficiaries Regarding Interest Taken by Bankers in Village Activities

District	*Keen Interest*	*Normal Interest*	*Least Interest/ No Interest*	*Total*
Baran	5	49	46	100
Bundi	7	51	42	100
Jhalawar	3	54	43	100
Kota	6	44	50	100
Total of the Region	21	198	181	400
	5.25%	49.50%	45.25%	100%

Table No. 7.43

Level of Services Rendered by Co-operative Banks in Comparison to CBs and RRBs

District	*Good*	*Bad*	*More or Less Same*	*Total*
Baran	76	3	21	100
Bundi	65	9	26	100
Jhalawar	82	3	15	100
Kota	70	8	22	100
Total of the Region	293	23	84	400
	73.25%	5.75%	21%	100%

Analysis of *table no. 7.43* reveals the level of services rendered by co-operative banks in comparison to CBs and RRBs. 73.25% respondents reported that the services rendered by co-operative banks were better than the services of CBs and RRBs; while 21% respondents mentioned that the quality of services of co-operative banks was more or less of the same quality. Only 5.75% respondents observed that the services of co-operative banks were poor than the services of CBs and RRBs. On the basis of above analysis, it could be said that the quality of services of co-operative banks was, on the whole, better than the CBs and RRBs.

Table no. 7.44 depicts the level of satisfaction of the beneficiaries from the work and behaviour of the bankers. Majority of the respondents (72.75%) reported that the work and behaviour of the bankers with them was satisfactory; while only 15.75% respondents mentioned that the work and behaviour of banker was unsatisfactory. 11.50% respondents did not disclose their mind on this aspect. The astonishing fact in this regard was that none of the respondents reported that the work and behaviour of the banker was extremely satisfactory and extremely unsatisfactory as well.

Table No. 7.44

Level of Satisfaction of Beneficiaries from the Work and Behaviour of Bankers

District	*Extremely Satifactory*	*Satisfactory*	*Unsatisfactory*	*Extremely Unsafisfactory*	*No Reply*	*Total*
Baran	-	77	13	-	10	100
Bundi	-	69	16	-	15	100
Jhalawar	-	74	18	-	8	100
Kota	-	71	16	-	13	100
Total of	-	291	63	-	46	400
the Region	-	72.75%	15.75%	-	11.50%	100%

Table no. 7.45 throws light on the dependency of beneficiaries on the type of sources of credit; *i.e.* institutional and non-institutional source of credit. The analysis of table reveals that 61% respondent beneficiaries obtained credit from the institutional sources; while 31% respondents fulfilled their credit demand from non-institutional credit sources. Thus, the role of institutional credit in the total requirement of credit was significant in the region. 7% respondents did not disclose their mind on this particular issue.

Table No. 7.45

Response of Beneficiaries Regarding the Dependency on the Type of Source of Credit

District	*Institutional Source of Credit*	*Non-Institutional Source of Credit*	*No Reply*	*Total*
Baran	56	35	9	100
Bundi	61	32	7	100
Jhalawar	60	32	8	100
Kota	67	29	4	100
Total of the	244	128	28	400
Region	61%	32%	7%	100%

Table No. 7.46

Response of Beneficiaries Regarding the Impact of SAA on Overall Development of Hadoti Region

District	*Increase in Income*	*Increase in Employment*	*Increase in Living Standard*	*Increase in Production*	*Increase in Assets*
Baran	80	76	64	77	60
Bundi	87	79	78	81	65
Jhalawar	78	73	59	72	58
Kota	91	84	81	86	70
Total of the	336	312	282	316	253
Region	84%	78%	70.50%	79%	63.25%

Table no. 7.46, elaborates statistically the resonse of the beneficiaries regarding the impact of SAA on an overall development of Hadoti region. The analysis of the table discloses the following facts :

1) 84% respondents reported an increase in their level of incomes;
2) 78% respondents reported an increase in the level of employment;
3) 79% respondent beneficiaries mentioned an increase in the level of production;
4) 70.50% respondents mentioned an increase in the standard of living; and
5) 63.25% respondents accepted that their assets have increased.

Thus, on the basis of above facts, it can be inferred that the impact of SAA on an overall development of Hadoti region was positive and favourable.

Table No. 7.47

Response of Beneficiaries Regarding the Success of SAA in Hadoti Region

District	*Highly Successful*	*Normally Successful*	*Unsuccessful*	*No Reply*	*Total*
Baran	57	32	2	9	100
Bundi	54	38	1	7	100
Jhalawar	61	30	1	8	100
Kota	69	17	5	9	100
Total of the	241	117	9	33	400
Region	60.25%	29.25%	2.25%	8.25%	100%

Table no. 7.47, presents the response of beneficiaries regarding the success of SAA in Hadoti region. The analysis of table reveals the following facts :

1) 60.25% respondent beneficiaries were of the opinion that the SAA was highly successful;
2) 29.25% respondents reported that the SAA was normally successful;
3) Only 2.25% respondents mentioned that the SAA was totally unsuccessful; and
4) 8.25% respondents in the region did not reply on this issue.

Thus, on the basis of above analysis, it can be generalised that the SAA has, on the whole, been successful in the region according to the opinion of beneficiaries, who are, infact, the real judge of this approach.

Table No. 7.48

Response of Beneficiaries Regarding Continuance of SAA

District	***Yes***	***No***	***Total***
Baran	87	13	100
Bundi	89	11	100
Jhalawar	83	17	100
Kota	86	14	100
Total of the	345	55	400
Region	86.25%	13.75%	100%

Table no. 7.48, presents the opinion of beneficiaries in statistical form regarding the continuance of SAA. As high as 86.25% respondent beneficiaries expressed their opinion in favour of continuance of SAA; while only 13.75% respondents did not support the continuance of SAA. Thus, the majority of respondents were in favour of continuance of SAA in view of its overall advantages to them.

□■□

Chapter 8

Problems, Suggestions and Conclusions

The year 1969 could be marked as the 'turning point' in the history of Indian banking when the perception and practices of banking witnessed 'sea-level changes' with the nationalisation of 14 major CBs and launching of LBs. The focus of banks shifted from 'class banking' to 'mass banking', 'urban banking' to 'rural banking', 'commercial banking' to 'social banking' and from 'credit worthiness' to 'purpose worthiness'. This rural and welfare innovative orientation of banking was primarily responsible for ushering in the new era in Indian banking. As stated earlier in previous chapters that many steps have been taken to improve the rural credit delivery system after the nationalisation of CBs. In the series of efforts, the last was the SAA - an innovative concept and most important policy initiative in the sphere of rural lending which was launched in 1989.

Though, the SAA is much better than the old LBs, even then it also suffers from many weaknesses, and confronted with many problems. Inspite of all pious intentions and efforts, the SAA could not prove as a fool-proof system nor became a 'grand panacea' for all ills of the rural credit management in India. Owing to the several severe weakness the panel of bankers of the Indian Banker's Association has suggested in 1998 that SAA should be abolished as it has resulted in a large number of unviable rural bank branches. The panel of bankers has further demanded that the banks and not the Government agencies should be given power to identify the beneficiaries since the present system has resulted in misuse of funds. The bankers, beneficiaries, academicians and the Government functionaries have evaluated SAA in their own way and they all agree that this policy approach also suffers from many shortcomings. The critics of the SAA raise fingers at the various impediments and the stymieing factors in the effective and glib of the SAA. These pertain mainly to the operational mode of the approach. Some of the most common hindrances in the smooth implementation of the SAA are assured and timely supply of non-credit inputs, effective co-operation and co-ordination of different Government agencies/ departments, meddling role of non-officials and natural short-comings of a non-competitive environment owing to monopoly operations in the service area. And, to top them all, there exists the bitter fact of the ever increasing aspirations of the common mass leading, generally to dismay among the people and thus, subsequently, nurturing the bane factor of corruption. Besides these, the lack of effective organisational and operational environment, *viz.* arrangement of credit institutions, skill formation in bank personnel, particularly the officials attending problems of rural masses, non-adequacy of man-power and supportive services/facilities at branch and block level, development orientation and motivation of persons managing the SAA and the various Government departments are also considered as the other major stumbling block to rural growth through SAA. Most of the problems, which are being faced by the credit planners and executors in the field are multi-dimensional in nature and which are mainly related to planning, implementation and monitoring of the SAA.

The author has attempted to trace-out certain important problems of the SAA on the basis of cross examination of beneficiaries, concerned bankers and Government officials through the field survey, structured interviews, personal discussions and on spot observations. These problems have been discussed below alongwith suggestions to overcome them :

PROBLEMS REGARDING THE FORMULATION OF REALISTIC CREDIT PLANS

Although the SAPs are formulated on sound principles and with utmost care as per the guidelines issued by the RBI, yet, the following key factors create obstacles in the path of formulating realistic credit plans :

(a) Paucity of sufficient and trustworthy data : The time for preparation of the village profile by banks is different from that of the actual credit extension time. The credit plans are chalked out on the basis of the background data given in the village profile based on the survey of villages. The data given in the village profile is neither adequate nor trustworthy. The background data used for chalking out of the credit plan was woefully insufficient as well as not reliable.

It has amply been observed by the author that the village survey profiles failed to produce primary and most readily available information regarding the command area villages. Though, there had been elaborate provisions in the survey proforma and the explanations and guidelines with regard to each and every point, yet, the village survey profiles either remain blank or denote 'No', 'Nil', 'N.A.', often quite impertinent and thus nullifying the sincere and dedicatedly noble efforts to nothing more than a routine carrying no weightage.

Most of the times, the infra-structural and resource base/potential related items (such as market, infra-structure, arrangement of institutional services, supply of non-credit inputs, factor cost of production etc.), of which information look difficult to obtain have been left unattended to in the VCPs. This leaves the VCPs as without database and unrealistic plan and makes the credit planning exercise as an entirely hollow exercise - an exercise which do not match with the ground realities.

The interactions of the author with various field functionaries in the region supports this fact that the data available is not only inadequate, but also unreliable, hence do not provide the true picture of the socio-economic environment of the concerned service area. Many times village profile contains a lot of irrelevant data, which are of no use. In the absence of sufficient, correct and reliable data, formulation of realistic credit plan even can't be imagined. Thus, the paucity of sufficient and trustworthy data poses a biggest hurdle in the formulation of realistic credit plans which match the ground realities.

- It is hereby suggested that if at all, BMs to make the credit plans more viable, realistic and scientific, they have to list out the following first :
- The prevailing schemes that are available to his branch;
- The schemes offered by other branches of a particular bank and other banks; and
- The schemes that ought to be renovated for the precise requirements of his area of operation.

The realistic credit projections based on the resource potential and needs of the specific area, too, should be given the foremost weightage. The lead banks of the concerned district are required thereby to compile and formulate background papers that must include block-wise elaborate developmental plans of the State Government and the same should be in an easy and ready access of the each branch of the concerned area under the beneficiary scheme. NABARD has been doing commendable job by preparing PLPs, but benefits of the same can be realised only if the same is expedited timely to the service area bank branches.

For realistic plan formulations, the LBO, DDM (NABARD) and BM may undertake joint inspection of the service area and deliberate on the methodology to be adopted for accessing the activity-wise credit potential of the service area on the basis of village-wise data. However, the credit plan should be prepared by the BM only and the endeavours of LBO and DDM should only be suggestive.

(b) Absence of perspicuous and precise guidelines : There are no clear-cut guidelines as regards how exactly the vast environmental data/ information collected by the BMs can be translated into the quantitative banking targets for ACPs. Since long-term perspective plan is not made under SAA, the branches were doing either over planning without phasing out the plan into the ACPs or just making projections; while effecting marginal increase over the preceding year's performance.

The concept of 'Performance Budgeting' that had been introduced way back in 1973, has yet to be implemented effectively at the grass-root level. Planning and budgeting are even yet no more than a cosmetic exercise in most of the branches of the region. The bank branches need to introduce the philosophy of performance budgeting and this should be implemented in letter and spirit.

(c) Lack of appropriate updating data : The field survey conducted by the author reveals that a general laxity on the part of the BMs is found in updating the data in time and only few of them have showed an urge to update them primarily because of the reason that updating of base data, which is often found unrealistic, take more than extra ordinary efforts and secondly the target oriented working is considered as the easiest outcome to avoid extra efforts. This, not only adversely affect the current financing, but also future plan formulation too.

Out of the 50 BMs interviewed 78% (39)) BMs have shown no interest in updating/ revising the data on the basis of socio-economic changes in their service areas. Consequently, the distorted information in tit-bits do not form an adequate and realistic base for review and formulation of credit plans. The Government functionaries were also not found displaying any interest to assist bankers in this regard. Thus, old and un-updated data has been found adversely affecting the quality of plan formulations.

It is suggested that a socio-economic household survey by an outside agency is required or instead of preparation of village profile through Government functionaries, the task may be entrusted to external agencies, such as CMIE (Centre for Monitoring of Indian Economy). This is expected to provide a valid database, which can be updated time to time by each bank branch as per its area of operation. Co-operation of researchers, students and teachers of schools and colleges, BDOs, Panchayats and Voluntary agencies can also be solicited for the updation task. The grass-root planning will become fructifying only when it has the backing of a computerised 'comprehensive depository of village level data' concerning various aspects and the same may be developed by DRDA.

The survey proforma also requires further elaboration and addition information so as to reduce the scope for any confusion among the users. It is also suggested that all the Government departments at block level should ensure their presence by attending BLBC meetings along with their plans/schemes and finalise credit plan after detailed discussions to integrate SAPs with developmental plans. Besides these, the annual VCP should factor the suggestions of a cross-section of people in the village, like – progressive farmers, educated youth and women, Sarpanch of the Panchayat and other responsible persons.

(d) Unmanageable area of operation : In some cases, the service area allotted to the banks is found unwieldy. The heterogeneity and long distances, which are found in Hadoti region due to its geographic and demographic situation, creates problem for the banks in some cases. The uneven roads, the hills and zig-zag paths also make the area unwieldy. The 'vicinity approach' of selecting the villages under SAA also affects the formulation of realistic credit plan.

For example, in Hadoti region, there were 47 service areas, which were serving more than 25 villages, which infact, were out of the reach of bank branches. Out of these, there were 8 service areas, which were serving more than 40 villages.

The allocation of villages amongst different banks and at times, even amongst branches of the same bank, changes abruptly with the change in the locational vicinity. It has been observed that the allocation of area is not done keeping in view the complimentary requirement of different areas, which affects the successful plan formulation and implementation. For example, a village where financing of tractors and other agricultural implements was done quite extensively by a branch was allotted to a different bank branch, whereas, the village where shops for tractor and other equipments was located as also the mechanic shops were financed was covered by the different bank branch. This creates problem not only at the time of realistic plan formulation as regards the overall requirement and credit potential of the area, but also adversely affect the recovery process.

In this context, it is suggested that new bank branches should be opened in the deficit pockets wherever feasible. In case of serving more than 25 villages by a branch, the regional offices of banks should identify the branches having population above 13,000 and approach to RBI for permission to open satellite branch or mobile services so that banking needs of the villagers are properly catered.

(e) Lack of experience and expertise : Majority of BMs posted in rural areas neither have proper knowledge of plan formulation methodology nor they are properly trained for this task, thus, making the whole credit planning process less effective and meaningful. It appears that the BMs are ill equipped to undertake economic surveys. Most of them neither possess the requisite academic qualifications nor do they have the experience and expertise. They lack in knowledge and skill which cannot be developed in a short span of time. Under the SAA, the Key person in plan formulation and implementation is the BM, who generally belongs to urban area. Lack of insight in branch officials about the rural economy greatly affects the quality of plan formulation, which the researcher has observed that 70% (35) BMs out of total 50 BMs interviewed of the region. It was found that bankers are interested in collecting and updating the data without putting their mind and heart in it. It was also observed that a great part of data is prepared for the purpose of target based financing and generated on the place of work, which is far from reality and adversely affect the whole process of credit plan formulation.

During the interaction, it was revealed that most of the banks provide training to their BMs through various induction courses, but such courses do not properly focus on village planning, survey and other aspects, which are pertinent to the requirements of the SAA. Generally, the BMs give priority to their day-to-day branch work and growth targets of the branch, *viz.* deposits, advances, profit, NPA reduction etc., which are given by their controlling officers. Collection of realistic as well as bankable data is extended least priority. Due to this lacklustre attitude, they normally do not attach much importance to collection of environmental data/information regarding backward and forward linkages and other infra-structural support available in the area.

To overcome the problem of experience and expertise it is suggested that special rural development training centres should established by all banks for rendering adequate and qualitative training practices. Rural orientation training programmes specifically meant for SAA should be organised by all banks at regular intervals for all categories of employees in regard to formulation, implementation and monitoring of credit plans under SAA.

It is acknowledged that the bankers have an important role to play in justifying their credit decisions and estimates of the targets at the BLBC meetings. Instead of 'Sporadic Lending', the 'Project Approach' to lending should be adopted to maximise and percolate the benefits to the needy. A positive developmental push is expected on the part of the bankers. The bankers would better have and incessant network of dialogue and liaison with different officials of the government and the rural households in his area of operation. It would be also advisable that the BM should attach his inspection 'on-the-spot' report with the loan application specifically commenting upon the justification for bankability of the activity or otherwise reasons for not promoting the same in the area.

PROBLEMS FACED AT THE ORGANISATIONAL LEVEL

Following are the main problems at organisational level :

(a) Network of rural credit : The major assumption of the SAA is that each rural branch is equally effective in all the villages allotted to it and should not be choosy in respect of social lending, by confirming itself to potential villages. This turns out to be the major flaw, since a policy of neglecting the backward areas and even in backward areas, financing only the high value loans in selected villages is not in line with the basic, spirit of SAA, which is infact, more equalitarian and impartial as between one village and another. The under banked and under development areas where the network of branches is not strong enough, some of the branches have been allotted a service area of over 30-40 villages or above. Due to large area of operations, having no correlation and cohesion between different agencies and thus, the problem of quality lending does not get solved.

It has been noticed in many areas that the co-operative societies have not been given adequate role to play. In Hadoti region, except in Jhalawar district, where the co-operatives were comparatively strong, the benefits of the co-operative network has not been utilised to maximum. The concept of service area casts a specific responsibility on the bank branches to look after the credit needs of service areas. However, this has raised the problem of organisational weakness of rural branches. The problem is quite menacing, where no branch has been opened by banks, looking to inadequate potential in that pocket. For example, 'Relawan' branch of HKGB is Kishanganj block (S.A. Code 99) of Baran district and 'Gainhu Khedi' branch of SBI in Bakani Block (S.A. Code 32) of Jhalawar district were having 57 and 55 villages respectively under their command areas. Due to lack of credit potential in both areas no bank was willing to open its branches.

With emergence of SAA, it was a commonly held doubt that the BMs may inculcate monopolistic nature and also that they might show a favourable indication to certain customers belonging to the prosperous class of rural community at the cost of the have-not's. The lack of competition element may lead to downfall in customer services, hence, the backward and the downtrodden may turnout to be the worst suffers. During the field visits and interactions with the beneficiaries, it was found that in Hadoti region, about 60% beneficiaries were from the middle and the upper income group. Apart from this, the villagers are forced to approach only a specific branch in their service area, which bars their right to select the best credit extension agency.

At present, a bank branch has to cover, 15 to 25 villages under its service area. It is suggested that present norm of 15-25 villages should be altered by devising a set of norms based on population, area coverage, infra-structural facilities, business potential etc. Going by the interaction with the bankers, it is felt that to make rural lending more effective and productive, the rural branches of the banks must be strengthened and the allotted area under the SAA should be restricted to 8-10 villages. But this has its cost too. In the present scenario strengthening and restructuring of the existing set-up of bank branches through inter-connectivity and computerised working environment, appears to be the best remedy to enable the BMs to (i) spare more time for credit planning; (ii) have complete record of the total indebtedness of service area; and (iii) assess potential for bankable economic activity in the area of operation.

In meeting and redressing the genuine credit needs of allotted villages under the SAA, the personal and specific problems of the branches like the shortage of staff should not work as barrier, since villagers have no other alternative source of institutional credit. Infact, the situation coupled with the attitude of indifference of bankers and erosion of institutional integrity indicates towards the need of competition in a service area.

Periodical and close monitoring by the controlling offices through field visits, strengthening the internal and external inspection system of branches, establishment of effective redressal mechanism through BLBCs and DLCCs and controlling offices of banks, solving the problems with regard to quality and quantity of manpower on a priority bases may be some of the solutions to bring about an effective curb on the menace of monopoly.

(b) Staff restraints : Fore more than a decade, there is no recruitment in banks barring few insignificant additions in certain cadres. Further, due to voluntary Retirement Scheme (VRS), declared by various banks in 2000-01 and 2000-02, there has been exodus of bank employees on a very large scale. The banks are finding it increasingly difficult to maintain the some standard of day-to-day service, which they used to offer in pre-VRS era. It is learnt that VRS schemes were launched and completed without proper manpower planning and identification of the possible vacuum in rural work places, where even the erstwhile position was not adequate. Hence, due to paucity of staff, especially the technical and rural oriented staff, the SAA continues to suffer on account of non-availability of the most vital input, the 'suitable manpower'. The rapid branch expansion has considerably strained staff resources of the CBs. Manning of rural outlets of banks is normally done as a ritual, since most of the banks have made 'rural assignment' mandatory for employees promotions. The officials, who do not have any background in loaning techniques due to lack of training and re-orientation are posted for two-three years, who often, do not undertake vigorous and judicious financing of bankable schemes due to lack of expertise and courage. Moreover, they know that they are in the rural sector for completion of 'rural assignment'. The situation is worse where no technical support is available,

The author observed that shortage of staff seems to be a major problem in most of the rural branches of Hadoti region. Generally, a rural branch has three staff members (manager, ledger-keeper-cum-cashier and peon). Although, the business volume in terms of amount handled by a rural branch is not much, but in terms of accounts, it has to handle quite a cumbersome task. A BM of a rural branch is, needless to say, over-burdened most of the time. He has to submit volumes of statements, reports, returns to headquarters, controlling offices and other government agencies related with development. As a natural out come of the tedious job requirements, he is hardly left with any time to visit villages for a periodic and timely supervision, follow-up of loan to ensure proper end use of credit, which finally culminates in the poor recovery of loans and dis-courages further financing.

Out of 50 BMs interviewed by the author as much as 86% (43) reported that villages allotted to them were more and difficult to manage in view of the inexperienced staff and resources available at their disposal. For example, in Digod branch of SBBJ, district Kota, which has 16 villages under its command area, only one officer was found posted. The officer was functioning as the BM and was also supposed to discharge the duties of accountant/payment officer as well as field officer, with more than 1000 advance accounts spread over an area of about 25 Kms. from the branch. Similar situation was noticed in Morak and Kherabad branches of the SBBJ bank. It was noticed that the BMs were so immensely engrossed with the routined work, that they hardly had time to attend to other matters, like development work. On the other hand, on semi-urban centres, lower allocation of villages in a service area was noticed, even when adequate staff strength and resources were available. For example, Ramganjmandi branch and Bhawanimandi branch of SBBJ, Anta branch of CBI in district Baran, Kunhadi branch of CBI and Kherabad branch of HKGB in district Kota, which were being served only one village. Hence, the situation reveals that the ability of bank branches in terms of staff and other resources to meet the credit needs of the allotted villages was not studied in depth while allocating the villages to a branch. In this context, it is suggested that there has to be a thorough re-organisation of the recruitment policy of the banks so that persons who are capable of planning the economic strategy for the villages are absorbed into the system. Banks should recruit/shortlist persons with rural bias, rural involvement and orientation and also having some kind of skills, which would enable them to conduct the surveys, do the planning; while at the same time function as excellent bankers. The new banker in the rural areas has to be an economist, a planner, a banker and an extension specialist all rolled into one. It is the call of hour that the rural branches must be adequately staffed to exploit the potential for lending, ensuring the end use of credit, recovery of bank dues, house-keeping and preparation of area-specific projects for social lending.

According to recommendations of the committee on Agricultural Lendings by Commercial Banks (CALCOB), the standard norm of 500 borrowers per Field Officer in all banks should be implemented. As the staff in rural areas are facing many problems and inconveniences, the role of IBA assumes a vital importance in making the rural service a prestigious and lucrative offer by providing suitable incentives like rural compensatory allowance, preference in promotion, transfer to place of choice after a stipulated term, reimbursement of educational expenses to the children for their study outside the rural areas, rent free accommodation, increased medical aid etc. The job of making arrangements for residential accommo-dation for BMs and other officers, at least for rural and semi-urban areas, should be accorded prime priority. On the contrary, in want of some of the basic facilities the rural service is considered, by most of the employees, as a punishment or at the most deprivation and sacrifice, which will ultimately adversely affect their working capacity and consequently banking activities. Infact, there is a genuine need to create an atmosphere, where the bankers working in rural areas feel motivated and committed to the development of rural areas.

The BM should inculcate in him skills of planner, public relation officer and the executor of his own plans as, needless to say, he is the hub of the procedure around whom revolves the whole process of credit planning. The number of villages for which credit plans are to be prepared is quite large at present. Hence, the BM has to be mentally and physically prepared to bear the tedious and demanding responsibility while carrying out his duties. He is to scan the economic environment of the allotted villages, their resources potential, the requirements of the villagers, potential for productive and viable economic activities and formulation of rural lending programmes based on the resource potential, locally available skills and infra-structural support. The BM should have intimate knowledge of the village economy and village population. He should ensure that credit flows to genuine borrowers for viable and income generating activities. It is also advisable that the BM should himself contact to beneficiaries and assist them in working out a viable enterprise.

(c) Lending procedures and discretionary powers : The inadequate discretionary powers with BMs as well as multi-layer decision making often takes more than the desired time in sanctioning of loans. The appraisal forms of the banks can be redrafted and the process be made transparent to reduce the disposal time of a loan application. The extant and complex procedure for sanction of loan affects the pace of lending. In many cases the discretionary power of BMs are not adequate. It was observed by the researcher that while the discretionary powers vested with the BMs of CBs was inadequate, the officers of Hadoti bank have to approach their Head Office frequently for sanction of loans for agri-culture equipments worth Rs. 2.00 lacs and above or crop loans of large amount. The time taken by Head Office acts as constraint on the progress of loaning and also dampens the enthusiasm of the BMs. It has also been observed that there was a considerable undue delay in sanctioning and disbursement of loans either on account of the incomplete applications or the applications lie pending/unattended by the BMs. This undue delay in sanctioning and disbursement of loans defeats the very purpose for which the loan is taken and it often leads to the problem of recovery of loans and misuse of credit.

The banks should display, over their notice boards or through brochures, full details about the papers/copies of the records etc. required by them for considering applications for a particular activity. This will help the villagers to prepare application forms as per the requirement of the bank and will obviate instances of repeated queries by bankers, thereby reducing the response time of a loan application. Simplification of loan application forms, documents and ensuring of a uniform system of procedures and documentation among the banks will go a long way in avoiding confusions among the villagers particularly among the illiterates.

The whole procedure and system of granting and disbursing of loans has to be transparent and should not impede active participation of the local people in developmental programmes. Loan applications should be expedited on a priority basis to conserve time and energy. The same can be achieved through organising credit camps where all concerned officials of relevant departments should congregate for the smooth and timely completion of formalities about the sanction and disbursement of loans. The Government sponsored programmes should be judiciously spread o ver the year to curb and avoid the tendency of rushing up the loan applications at the fag-end of the year. The loan disbursal programmes too need a careful planning. This would render the banks more competent in attending to the need and requirement of the loan applications in a better way and thus, in the process, improving the overall quality of lending.

(d) The Problem of Co-ordination : Though, co-ordination between various government agencies/ departments and financial institutions is a *sine-qua-non* for the successful formulation and implementation of credit plans, but interaction held with bankers and concerned officials of various govt. agencies/ departments in Hadoti region, it is reveals that there was an absence of co-ordination among the financial institutions, the government departments and other concerned agencies operating in the area.

The problem of co-ordination among various agencies involved in credit planning is crucial, which appear in the following forms in the region:

(a) Among financial institutions : Co-operatives were not in position to provide the lending programmes as there records were not prepared village-wise. Therefore, it is suggested that the records of the co-operatives should be prepared village-wise for chalking out realistic lending programmes as and when required. Any amount of sophistication in preparing VCPs solely by CBs/RRBs cannot ensure the realism in them unless the consideration of share of credit being provided by the co-operative at the village level is incorporated. The researcher has seen personally during her field visits of the region that there was no systematic demarcation of area of operation among the various financial institutions. This lack of systematic demarcation of area among the financial institutions, often, lead to the problem of over financing, which in its own turn creates the problem of recovery and rising non-performing assets. This was found true, to a great extent, in the region. Therefore, it is suggested that the proper harmony and co-ordination among different financial institutions operating in the area should be ensured as early as possible. The BLBC can play a vital role in this regard by extending help in making proper demarcation of service areas among bank branches. If, this is done in an earnest manner, it will definitely reduce/avoid the concentration of loaning activities only in a few developed villages. It is a commonly held and practised notion that the financing is hassle free to reach affluent areas/classes. But sadly enough, this is done at the cost of neglected and backward areas/communities.

The problem of Co-ordination between the CBs including RRBs with the Co-operative banks was more acute in the region because of lack of Co-ordination and understanding between them regarding their lending activities. Co-operatives were not in position to provide the lending programmes as these records were not prepared village-wise. Therefore it is suggested that the records of the co-operatives should be prepared village-wise for chalking out realistic lending programmes as and when required. Any amount of sophistication in preparing VCPs solely by CBs/RRBs can not ensure the realism unless the consideration of share of credit being provided by the co-operatives at the village level is incorporated. Besides these, there were problems concerning the issue of "No Dues Certificate" and sharing the information about the borrowers, which resulted into the problem of over-financing and repayment of loans.

(b) Overlapping roles of LBO and DDM : The problem of overlapping roles of LBO and DDM in different districts of the region was observed by the researcher. When the researcher contacted the LBOs and DDMs and talked with them in regard to their respective roles, they both were critical of each others role. Thus the problems of super-imposing the personality and authority on each other emerged. It is, therefore, suggested that to avoid the overlapping roles of the LBO and DDM, their roles and mutual relationship should be clearly spelt out. The LBO should envisage the DDM as an expert available to guide and smoothen his work instead of opposing his presence. If the DDM spends more time in the district, he would be of more help than LDO who is by and large, only an occasional visitor and hasn't much insight of the district's economy. In this regard NABARD officials are much more knowledgeable and helpful to the LBO. Some steps should be taken to develop a new work culture wherein DDM should act as friend, philosopher and guide to the LBO instead of acting and feigning as an overbearing supervisor.

(c) Between Government Agencies and Banks : Owing to the lack of appreciation of mutual dependence, most of the government officials, by and large, have a notion that their role is confined only to government sponsored schemes. They didn't identify seriously the importance of linking credit with other non-credit inputs and linkages for the credit routing through bank's credit plans outside the government sponsored schemes. The Govt. officials working at block level, often, feels that their role extinguishes after sponsoring of applications under government sponsored schemes. The Government officials and bank official differ in their perception in regard to the financial viability of a particular scheme. The Government officials do not attach much significance to this aspect and the bank officials generally display a conservative attitude in this regard. Under the SAA, the bank and the government officials have to work in harmony with each other, but manytimes the outlook and approach of the two are not in cohesion. There were a tendency on the part of the Govt. agencies to dump cases on the bank branches for providing credit much in excess of the credit plan targets. Proper and well knit cohesion among the functioning of officials of financial institutions and Govt. agencies is a *sine-qua-non* for the successful formulation and implementation of the credit plans under the SAA. In this area too, there are practical problems because of inadequate understanding of mutual dependence. The goal of co-ordination among the officials of financial institutions and the Govt. officials and also enhancing their awareness about the DCP could be achieved by holding district level workshops at frequent intervals in each district as decided by the high power committee on the LBS. Such meetings will definately create a congenial atmosphere of mutual trust between them.

Lead banks should organise programme for both the bank and Govt. officials after some regular intervals, which should include inputs on the credit plan concept, development of agriculture and small scale industries and financing of these activities, so as to enable them to have a sense of appreciation of each others role and to develop uniform approach.

The availability of non-credit inputs such as seeds, fertilizers, pesticides, marketing, technology and irrigation extension support is essential to make bank credit productive and these are made available by the Govt. agencies/ departments. Therefore , it is further suggested that to remove conflicting ideas among bank and Govt. officials, joint seminars and training programmes of all the functionaries of concerned agencies should be conducted by NABARD, so that the BMs, BDOs, LBOs, DDMs, representative of DICs, fisheries, sericulture deptt., and agriculture officers etc. can have an interaction from time to time for understanding each other's role properly. This would certainly develop a team spirit and would work as a guiding and motivating factor in working as a well knit team goals in unison to achieve common goals.

Teams consisting of Govt. officials and credit institutions should be built up at district and block levels for this purpose. Since, Govt. district authorities have a significant role in the formulation and implementation of DCPs, therefore, team spirit can not be overlooked. As the DCP is based on the DDP, therefore, the district authorities must see that those projects/schemes of the DDP, which form the basis of the DCP are incorporated and implemented on a priority basis. The another crucial area, where Govt. officials can assist the banks, is in the recovery of loans. Recovery of loan is a vital problem of DCP management, which can be substantially reduced, if only the Govt. officials at district level are willing to extend their support whole heartedly to the bank officials. 'Special recovery camps' should be held at regular intervals with appropriate backing by the district administration.

The present grass-root level set-up needs to be refurbished so as to make the role of DICs more effective and meaningful. It's Industrial Extension Officers/Project Development Officers are required to carry out studies in their respective areas in order to chalk out location specific schemes which are economically viable and technically feasible.

(d) Alignment of DCP with DDP : The other important problem observed by the researcher during the survey work was lack of proper dovetailing of DCP with DDP. There were many missing links in this regard.

For realistic formulation of DCP, it should be based on DDP. To formulate DCP, Govt. programmes and infra-structural resources in the area are to be taken into account. But, the Govt. Agencies are not ready with the development plans before finalisation of the BCP for its area of operation and thus, the alignment of the DCP with DDP could not be materlized. The BCPs are generally given a nod of formal approval without ensuring detailed discussions or sometimes even without attendance of all the development agencies at the block level. More than 50% of the Govt. Officials interviewed by the researcher reported this hard fact that they had seen the credit plans only at the BLBC meeting while formally approving the same. This clearly reveals that the involvement of Govt. Officials in the finalisation of credit plans was not up to the desired level and it was sheer formal at the approval level.

The Govt. departments and district officials generally do not prepare the DDP, which suits to the need of financial institutions, hence banks face various types of difficulties at the stage of formulation of DCP.

One of the major problems is related to the availability of necessary, adequate and reliable data/information from the Govt. departments engaged in the activities covered under DCP. The problem, often, worsens as district credit planning has to be undertaken as an exercise supplementary and complementary to the district developmental activities of the Government. Non-availability of well chalked out DDP and also elaborate details about various development schemes covered under it was also a serious barrier in the preparation of an expedient DCP.

Besides above mentioned problems, many difficulties were observed in such alignment by the researcher in the region.

Some of them are as follows :

i) All the districts in the region did not have proper DDP. Infact, what was available in the name of DDP was an abstract of departmental programmes, but not an integrated and balanced DDP in which linkages of various sectors and sub-sections were properly studied and development targets worked out on the basis of such linkages.

ii) Departmental programmes for districts, which were finally approved at the State level, didn't focus on developmental requirements of the district concerned were prepared, but often on the considerations of resources availability. Besides that, departmental plans were generally not broken down block-wise for readily and prompt implementation.

iii) The credit planners didn't bother even to examine the Govt. schemes before accepting them whether these satisfy the basic tenets of credit extension or area specific requirements. Not only this, the schemes formulated by credit planners themselves were also not rational in terms of their suitability.

Thus, the DDP is to provide the foundation of DCP, but it is disquiet to mention here that the proper DDPs were not available in all the districts of the region. The assumption that the DDP and DCP should work in harmony for producing a synergistic results has remained an elusive dream that has yet to be realized.

The development of infra-structural facilities plays an important role in successful implementation of DDP and DCP both. Basic infra-structural facilities include transport, communication, storage, processing, marketing etc. The financial institutions have a limited role in providing such facilities by acting as purveyor of credit. A 'multi-agency approach to development' is aspired to have the desired impact of a particular project. Therefore, attempts must be made to create and develop a district-level planning and development forum, where banks, Govt. agencies local self Govt. bodies, Voluntary social organisations, educational institutions, Corporate and Urban elite interested and involved in development are brought together on a common platform for developing and implementing the programmes of development. If credit plans are to be virtually successful then, the economic plans of the Govt. and the banker's plans will have to operate in tandem. If such linkages is established, then, it will definitely be possible to involve the financial institutions and government agencies in the growth agencies process in a more effective and efficient manner. Ultimately, any programme of development is a collective venture of all participating agencies, therefore, their deep involvement and sense of belongingness are pre-requisites of any successful planning.

(e) Co-ordination between DLCC and BLCC : The DLCC has no formal authority to enforce the decisions taken in its meetings as it is only advisory body. The meetings of DLCC are often attended by junior bank officials, who have no authority to commit on behalf of their institutions. The DLCCs were established as a common forum of district authorities, Govt. developmental agencies and the financial institutions to adopt and encourage co-ordinated approach on their part in a joint effort for the development of the district. Although, there is a considerable improvement in respect of coverage, contents and participation of the agencies concerned, yet, the main agenda of the meetings still continues to be an evaluation of progress in respect of Govt. sponsored programmes only. The aspects related to overall development of the area were not given due weightage during the course of discussion.

In practice, for the improved functioning of the DLCC, following measures may be adopted :

i) The DLCC should review sector-wise, scheme-wise and bank-wise progress made in the implementation of DCPs.

ii) The active participation in the DLCCs should be voluntary instead of being a forced one, as is the general case. The banks themselves should feel a sense of moral obligation in being answerable to DLCC despite the bitter fact that the DLCCs hold virtually no command over banks.

iii) There should be detailed discussion in the DLCC on the issues such as deficiencies in infra-structure arrangements for different programmes and for an explicit guideline to fix the responsibilities of different departments/agencies for making available the requisite infra-structural facilities so as to make banks competent enough in co-ordinating with different agencies for extending credit facilities and also their performance can be monitored effectively.

The DLCC should discuss the magnitude of credit deployment for the district and the required non-credit inputs for block-wise and service area-wise. A cohesive planning is the need of the hour at the micro-level and multi-level approach for providing effective linkage. DLCC should attempt a co-ordinated and harmonious working approach in the service area with the overall development plan of the district. The plan for non-credit inputs should, preferably, emerge from the village level and proceed to the BLBC for it's onward submission to the DLCC for it's swift and effective implementation. The provision of non-credit inputs should be examined, revised and monitored at regular intervals at all levels of credit planning.

(f) Inapt Monitoring mechanism : The purpose of monitoring is to locate the gaps in implementation of credit plans and apply corrective measures. Lack of proper monitoring system of performance of SAPs was observed as a another major problem of SAA. The present set-up of monitoring the progress under SAA does not take into account the primary motto of linking bank credit to increase in production and productivity. Hence, there is need for ascertaining the linking of the bank credit with the production, productivity and income. For this purpose the researcher proposes to undertake studies to watch the incremental output effect of the credit, which was extended to a particular activity/scheme. In this regard the RBI should formulate a suitable format for the assessment of yields in crops emanating from bank credit and similar assessment in other segments of operation should also be done. The banks should also develop their own guidelines/mechanism for assessing the increase in production, productivity and income of the credit supplied to the borrower at their own level. They may undertake such periodical studies through an independent cell within the bank comprising of experts. Such independent research cells should be established at the district head quarters. It would not be out of place to mention here that the guidance and help of university professors from the department of commerce and economics can also be obtained in this regard. These expertise assessment studies should pin point the shortcomings in the implementation of credit plans and should also suggest appropriate remedial steps to overcome them.

Apart from such studies, more effective periodical monitoring than at present should be done through the interpretation of data is also necessary by the BLCC at the block-level and by the DLCC at the district-level. The controlling offices of the banks should also undertake such monitoring at their own level. The review of credit plans in BLBC and DLCC meetings should include, besides the other, the progress made in the commitment of non-credit inputs also, which is not being done at present. For bringing more effectiveness, the State Government should monitor not only it's sponsored/subsidy linked schemes, but should also review all other activities pertaining to rural development. This is necessary for enlisting government support because development has to be adjudged as a joint endeavour of all concerned and more particularly of the State in view of it's welfare role. Greater follow-up is required at the district level so as to put an effective check on the stymieing factors retarding the effectiveness of bank credit.

The LBO should make frequent inspections/visits in the district to get first hand information of the progress made in the implementation of BCPs and to guide the BMs in their proper implementation and addressing the other problems. Frequent field visits by the BMs at pre-sanction and post-sanction stage of loan on an-on-going basis mandatorily also is suggested for effective supervision, monitoring and success of credit plans.

At present, supervision and follow-up of small borrower accounts are being monitored by bank officers only. For making it more effective, the bank may contemplate to evolve a "Supervisory team" system at their regional/head office level. A cohesive Management Information System (MIS) with internet connection is the need of the hour for speedy and timely monitoring and follow-up action. Computerised data should be provided by the NABARD to the credit agencies for review of credit plan and for initiating suitable remedial measures, as timely review rests mainly on how swiftly and precisely performance data is compiled and made available to the concerned agencies.

Problems Regarding the Integration of Credit and Non-Credit Inputs

Without proper infra-structural support and forward/backward linkages, only credit input cannot bring about the magic of rapid development. Merely the availability of credit input without proper matching of non-credit inputs, may not increase productivity, production and the level of income to the desired extent. But, unfortunately, the integration of credit and non-credit inputs could not be established in all the district of the region. For example in most of the SAPs, crop loan for high yielding varieties have been contemplated, but the non-availability of any or more of the requisite inputs like seeds, fertilizers etc. adversely affect the implementation of the scheme. The non-availability or inadequacy of a single input may retard the implementation of a number of related schemes.

At the time of launching of an activity the availability of minimum infra-structural facilities, extension services and credit input are essential for its success and absence of any one would result in the failure of the activity. It has been observed by the researcher during her field visits that in Hadoti region, some schemes were nipped in the bud as 'spatial integration' of infra-structural facilities, extension services and credit were, sadly enough, altogether missing. Some of the borrowers defaulted on account of non-availability of apt marketing facilities of their produce. Dairy development scheme is an eye opener example in this regard, where disorderly lending without keeping in consideration the availability of veterinary service, continuous supply of proper breed cattle and an arrangement for purchase, collection and transportation of milk has culminated in an uneven success of the scheme.

It was further observed that the sample branches did not specify any non-credit inputs and linkages to be provided by credit agencies in their plans, which is a pre-requisite of success of their credit plans. Even today, there is no provision to specify non-credit inputs and linkages in the SAP proforma as well. This needs to be incorporated immediately. The branches have taken into consideration only the prevailing level of infra-structure, non-credit inputs and linkages; while chalking out their credit plans.

The district authorities would have to ensure that the primary requisites of a crop loan; i.e. timely and sufficient supply of fertilizers, seeds, pesticides are met with adequately and timely. Hence, it is essential that the infra-structural facilities and other non-credit inputs, which directly affect the level of progress attained under certain schemes, should be given due preference and efforts should be made to streamline the required services of various agencies and make them easily accessible and available in the service area of the concerned branch.

Cattle fairs/ purchase camps should be held for the borrowers who are the main beneficiaries of the financing for plough animals, milch cattle, sheep and goat so as to make them available the improved quality breeds. The vaccination and other facilities should also be made available and good breed bulls should also be provided. More distribution outlets for availability of diesel and abundant service facilities for the diesel pump sets and tractors have to be ensured for the optimum utilisation of credit in rural areas. For supply of better seeds, seed processing units need to be set-up and more supply points should be opened for timely availability of quality seeds, fertilizers, pesticides etc. Moreover, some more milk collection routes should be identified and exploited to the maximum.

Bank should specify, in clear terms, the non-credit inputs and linkage at the time of approval of SAPs by the BLBCs and should be ensured to get commitments from Govt. agencies so as to enable the BLBC to review the flow of non-credit inputs and linkages also alongwith the credit flow. Steps must be initiated to improve SAP proforma by including activity-wise non-credit inputs and linkages be specified by branches as a pre-requisite to their plan. With the inclusion of these, the review of non-credit inputs and linkages by BLBC will become smooth and realistic. Whenever an activity demands infra-structural facilities, the scheme should be floated in and around such areas where both extension and credit are easily available. In case of HYV programme, it may be beneficial, if the agriculture department in consultation with credit institutions decides the villages to be covered and provide the necessary inputs and the extension machinery is well geared-up for this purpose.

The expected development of industries too relies on the availability of infra-structure contemplated in there with the development plans. To improve the quantity of lending, the minimum infra-structure is required for forward and backward linkages of financial activities; *e.g.* for rural industrialisation, availability of raw materials, power, transport, communication and market are to be ensured before the plan implementation. In this regard the Govt. can play an important role in developing infra-structural facilities. After the development of infra-structural facitlities by the Govt., only then that the banks will be able to show a marked progress in their service areas.

Problems Regarding Extension Services

(a) Lack of improved farm practices : The basic objective of the SAA is to bring about overall economic growth through institutional credit input in rural sector by improving the quality of lending. However, tendency to resist improved techniques and fear to use high yielding seeds or high breed cattle, are still working as snag to aggrandize the optimum benefits as regards production and productivity in agriculture and allied activities, even when the timely and adequate credit support is ensured.

The present study has revealed this fact that a large number of small farmers did not make use of improved farm practices. In this regard the position of district Jhalawar was worst, where as much as 57% of farmers interacted by the researcher were not using improved farm practices followed by district Baran (52%), district Bundi (40%) and district Kota (35%). Lack of education and easy accessibility of credit and risk taking capacity all together have deprived the farmers of the region in using improved farm practices. The knowledge of better methods of cultivation and adoption of these can definitely increase the production, productivity and incomes of the farmers. For materialising it in practice, the proper extension work is needed for using high yielding varieties of seeds and improved cultivation practices. The extension workers in the service areas have to persuade the farmers to adopt modern scientific techniques of cultivation.

(b) Lack of Awareness : The another important problem of credit plans in the region was lack of adequate awareness about the various schemes and facilities available in service areas to the rural people. Although, the State Government is trying its level best, inspite of that beneficiaries were not aware fully. No plan/scheme for development could succeed without active involvement and participation of the people for whom it is meant. For enlisting genuine participation of local people, the knowledge and awareness of the schemes/policies/plans/programmes is a must. Therefore, it is strongly felt that the benefits of the credit plans and the provisions of the schemes be publicised from time to time properly and the prospective beneficiaries of the credit plans should be made conscious of the facilities they could derive from them. For creating awareness among the masses, the level of literacy becomes crucial. The data of literacy of different districts of the Hadoti region reveal this fact that the percentage of literacy is far-far below the cent-percent mark.

According to census 2001, district Kota was on the top (74.45%) in in terms of percentage of literacy in State of Rajasthan; while the literacy percentage of Baran, Jhalawar and Bundi districts were 60.67%, 57.98% and 55.80% respectively. Keeping in view the national average (65.38%) and Rajasthan state average of literacy (61.03%), there is too much scope in Jhalawar, Bundi and Baran districts of region to enhance the level of literacy level to make proper use of extension facilities available and for creating full awareness among the rural people. The researcher has come to know through the interaction with the people of the region and also from the field survey about this amazing situation that still today, after 50 years of planned economic development in the region, about 32% rural indebtedness is of the non-institutional sources of credit; *i.e.* out of the fold of institutional credit. About 65% of the beneficiaries whom researcher interacted in the region were not aware of the credit delivery system under the SAA, though 33% of them knew the allotment of their villages to a particular bank branch. At the same time, around 28% beneficiaries raised doubts about the ability of particular branch in meeting their credit needs.

This clearly indicates that still, the concept of SAA and procedures thereof, are not known and new to the rural people. In the absence of such awareness and extension work, there remains a low level of credit absorption capacity in rural areas of the region. Due to absence of adequate and proper campaigning and publicity by the banks about their various credit schemes and complex procedural formalities involved in them, the borrowers feel shy of them and also in availing of credit facilities from institutional channels of credit.

Various extension programmes like group meetings, general meetings involving Govt. agencies and experts, visiting farms and homes, involving in social functions, exhibiting film shows and slides, educating though local leaders, voluntary agencies etc. can be taken-up on the pattern of NABARD pilot projects so as to enable the bankers identify themselves with the people and build confidence among them to achieve their involvement freely. Besides these, the following steps may be taken for enhancing awareness level among the rural people. The Lead bank may also conduct entrepreneurial development programmes where there is potential for industrial development and absence of entrepreneurship. The DIC and district authorities should also assist in this matter;

- A list of schemes for which bank finance is available may be displayed in local language at weekly markets;

- Meetings of borrowers at the village level may be arranged in order to explain the various schemes of banks; and
- The details of the various scheme can also be publicised through brochures and other method like camps etc.

It was observed by the researcher that the large number of borrowers in the region were of the opinion that the bank should undertake 'extension education service' to create awareness, as the extension service provided by the Govt. agencies was not specific as well as adequate to the credit schemes of the banks.

It is suggested that creation of awareness among the rural people through the bank staff to be made a part of banker's new role. The issue should receive adequate attention. The success of SAA basically rests on the shoulders of the BMs, who should have the necessary motivation and involvement in performing this task. For this, skills of the BMs need improvement in translating the plan perception into concrete plans and for their proper implementation.

Problems Regarding Overdues and Recovery

Mounting overdues and default in repayment of loan extended by the financial institutions is a grave problem not only in Hadoti region, but throughout the country. There are many factors behind the roots of this problem. The factors which are responsible for poor recovery of loans may be classified as under :

S.N.	*Factors*	*Causes*
(a)	Natural Factors	Natural calamities, economic recession, change in Govt. policies etc.
(b)	Deficiencies of the credit delivery systems	Improper identification of borrowers, delay in sanction of loans, inadequate system of monitoring, diversion of funds etc.
(c)	Human indiscretion	Erosion of repayment ethics, wilful default socio-political systems etc.
(d)	Legal process	Faulty legal system, absence of proper legal frame-work for non-payment of bank dues etc.
(d)	Globalisation	Increasing competitive market pressure, lack of comparative advantage, inadequate technical know-how, unskilled labour force.

A default in loan repayment can be classified broadly into three categories :

(i) **Technical default** - These are defaults, which occur due to change in legal/statutory laws, deficiencies of the credit delivery system, faulty legal process etc.

(ii) **Genuine default** - These are defaults, which occur due to natural factors, change in borrowers preferences and market downfall etc.

(iii) **Wilful default** - These are such defaults, which arise due to discontinuance of debt servicing burden; *i.e.* non-payment of principal and interest amount, inspite of the fact that they are capable of doing so. These types of defaults arise basically due to the deliberate non-payment of the amount of loan and interest their own.

The rate of default in recovery of bank loans has an intrinsic relationship with the :

(a) Success rate of ventures financed out of bank funds as per the projected parameters;

(b) The feasibility and happening of the events crucial/supportive to the project;

(c) The collection mechanism of financing agencies;

(d) The overall indebtedness of the borrowers;

(e) The political environment of the area;

(f) The need for further financing etc.

Inspite of all pious intentions and best efforts by the Government of India, RBI and the State Governments, the problem of recovery of loans is still persisting and it is one of the biggest problems of institutional finance ultimately resulting into mounting NPAs. The gravity of this problem can be judged from the present recovery position of loans. The recovery position of loans was only 65% in the whole country; while it was 63.53% in the state of Rajasthan at the end of June, 2000. The recovery position of loans in Hadoti region was 63.49%, which was slightly less than the all India and the State of Rajasthan recovery percentage. Thus, the trend of recovery of loans was more or less the same at all above mentioned three levels.

Table no. 8.1 depicts the position of recovery under priority sector advances in Hadoti region and in the State of Rajasthan during 1995-96 to 1999-2000. The analysis of this table brings out this fact that the recovery position under priority sector advances in the region as well as in the State of Rajasthan is improving over the years. This can be substantiated from the figures of different districts in Hadoti region. The percentage of

Table No. 8.1

Position of Recovery under Priority Sector Advances in Hadoti Region and in the State of Rajasthan (19995-96 to 1999-2000)

YEAR	BARAN (Rs. in Lacs)				BUNDI (Rs. in Lacs)				JHALAWAR (Rs. in Lacs)			
	Demand	Collection	Over-dues	Recovery %	Demand	Collection	Over-dues	Recovery %	Demand	Collection	Over-dues	Recovery %
1995-1996	7385	4468	2917	60.50	4477	2487	1990	44.00	1583	606	977	38.31
1996-1997	6483	3751	2641	57.80	4060	2391	1669	59.00	1969	777	1192	39.46
1997-1998	7634	4303	3331	56.40	4409	2654	1755	60.00	5684	3959	1725	69.70
1998-1999	6456	3452	3004	53.48	4708	3065	1643	65.00	6273	4391	1882	70.00
1999-2000	5766	3591	2176	62	4021	2667	1354	66.00	7645	5368	2275	70.22
TOTAL	33724	19565	14159	58	21675	13264	8411	61.20	23154	15101	8053	65.22

YEAR	KOTA (Rs. in Lacs)				TOTAL of the Region (Rs. in Lacs)				STATE of Rajasthan (Rs. in Crores)			
	Demand	Collection	Over-dues	Recovery %	Demand	Collection	Over-dues	Recovery %	Demand	Collection	Over-dues	Recovery %
1995-1996	6572	2252	4320	34.00	20017	9813	10204	49.00	1231.62	680.27	551.35	55.00
1996-1997	5011	1761	3250	35.14	17523	8680	8843	49.53	1441.93	838.18	603.75	58.00
1997-1998	7472	2955	4517	39.50	25199	13871	11328	55.00	2122.27	1277.40	844.87	60.20
1998-1999	8149	4224	3924	51.84	25586	15132	10454	59.00	2354.41	1456.20	898.51	61.85
1999-2000	11201	7133	4068	63.68	29323	18620	10703	63.49	2424.91	1540.59	935.66	63.53
TOTAL	38395	18325	20070	47.72	117648	66116	51532	56.20	9575.14	5792.64	3782.50	60.50

Source:

- *Agenda papers of SLBC meetings (from 64th meeting to 74th meeting)*
- *DCP & PLP (year 1999-2000 to 2001-2002) of Baran, Bundi, Jhalawar and Kota Districts.*

recovery in district Baran was 60.50% in 1995-96 which increased to 62% in 1999-2000. The improvement in the recovery position of district Bundi was far better than the district Baran. The recovery percentage of district Bundi was 44% in 1995-96, which went-up to 66% in 1999-2000, thereby denoting a substantial improvement of 22 points. The recovery percentage in district Jhalawar was only 38.31% in 1995-96, which increased tremendously to a very high level of 70.22%. The recovery percentage of district Kota was also very low (34.1%) in 1995-96, which surged-up to 63.68% in 1999-2000. On the pattern of different districts of the region, the recovery percentage of the Hadoti region has also improved from 49% in 1995-96 to 63.49% in 1999-2000. If we look at the recovery figures of the State of Rajasthan, we also find some improvement. The recovery percentage which was 55% in 1995-96 soared-up to 63.53% in 1999-2000. The worth mentioning point here is that the recovery percentage of the Hadoti region and the State of Rajasthan is more or less the same in the year 1999-2000. Undoubtedly it is a ray of hope for bankers to recycle the funds in a meaningful way, but at the same time mounting overdues continue to cause a serious concern. The irony of fate is that banks are sacrificing a handsome amount towards compromise and are compelled to write off loans every year.

A sincere effort was made by the author to locate the factors responsible for the poor recovery of loans in Hadoti region. On the basis of the response of borrowers and BMs, the main reasons for poor recovery of loans have been identified, which are explained as under :

1) **Scattered Lending :** Scattered lending was one of the reasons of poor recovery of loans in the Hadoti region. This is evident from this fact, which has also been observed by the researcher during her field visits, that the area covered by some of the branches in the region was even exceeding 25-30 Kms. For example, Digod, Chhabra, Baran branches of SBBJ were having the area more than 25-30 Kms. under their jurisdiction. This created the problem of effective supervision of the end use of credit. The problem of distance and scattered lending in the service area, often, results into the problem of irregular and ineffective supervision, monitoring and follow-up action on the part of BMs. Owing to unmanageable distance factor and scattered lending, bank officials many times find difficulty in having close-eye watch on the resultant generation of income from an activity/scheme on a continuous basis, which ultimately leads to non-repayment of loan.

2) **Large number of loan/ borrowal accounts :** The author observed that some bank branches in the region are working for about last 30-35 years. Due to their long existence, the area of operations has not only crossed manageable extent, but a large number of borrowal accounts have also been added to their work load. Thus, the number Fact of loan accounts became unmanageable for a branch. Besides that, the poor record of recovery has restricted liquidation of old borrowal account. Though, the RBI during the year 2000-01 had declared "One Time Settlement" (OTS) scheme, inspite of that there has not been much reduction in the number of loan accounts with most of the branches in the region. Still some branches of CBI and SBBJ were having borrowal accounts far in excess of their capacity. For example, Digod, Baran, Chhabra branches of SBBJ were handling 1050, 2600 and 2500 loan accounts respectively; while the branch of CBI was having as much as 1100 loan accounts. This position coupled with scattered lending led to poor follow-up by banks which adversely affected the recovery of loans.

3) **Lack of financial discipline :** Lack of financial discipline in the banking industry is one of the main reasons for the poor recovery of loans and increasing intensity of default. Due to lack of strict financial discipline, due weightage is not given to the technical feasibility and economic viability of schemes/activities at neither pre-sanctioned nor post-sanctioned stage of loan. This ultimately results into the failure of projects or lack of generation of expected return, which in turn increases the intensity of defaults. Lack of proper check on end use of credit leads to either diversion of funds for some other purposes or mis-utilisation of funds, which ultimately reduces the repayment possibility of loans as it has an adverse impact on generation of incremental income.

4) **Un-competitive capital infusion and incremental income :** Most of the financing in rural areas is done with fear psychosis of possible default and in turn it creates the problem of un-competitive capital infusion (under financing). Due to this problem, the economic activity financed becomes unviable. Consequently, the recovery of loan gets affected adversely because either of poor performance or failure of generating incremental incomes envisaged in the plan. This leaves inadequate surplus to meet the repayment obligations. The lower than the required level of capital needed for the activity do not generate the envisaged level of income, at times, it even vanishes and becomes the victim and get marginalized by large players having larger

capital base and hence the market share. In nutshell, the competitive edge of an activity remains weak due to under financing of it.

5) **Wilful default :** The researcher has observed during her field visits that due to lack of timely and stringent action against wilful defaulters, even the borrowers who are making envisaged income are defaulting and polluting the credit discipline in villages. The recovery climate has been so vitiated that even regular loan repayers sometime withhold repayments in anticipation of write offs- an expectation aroused by announcements of interest subsidy/waiver by some State Governments particularly the loan waiver scheme 'Agriculture and Rural Debt Relief Programme' (ARDR Scheme), 1990-91 in the past and recently the OTS scheme are considered responsible for creating the mentality of wilful defaults. The feeling has reached to an extent that in a loan disbursement camp organised at Atru in district Baran, one borrower who received the cheque for loan, asked about the period after which the loan disbursed to him on that day would be waived or settled. This sounds that the situation is very grave and no act of the central planners or bankers should lead to a feeling amongst ranks and file that the public money can be misused.

6) According to the latest report of RBI on "Trend and Progress of Banking in India 2000-2001", gross NPAs of SCBs stood at Rs. 63833 crore at the end of March, 2001, up from Rs. 60408 crore at the end of March, 2000. Similarly Net-NPAs have gone-up to Rs. 32468 crore as on end of March, 2001 from Rs. 30073 crore at the end of March, 2000. The main reason behind this sharp rise in NPAs at a time when banks are increasingly exploring risk-management mechanisms is that of "wilful defaults".

7) **Pendency of large number of court cases :** The provisions of State Govt.'s support in recovering bank's dues are primarily stipulated in the RACO (ROD) Act, 1974, wherein competent revenue authorities are equipped with adequate powers in this regard. The enactment of the act itself provided bankers increasing impulses for collecting their amount in totality. But this could not happen due to faulty legal system. A huge amount of loans still remains with the borrowers and the same is mounting year after year. Though, bankers have filed numerous cases with various revenue authorities, but decisions are still awaited. A large number of cases were lying pending with the revenue courts filed under the RACO (ROD), Act, 1974 in the Hadoti region as well as in the State of Rajasthan. Recovery position under

RACO (ROD) Act, 1974 in Hadoti region and in the State of Rajasthan as on March, 2000 has been depicted in *table no. 8.2.* The analysis of table reveals clearly that around or more than 80% cases filed under the said act were lying pending for settlement in all four districts of the region. For the whole State of Rajasthan, the percentage of cases lying pending was also on the same pattern of Hadoti region, which was more than 80% (86.62%). Unnecessary long delays in decisions of such cases have an adverse impact on 'repayment culture' of the loanees. The borrowers feel that no action is going to take place against them, hence they do not bother in repaying their dues on time.

Table No. 8.2

Recovery Position under RACO (ROD) Act, 1974 in Hadoti Region and in State of Rajasthan

(As on March, 2000)

Particular	*Baran*	*Bundi*	*Jhalawar*	*Kota*	*Total of the region*	*State of Rajasthan*
Cases Filed	7982	7495	5068	8120	28665	167263
Decreee Executed	1317 (1650)	1379 (18)	1026 (20)	1056 (13)	4778 (16.67)	22379 (13.38)
Cases Pending	6665 (83.50)	6116 (82)	4042 (80)	7064 (87)	23887 (83.33)	144884 (86.62)

Note : Figures shown in brackets indicate percentage of cases filed.

Source: Agenda papers of 74th meeting of SLBC, Rajasthan, Convenor, Bank of Baroda, Jaipur.

8) **Political Interference :** An impression has been created by local leaders in the minds of villagers that the loans given by banks are in the nature of 'government support' and therefore, need not be repaid. The local leadership has often been fanning this notion among the gullible borrowers to sub-serve their own vested interest, resulting in low recovery of advances. It also creates an unfavourable atmosphere of recovery. Political interference in loan melas, encouraging defaults, pressurising bank officials to extend credit for unviable activities.

9) **Other reasons for poor recovery :**

(i) In certain cases, income generation from the activity/scheme was not upto the desired extent, hence poor recovery prevails.

(ii) It has been seen by the researcher that as many times, bankers report to casual approach for lending to achieve the targets given to them under government sponsored schemes without consideration of viability of schemes, which results in weak follow-up and in-built skeleton recovery.

(iii) An un-co-ordinated approach of bank and government officials was also found responsible for poor recovery in many cases in Hadoti region.

(iv) Crop failure in the wake of unprecedented drought in continuation for the last three years has created an alarming poor situation of recovery in the State of Rajasthan and also in Hadoti region.

Hence, whatever reasons may be assigned to low recovery, but it retards the path of recycling of funds and come in the way of fresh lending. Overdues prevent banks from recycling their funds effectively and also continuous defaults tend to demoralise the field staff of the banks. The poor recovery position of banks affects their entitlement for refinance from NABARD, therefore, now banks are hesitating increasingly in providing further loans specially under the Govt. sponsored schemes.

In view of the above mentioned facts, it is suggested that the timely recovery of loans and strict credit discipline is of utmost importance for all credit institutions not only in the interest of financial institutions themselves, but also in the interest of rural economy. Equally important is the need for a mechanism to take due care of the non-wilful default arising out of natural calamities or other adverse factors beyond borrower's control, which make timely repayment difficult. Recovery of bank loans has assumed more importance after the introduction of prudential norms (1992-93). Presently, recovery of loans is considered as a most important parameter for measuring the efficiency and profitability of a bank. (Over the years, a mistaken notion was formed that 60% recovery could be considered as a benchmark for good performance, where as recent studies have shown that for financial viability and sustainability of credit operations, the recovery performance would have to be considerably higher; *i.e.* around 90%). While banks own the primary responsibility for proper identification of borrowers, careful appraisal, close monitoring and building-up relationship to enforce proper credit discipline among the borrowers, but simultaneously the State Governments have the responsibility for creating a conducive climate for recovery of loans. In practice, the problem of recovery of loan should be considered as an integral part of credit management and not treated as an isolated problem as has been the case so far. To reduce the intensity of recovery problem, it is suggested that :

- Bank staff should take adequate precaution and interest in guiding the borrowers regarding successful completion of financed activity and tell them the importance of recovery by making them understand that the timely repayment of loan is in their own interest. It is not so significant that how many persons have been advanced loans, but what is more important is that how many of them use the bank's funds properly, so that they could become gainfully employed, earn a livelihood and repay the dues timely.
- The suggestions of the Expert Committee on Bank Frauds under the Chairmanship of Dr. N.L. Mitra should be implemented in letter and spirit. The committee has suggested both the preventive and curative aspects of bank frauds and has recommended for inclusion of bank frauds (which also covers mis-utilisation of bank funds) as a criminal offence and amendment in Indian Penal Code by including a new chapter on financial frauds; amendments to the Indian Evidence Act to shift the burden of proof on the accused person and special provision in code of criminal procedure for transferring the properties involved in financial fraud and confiscating unlawful gains. The committee has also deliberated on the issues relating to introduction and development of 'Best Code Procedures' by banks.
- One day in a fortnight should be fixed by the SDM for disposal of cases filed under RODA at each Tehsil centre in the district for speedy settlement of cases. Suitable amendments be made in the RODA so that the cases to the designated authority should not become time barred. The Act should cover non-agricultural advances also and the guarantors alongwith borrowers should be made responsible for recovery of the dues. The remedy of borrowers to approach civil-courts, pending proceedings under RODA, should be restricted/ suspended like in cases before Board of Industry and Financial Reconstruction (BIFR), where financing agencies are restricted to continue with the civil suit without the permission of the bench of the BIFR.
- The system of permitting concessions in interest rate for prompt repayment of loans on due date or before time should be introduced as an incentive to develop regular repayment ethics among the borrowers.
- The pre and post disbursement inspections should be conducted in an exhaustive manner to look into the weaknesses in the proposal and ensure correction/rectification in the scheme at an

appropriate time. The golden rule is "if the loan is good, the recovery would be good".

- Appointment/deputation of recovery/revenue officers at selected districts should be made where large number of cases are pending under RODA, so that the cases are cleared on priority basis.
- Lok Adalats on the pattern of other cases should be held in different parts of the region to reduce the number of pending cases lying with the courts.
- It is also suggested that all the lead banks and lead district managers to activise recovery campaign through joint publicity with the help of district authorities to create awareness amongst borrowers/defaulters. The efforts should be made to propagate the 'repayment ethic' among the borrowers and a climate for the appreciation of values of 'sound use of credit' should also be created through the use of all kinds of media.
- Govt. officials at the district level should accept RODA cases without limiting their number and dispose of them expeditiously.
- BMs should invariably attend the recovery camps organised by the district level authorities.
- Joint recovery teams should be formed, in which Tehsildar/ Revenue Inspector/ Patwari and Bank staff jointly expedite the execution of decrees under RACO (ROD) Act, 1974.
- Special notice should be issued to defaulters from time to time to repay loans duly signed by the Tehsildars.
- Sincere, energetic, dynamic and dedicated outstanding officers in the filed of recovery should be identified as 'Nodal officers' for intensive recovery purpose and they should be assigned the duty to accelerate the recovery campaign in a specified area.
- The bank staff should be mobilised and motivated to improve recovery position in their respective area of operation. Following steps may be suggested to mobilise and motivate the bank staff:

    (a) Performance of recovery should be given weightage in placement of officers of the branches of their choice.

    (b) Running shield / Trophy for branches showing outstanding performance in recovery should be introduced alongwith individual certificates.

(c) Staff and branches with excellent performance in recovery were given suitable coverage in Bank's periodicals to highlight their role and to induce others in improving their performance for recovery of loans.

(d) Regular interactions of top functionaries of the banks should be held with the staff by holding workshops/ seminars of BMs/ Field functionaries and others.

If above mentioned suggestions are implemented truly, it is hoped that it will bring reorientation in the attitude of bank staff and improvement in the level of their commitments towards their role.

- During the filed survey, it was noticed that payments made to 'third parties' out of the loan amount creates hurdles not only in purchase of quality assets, but also makes the recovery difficult. Under dairy loans, loans for plough animals, carts etc., it was observed that the assets of poor quality were purchased by the beneficiaries at higher cost to make 'third party' payments possible. There should be strict action against erring officials and the machinery facilitating such practices, since the very premise of welfare banking is thwarted by such mal-practices. Therefore, it is suggested that the banks should be permitted to provide credit facilities in cash, so that the beneficiary can have the best assets at reasonable prices by reaping the benefits of the competition that prevails presently in every sector of life. Introduction of Kisan Credit Card (KCC) scheme which was introduced in March, 1999 is a good example to quote, whereby the beneficiary has been extended the privilege to enjoy the freedom of meeting his input needs from the sources, he finds the best. The right choice is a must which can be ensured by delivery of bank credit through cash components or near cash components like 'credit cards'.
- It is suggested that BM should be given 'Magistrate power' to confiscate and sell the properties of the borrower for requisition of the bank use. On the basis of the recommendations of the Narsimhan committee, a bill to such effect has been placed before the cabinet for the due consideration, but has yet to get the formal approval. A sense of urgency as well as exigency is desired on the part of the Government.

- The political parties should not include the loan waiver schemes in their election manifesto and nor should publicize that they will waive the loans of farmers, if voted to power as has been the practice in past.

Problems Regarding the Implementation

The overall attitude of all concerned with the implementation of the SAA look mechanical rather than innovative. The fear of poor recovery is one of the major factors behind the reluctance of bankers and to approach new borrowers for development lending in Hadoti region. Out of 50 BMs interviewed as much as 78% (39) BMs have expressed the fear of poor recovery of loans, which has adversely affected the pace of fresh lending. Another major difficulty normally faced by banks in the field of successful implementation of SAA is that many bank branches are not well tuned to handle rural lending. As a result, the persons residing in the service areas allotted to such branches are being served neither by the service area branches nor by the branches which were earlier financing in these villages for fear of violating the instructions of RBI on SAA. This creates as the main stumbling block in effective flow of credit in villages.

As already analysed in *Chapter VI* in *table no. 6.4*, the number of villages allotted to many bank branches has been between 15 to 40, making it altogether difficult for BM to play his role as a 'solitary development agent'. In some of the cases in Hadoti region, where a branch has been allotted only 1 village and in contrast to it, another branch has been allotted 57 villages at the other extreme. Thus, the way banks are forced to adopt-villages compulsorily without proper and prior thought to the existence of development projects or any useful socio-economic infra-structure, tells that normal economic principles are undermined or totally sacrificed.

Quality of lending can be ensured and gauged from the efforts of recycling of funds which includes repayment of loans on time as per scientifically work out repayment schedules and mobilizing deposits will have to be augmented rather than depending on the head offices. It is worthwhile to mention here that the quality of lending needs mobilisation of savings from the beneficiaries who have been benefited out of bank loans, which has not been given any due priority as yet. This asks for developing new deposit mobilisation schemes and concerted efforts for the same.

To counter this stymie, district agriculture departments in all the districts concerned should sponsor sufficient applications for crop loans to the commercial banks and special camps for the same have to be organised by the agriculture department. The borrowers wishing to get loans should be helped by organising special camps from time to time. A camp calendar, prepared by authorities, would serve a great deal in this direction. The Govt. initiative to cover all eligible borrowers under 'Kisan Credit Card Scheme' within next three years should be given shape in letter and sprit by the banks.

At the village, branch and block level, the task of estimating potential for growth in various sectors, fixing targets taking into account all relevant aspects and arriving at realistic, forward looking and balanced budget is enormously complex and time consuming and can not be carried out without the help of powerful computer. Therefore, it is suggested that a competent computer network should be established at the branch level for preparing scientific and realistic plans and to implement them properly.

For better and effective implementation of credit plans, review of past performance is essential because apart from assisting in the formulation of a greater realistic operative action plan, it also helps in the allocation of operationally meaningful targets between the individual financing agencies. Bank should keep at bay under financing activity at it generally leads to default in repayment of loan by the borrower. They should also refrain from over extending their credit beyond their own resources and those which they can legitimately expect by way of refinance.

It is pertinent to mention here that though, the credit and non-credit inputs for backward and forward linkages are vital inputs and a *sine-qua-non* for development, but the people's participation is equally important and essential input for rural development. Therefore, there should be an active and meaningful participation of people for whom the credit plans are prepared and implemented. Participation by people at large in any poverty alleviation programme can be feasible only when people come to know what these schemes are and what is the formal procedure for availing the benefits of these schemes. Therefore, there is a need to publicise various social banking programmes and simplify the formalities regarding the bank loans. To improve active participation of people, it is suggested that the banks with the co-ordination of LBO should develop awareness in beneficiaries by suitable methods like arranging some audio/visual informative and entertaining programmes at places of gathering of village people in their own language.

Problems Regarding Attitudes

It has been observed that the problem of attitudes is one of the serious problem of bank personnel working in rural areas which is adversely affecting the whole credit planning process in the Hadoti region as this has affected the spirit of involvement of the BMs and their staff and they could not be deeply involved in their service areas. In practice, the attitude of bank staff to the credit plan and commitment under it, needs to be changed radically.

It is needless to emphasise that active involvement of BMs at rural and semi-urban centres is one of the essential condition for the success of SAA. The same, however, remains dependent on paucity of the staff and shortage of time at the branch level, as well as the general apathy of banks personnel towards rural life. The researcher has observed that there is a problem of low motivation and of low morale among the rural bank employees. It was also noticed that there was also lack of dedicated personnel who could take up the challenges regarding productive rural lending. Out of 50 BMs interviewed by the researcher, as much as 82% (41) BMs have mentioned that working in rural areas is a tedious job as there is lack of basic amenities of life; such as transportation, medical-aid, education for children, recreation, accommodation etc. Due to lack of these facilities there was a general reluctance among the staff to be transferred to rural areas.

Apart from above mentioned problems, lack of proper career planning and lack of proper personnel policies in banks are yet another critical factor which adversely affect the entire success of the SAA. It was disappointing that persons posted to rural branches do not have their heart, mind and soul to work at these places. Most of them go to rural areas only to complete their rural assignment.

It was further observed that most of the bank employees are urban cultured and urban biased. Due to lack of rural background, they do not understand the real rural problems and also are not interested in knowing them as they feel that they are only for little time in rural branches. Even where the rural posting is accepted, the tendency on the part of the staff is to have residence at the nearest urban place and to commute daily to the rural branch from their urban residence. This reduces their effectiveness at the rural branches. Unless one stays at the place of work, one hardly will be acquainted with the area of operation to do justice.

The banks are to move towards a system of decentralised micro-level planning, therefore, for taking into account the various aspects of rural reality, sincere involvement, devotion and committed attitude are required on the part of the BMs and other bank staff. The BM should behave with villagers in a manner, so that they treat him as a 'friend in need' and a person, who is genuinely interested in upliftment of their well-being. The commitment level of bank staff should be such that with their intimate-knowledge of villages served by the branch, they should be able to resist the pressure from the sponsoring authorities and politicians in respect of loan applications sponsored for non-viable activities. It is vital to note that skills can be developed through training, but commitment to the cause will have to come within. This sense of commitment should be there not only among the bankers, but among all concerned.

Attitudinal changes and reorientation of BMs of rural branches are required to be fortified with a certain measure of idealism, ready to face the inconveniences of rural life. It is suggested that bankers should take rural lending as a mission and fulfil their responsibility by providing credit to all needy persons in service area as per their requirements. They should also take into account the inter-linkages between various economic activities sought to be financed so that regular investment can have a multiplier effect on the generation of income and employment. It is high time when the banks should attach due importance to successful credit expansion by an official to his career profile. At present, confidential reports in banks do not have a weight for performance in rural sector vis-à-vis urban or metro centres. The mandatory assignment of two years in rural areas is not considered sufficient to address the issue. It is suggested that instead of minimum period of stay, the assignment should be to achieve minimum credit expansion targets alongwith minimum recovery successfully in rural areas.

Apart from above mentioned, another important cause regarding the attitudinal change in BMs has also come into notice during the survey. Out of the 50 BMs interviewed 82% (41) have the opinion that SAA has lost its Charisma.

The SAA was introduced at a time when banks were not even aware of NPA norms. The SAA had envisaged co-ordinated and integrated approach for lending to the rural masses. Due to change in accounting method of profits after introduction of prudential norms, *w.e.f.* 31.3.92, the bottom line of most of the banks experienced the brunt of this change in their income earnings. This clearly indicates that the scheme has lost its focus, in respect of concentrated efforts and integrated lending in the eyes of bankers. The reason for such a change in attitude of bankers can be attributed to a shift in philosophy from social banking to viable banking. This change in attitude of bankers is due to stringent NPA norms which over the years have become more strict.

In view of the stringent norms of NPA and deteriorating position of recovery, besides many other problems, compelled bankers in adopting a cautious approach in extension of credit to the rural people. Now the bankers have started assuming that financing in rural areas has become an unattractive and unviable proposition. Earlier the bankers were equally concerned about the success of the venture as well as feasibility of recovery. However, with change in the banking atmosphere due to loan waivers, OTS scheme and strict NPA norms, the main concern of banker now is, the recovery of loan granted to the beneficiaries.

Undoubtedly, there has been a change in banking systems, processes, practices and priorities during the last decade. Under the changed circumstance the bankers are required to gather the intensity of dynamism and change in work culture accordingly to cope up with the changes. They should accept and practise the new concepts and philosophy of the innovative banking in its true practical sense. While the bankers expectation to have a regular repayments from the borrowers is considered legitimate, their high commitment level and active involvement in rural planning and execution of schemes is also considered a justifiable aspiration of the rural masses.

OTHER PROBLEMS

(a) **Regarding the proper identification and selection of beneficiaries:** The most important aspect in effective credit planning is the proper identification and selection of beneficiaries, the credit planning is indeed meant for. At present, the procedure and method of identification and selection of beneficiaries is full of flaws. It has been criticised not only by the bankers, but also by others too. The author has interviewed 50 BMs in knowing their opinion regarding the criteria and procedure of selecting the beneficiaries of credit plans. Out of the total 50 BMs interviewed, 66% (33) BMs have criticized the procedure of selecting the beneficiaries on the ground that the banker has no say at all or least say in selecting the beneficiaries under Govt. sponsored schemes. 70% (35) BMs also highlighted this fact that so many undeserving candidates are also selected due to political pressure/ interference without any adherence to norms. 36% (18) BMs were of the opinion that due to short duration of credit camps (Loan Melas), proper selection of beneficiaries was not possible, whatsoever the selection criteria may be.

Apart from these problems, sponsoring agencies didn't forward loan applications evenly throughout the year, so that they could be processed/scrutinised accurately without pressure of time. Generally, it has been the practice in Hadoti region as very much similar to other parts of the country that only in last few months of the year, the process of identifying and selecting the beneficiaries in large numbers start and get momentum at the fag end of the year. Thus, selecting the proper beneficiaries becomes very difficult due to paucity of time and pressure of fulfilling the targets. Under such a situation, banks get loan applications in bunches from sponsored agencies, which ultimately leads to disbursement of loans without proper and thorough investi-gation of viability of the scheme/activity for which loan is sought. Further, in a very short period of time, it is not possible to judge the attitude and aptitude of the borrower and his/her credit worthiness. This whole situation throws the banker in hot waters by creating the paradoxical situation in which banker has no say or little say in selecting the beneficiaries; while he is held fully responsible for non-repayment of the loan. It is, therefore, suggested that the banker's judgement in selecting the beneficiaries should be given more weightage than any other factor as ultimate responsibility of recovery of loan is of him/her. The another point of submission in this regard is that a transparent and objective suitable criteria should be evolved, so that undue bias and influence in selection of beneficiaries may be avoided as far as possible.

(b) Delay in release of subsidy : The another problem is of unnecessary delay in releasing subsidy by the sponsoring agencies particularly under the poverty alleviation programmes of Govt. This causes a wide time-lag between sanctioning and disbursement of loans. 78% (39) BMs out of total 50 interviewed by the author, made complaint pertaining to this problem. For overcoming this problem, it is suggested that the CBs be made sole agency to implement subsidy-linked social lending programmes so the loan sanctioning, disbursing and subsidy releasing authority remains one and the same. The alternative suggestion to this problem can be submitted for consideration is that some competent Govt. official such as BDO at block level should release a lump-sum amount in favour of BM against subsidy head so as to reduce the delay in disbursement of loan.

(c) **Lack of sufficient and qualitative training facilities :** The author has observed minutely during her field visits that the facilities available for training of bankers in Hadoti region were appallingly insufficient. Not only this, the quality of training imparted to them was also not up to the mark and as well as of no much use in view of the work performed by the bankers in practice. Even at present, most of the bankers are conservative in their practical approach and for them banking resolves around only two parameters (words); *i.e.* deposits and advances, hence making their approach parochial.

Unfortunately, training and manpower development arena are such which generally get lukewarm response and low scale of preference in the list of priorities of top management of banks. Infact, human resource development should get topmost priority in the eyes of top management of banks. The need for training cannot be over emphasised as most of the bankers are ill equipped in skills of credit plan formulation, implementation and monitoring. The basic purpose of imparting training to rural bankers should be to equip them with the skills in credit plan formulation and their implementation. Besides that, the training should be scheme specific/project specific so as to translate the potentials into realities. Therefore, it is suggested that special training centres should be opened-up for providing training to bankers specially in the sphere of rural credit planning, rural development and technical feasibility and economic viability aspects of different schemes/activities.

The techniques of economic survey and methods of completing village profile, innovations in banking practices and norms ought to become the foundation stones of training programmes of the banks. The benefit of the expertise available with the NIBM should be availed of for updating and revolutionising the training programmes and their execution. The periodical training, which is to be imparted to rural bankers, should be in fine tuning with the dexterity for better appraisal and supervision of loans on the basis of NABARD pilot project which is being in force at present. State level workshops for LBOs and DLOs should be organised at least once in a year so as to have healthy interaction among the officials for sake of understanding and appreciation of mutual roles of each other, which help in translating the useful ideas into practice emerges out of deliberations. Besides all this, what is more important is the change in the attitude of bankers towards rural people and rural development. For it, rural orientation training programmes should be organised at some regular intervals for all categories of bank staff. This reorientation of mind will definitely have a positive impact on the quality of lending and would also reduce the incidence of default in loan payment.

Likewise, the need of imparting training to beneficiaries of credit plans cannot be over-emphasised. Unfortunately, so far no bank in the country has initiated any action plan in this regard. If the suitable training is provided to the beneficiaries about the technical feasibility and economic viability aspects of the schemes for their benefit, ethics of repayment of loan and above all, the re-orientation of mind of the beneficiaries, so that they can understand the role of credit plans and bankers as well. If, the training imparted to beneficiaries enables them to understand this fact that the interest of banker lies in the interest of beneficiaries, most of the problems of credit planning will reduce significantly, if not eliminated at all. Undoubtedly, the trained beneficiaries are able to extract better results from the activity financed by a bank. Therefore, it is submitted that it is a highly opportune time to give a concentrated thought to this idea that before providing credit to the borrowers, some kind of training should be imparted to them. Such training will definitely change the mind set of the borrowers, which will ultimately help in effecting proper end use of credit and improving the recovery position.

(d) Low level of Literacy and Education : The another problem, which confronts to the rural credit planners is the low level of literacy and education, which in its own turn creates hindrance in inculcating the full awareness about the credit plans, without which the maximum benefits of such plans cannot be derived. The level of education has an important bearing on the knowledge, outlook and mind set of a person, which determines the method and pattern of performing a task. The educated people really understand the benefits which they can derive by seeking finance for several bankable schemes, which are in force. It is well established fact that the level of education is positively co-related with the resultant incremental income from the schemes financed by banks. This reveals that the educated borrowers make better, efficient and optimum use of bank credit in comparison to the illiterate and educated one. The literacy percentage in Hadoti region, according to the provisional figures of census 2001, was around 62%, which was lower than the national literacy percentage (65.38%). Not only this, the percentage of people were qualified upto the secondary level and above was very low (18.50%). Owing to these factors, the level of awareness of the people of Hadoti region, was also low. Therefore, to make rural lending more productive and purposeful, it is suggested that the young and literate farmers and other such borrowers should be accorded higher preference in granting loans. The author has personally seen that the young literate and innovative farmers have made better use of credit than the illiterate and old farmers. It was also found during the field visits of the author that most of the literate and educated farmers have adopted modern and scientific methods of cultivation, therefore, agriculture has become a profitable venture for them and they are able to repay their loans timely. Thus, it reduces to incidence of default in loan repayment automatically.

(e) **Lack of diversified lending :** The author has observed and also the figures of amount of loan disbursed in Hadoti region speak this truth that more emphasis was given to the dairy farming in sanctioning of loans. There are many other activities allied to agriculture in the region such as piggery and poultry farming, fisheries, seri-culture, horticulture etc. which have tremendous potential for development, but have not been given due attention to tape their full potential. Thus, the credit disbursement was concentrated mainly to one single activity; *i.e.* the dairy farming; while neglecting the others. Thus, in view of the above facts, it is suggested that all sectors which have sufficient potential for development should be developed by drawing suitable bankable schemes for them and providing them adequate amount of credit and non-credit inputs timely.

(f) **Lack of people's active participation :** Any planning whether related to credit or development is unlikely to be successful and sustainable, unless people for whom it is meant, have stake in their own development. Popular and active participation enriches the planning process by checking the reliability of data, ensuring commitment of the people to targetted projects for the rural sector basing the proposals on the judgement of the people affected by the programmes. Besides that, people's involvement ensures strict supervision at the cutting edge of the level of administration. It can alone avoid duplication, minimize delay and ensures easy accountability. As a result of participation, the rural people are in a better position to assess their rights and respon-sibilities. Thus, as a result of participation, the talent pool becomes larger. **Balwant Rai Mehta Committee** has rightly observed that "rural development and rural welfare are possible only with local initiative and local direction". This is possible only with people's participation. The main objectives of people's participation are better planning and implementation of credit plans, mobilisation of additional resources for rural development and empowering the people, particularly, the poor to play an effective role in rural development. But the unfortunate part of the story of SAA in Hadoti region is that people's participation was terribly lacking and people were found to be indifferent about credit plans and schemes for their benefits. Apart from this, the credit planners and executors didn't take an initiative in enlisting the participation of people by winning their confidence in rural credit delivery system. Therefore, the need of the hour is that people's partici-pation needs to be ensured earnestly in all spheres of credit planning so that people not only know what is good for themselves, but also have the power to go about getting it done themselves. It is cent-percent true that the people, for whom all the schemes are chalked out, had not been consulted either for diagnosis of the problem or for the prognosis of the schemes. In the rural sphere the Participate Rural Appraisal (PRA) technique is recommended for better understanding of rural problems and finding out their feasible solutions. This technique may serve as catalyst for local and external elements to introduce positive change in the system. If this is implemented sincerely, this would go a long way towards increasing the efficacy and acceptance of the programmes on one hand and reducing the operational and administrative cost, on the other.

Ensuring people's participation is a difficult task for various reasons. Some of the reasons are non-involvement of the community and local leaders, lack of education and awareness among the rural people about various programmes, village factionalism and rural power structure, apathy of bureaucracy and inadequate use of the mass media. Inspite of all these problems, some way has to be found out for winning the confidence and seeking the active participation of the rural people.

The success of SAA rests mainly on how sincerely and in a concerted manner the credit plans are formulated and executed at different levels by the policy planners and executors. Besides this, the other important contributing factor in the success of SAA is the sense of belongingness and dedication of bankers and district development officers, which they put in together with a sense of mutual understanding and appreciation of each others role. This type of cohesive approach of bankers and district development officers with a deep sense of involvement and positive mind set can alone ensure the grand success of SAA. The voluntary acceptance of roles by all concerned in credit planning exercise is the key to success of SAA. The SAA can prove to be a boon to rural people in uplifting their well-being only when its conceptual and practical obstacles are removed as earliest as possible by adopting well chalked out strategy drawn by both bankers and development officers for properly dovetailing of DCP with DDP rather than on the basis of fire-fighting approach. The last and ultimate factor in this regard is the genuine love and involvement of the people for whom the whole credit planning exercise is done and meant for. Any plan, howsoever it may be well chalked out, cannot meet its fate of success without the active participation and deep involvement of the people. Therefore, some work plan and calendar of activity should be prepared and implemented in a time bound manner for enlisting the support of rural people. The foot impressions created by the NABARD in this regard through Vikas Vahini Volunteers (VVV) scheme should be replicated with a sense of wisdom vigorously in SAA too.

Effective monitoring at the pre-sanctioned and post-sanctioned stage of loan is also an essential condition for the success of SAA, which has to be ensured by all means through. If only we could keep the stymieing factors, in its way as mentioned in this chapter, at bay and categorically curb the shortcomings in the formulation and implementation of the SAA in the wake of suggestions stated above, SAA will become a role model for rural development strategy as this would serve as a lamp post of the path for growth of rural economy of the country and set an example that would enlighten the other developing countries as well as they too, would follow suit and tread the path shown by us in order to extricate the poor from the pathetic state of affairs and would serve as a milestone on the road leading to a successful and dazzling socio-economic revolution.

In nutshell, if the suggestions, as stated above, are implemented with great zeal and fevour as well as in letter and spirit, the author has an unflinching faith and belief that it would bring about a positive and healthy change in the functioning of the SAA, particularly when they have to combat some blocking factors in its smooth functioning. If at all, these cannot be eradicated, then at least would definitely be curbed to a great extent.

Testing of Hypothesis

The author has tried her level best to test the hypothesis of the present study, which is presented below :

1) The inferences drawn from the study approve this hypothesis that "the credit plans framed under the SAA have been successful in creating and enhancing the awareness about the use and importance of institutional credit among the rural people in Hadoti region." The logistics behind supporting this hypothesis are as under :

   (i) There has been continuous increase in overall targets of credit plans during the period of the study in the region. A consistent rise in the targets of credit plans was visible year after years as per the details of table no. 6.6 in chapter VI of the present study. The increase in overall targets of credit plans in the region has been impressive as these jumped-up by 373% over the base year figure. Thus, denoting 4.75 times increase.

   (ii) The average annual growth rate of targets in the region has been 41.66% during the whole period under investigation. Indeed, this is an impressive growth by all means.

   (iii) An overall increasing trend has been witnessed in the absolute amount of achievement of credit plans. The achievement has gone-up by 371.60% during the whole period of study, thereby, depicting a growth of around five times over the base year. This could again be termed as extremely satisfactory.

   (iv) The average annual growth rate in achievement of credit plans has been of the order of 41.28% during the whole period of study, which could be said as excellent.

   (v) The performance of CBs in financing to priority sectors in the region has been excellent as the performance in Baran, Bundi and Jhalawar districts of the region has been around double of the prescribed norm of 40% of total advances. In case of district Kota, the performance hoovered around the prescribed norm. Thus, the performance of CBs in the whole region has been more than the prescribed norm.

   (vi) The performance of CBs in financing to direct agriculture in Baran, Bundi and Jhalawar districts of the region has been at least around three times of the prescribed norm of 18%. In case of district Kota, the performance hoovered round the prescribed norm. Thus, the overall performance in this regard in the whole region could be said as splendid.

(vii) The performance of CBs in financing to weaker sections of the society in the region has been excellent in Baran, Bundi and Jhalawar districts, as it was at least three times more than the prescribed norm of 10%, but in district Kota it hoovered round the prescribed norm. Thus, the overall performance in this regrad has been excellent in the region.

(viii) The absolute amount of total advances has increased more than double.

(ix) 61% respondent beneficiaries reported that they obtained credit from institutional sources. Thus, the role of institutional credit in the total requirement of the credit in the region has increased, which is significant in view of the agrarian and backward economy of the region.

2) The findings of the study expressively approves this hypothesis that "the credit plans formulated and implemented under the SAA have been successful in enhancing the share of institutional credit in the Hadoti region." The approval of hypothesis can be substantiated by the following facts :

(i) The share of institutional credit in the total credit of the region, was 61%, which has increased over the years.

(ii) Around 57% beneficiaries have reported this fact that they could repay their loans timely because of generation of sufficient income from the activity/scheme for which they have obtained the loan from financial institutional operating in their area. This is a positive indicator of increasing share of institutional credit in the region.

(iii) Around 2/3 (67.58%) beneficiaries accepted this fact that they got sufficient amount of loan as per their requirement from financial institutions operating in their area.

(iv) Around 2/3 (70%) beneficiaries could repay their loans timely which speaks itself that the use of institutional credit was highly beneficial to them and also they wanted to avail more credit facility from the financial institutions.

(v) Around 86% beneficiaries were in favour of continuance of SAA because of easy and ready access to the institutional credit, which has reduced their dependency on non-institutional sources of credit and could make them free from the clutches of money-lenders.

3) An overall critical appraisal of SAA in Hadoti region approves this hypothesis that "the SAA have been successful in enhancing the credit absorption capacity in the region." The following facts support and subscribe this point of view :

(i) There has been tremendous and continuous increase in absolute targets and achievements of credit plans during the period of investigation as stated earlier while testing the hypothesis number 1.

(ii) The overall credit deposit ratio of the region for the whole period of the study was around 65%, which was marginally higher than the prescribed norm of 60%. The credit deposit ratio of the region has been higher than the prescribed norm in most of the years of the period of study.

(iii) The absolute amount of total advances in the region has shown a consistent growth as this has increased from Rs. 40134.72 lacs in the initial year to Rs. 95642.89 lacs in the final year of the study, thereby depicting an improvement of 138%; *i.e.* more than the double. The average annual growth rate of total advances in the region during the period of study has remained at reasonably good level of 15.37%.

(iv) The overall performance of CBs in financing to priority sectors in the region has been much higher than the prescribed norm of 40% to total advances.

(v) The overall performance of CBs in financing to direct agriculture has been substantially higher than the prescribed norm of 18% of total advances.

(vi) The overall performance of CBs in financing to weaker sections of society in the region has been significantly higher than the prescribed norm of 10% of total advances.

(vii) Yearly targets fixed for agriculture and allied sectors in the region have increased from Rs. 4937.57 lacs in the base year to Rs. 24680.30 lacs in the final year of the study, thereby registering a growth of 340%; i.e. about five times. The average annual growth rate in targets of this sector has been about 44%, which could be termed as excellent.

(viii) The targets fixed for industrial sector in the Hadoti region have increased from Rs. 1160.23 lacs in the base year to Rs. 3271.30 lacs in the final year of the study thereby depicting a growth rate of 182%; i.e. around three times. The average annual growth rate in targets for industrial sector has been 22.22%, which could be termed as satisfactory.

(ix) The targets for tertiary sector in the Hadoti region has shown a quantum jump from Rs. 932.77 lacs in the beginning to Rs. 5438.35 lacs in the final year of the study, thereby registering a robust growth of about 483%; i.e. around six times increase.

(x) The average annual growth rate of achievements in all sectors in the Hadoti region together has been 41.28%, which could be termed as impressive.

4) An overall evaluation of SAA in the Hadoti region approves this hypothesis of the study that "the credit plans constructed and implemented under the SAA have been successful in raising the level of income of the people in the region." Following facts can be advanced in favour of the hypothesis :

(i) 84% of the beneficiaries has expressed their opinion that their level of income has gone-up due to the credit facilities received from the financial institutions operating in the region.

(ii) Around 3/4 BMs reported that the level of income of beneficiaries in the Hadoti region has gone-up. Though, the opinion was divided about the degree of increase in level of income.

(iii) In view of the above mentioned facts, it can be deduced that the standard of living of the people in the region has increased during the period of investigation, which was also visible through the changes which have taken place in different economic parameters in the region.

(iv) 71% beneficiaries reported this fact that they have repaid their loans out of incremental income generated by the activity undertaken by them through the credit received from the financial institutions.

(v) 57% beneficiaries could repay their loans timely as stated by them because of generation of sufficient level of income as referred earlier.

5) The findings of the study approves this hypothesis that "the recovery position of loans has improved in Hadoti region due to the implementation of SAA." This can be substantiated by the following points :

(i) The recovery percentage under priority sector advances in the region, which was 49% in 1995-96 has increased substantially to a level of 63.49% in 1999-2000. Thus, denoting an increase of 14.49 points.

(ii) Like-wise the region, district-wise recovery percentage has also gone-up in all districts of the region. Recovery percentage in district Bundi which was 44% in 1995-96 has increased to 66% in 1999-2000. In case of district Baran, the recovery percentage has gone-up from 60.50% to 62% in the same period of the study. The recovery percentage in district Jhalawar has improved substantially from a low level of 38.33% in 1995-96 to a very high level of 70.22% in 1999-2000, thereby denoting, an increase of 32 points. Almost the same pattern of improvement in recovery position was also observed in district Kota wherein percentage of recovery has soared-up from 34% in 1995-96 to 63.68% in 1999-2000, thereby depicting an increase of around 30 points.

Findings of the Study

Some of the important findings of the study are as under :

1) The total number of all types of bank branches in Hadoti region were 379 at the end of March 31, 2000, out of which 56% branches were in rural areas and 25% branches were in semi-urban areas. Thus, 81% branches in Hadoti region were in rural and semi-urban branches. This shows that SAA in Hadoti region has given due emphasis for the banking development in unbanked and backward areas of the region, which helped in promoting the development of rural communities.

2) The average number of villages served by a service area branch in Hadoti region was well within the range of number of villages fixed by RBI; i.e. within 15 to 25 villages. The average number of villages served by a service area branch separately in all four districts in the region was also within the norm fixed for a service area at the national level.

3) Out of 244 service areas in the Hadoti region, 46% service areas were having below 15 villages, 35% service areas were having villages between 15 to 25 and 16% service areas were having more than 25 but upto 40 villages. Only 3% service areas were having more than 40 villages in their jurisdiction. Thus, 81% service areas were having the number of villages either below the prescribed norm or within the prescribed norm for a service area in the region.

This indicates a pleasant situation in the region in terms of number of villages served by a service area bank branch.

4) The overall performance of credit plans in the Hadoti region was satisfactory as the percentage achievement was slightly less than 100%. Besides that, there has been continuous increase in absolute amount of both targets and achievements of credit plans in the region, thereby depicting a healthy growth path. The overall performance of credit plans in different districts of the regions too were also satisfactory. The achievement of credit plans in Baran and Bundi districts was more than 100%; while the achievement of district Kota was slightly less than 100%. The performance of credit plans in district Jhalawar was moderate. The overall performance of credit plans in Baran, Bundi and Kota districts was higher than the whole region, but it was lower in district Jhalawar.

5) The overall performance of credit plans in agriculture and allied sectors in Hadoti region has been excellent, as the overall achievement has exceeded 100%. An overall upward trend was clearly visible in terms of absolute amount of targets and achievements for this sector in the region. The district-wise overall performance of credit in plans agriculture and allied sector has been excellent in Baran, Bundi and Kota districts of the region, as this was more than 100%; while it was satisfactory in district Jhalawar where it was marginally less than 100%. The performance of credit plans in agriculture and allied sector was higher in district Baran and Bundi in comparison to the whole region; while it was lower in district Jhalawar and Kota.

6) The overall performance of credit plans for industrial sector in Hadoti region was modestly satisfactory (82.60%). On the whole, an increasing trend has been observed in the absolute amount of both targets and achievements in industrial sector in the region. While evaluating district-wise overall performance of credit plans in industrial sector, we find a lot of variations. On the one hand, the performance of credit plans in district Bundi was excellent as it exceeded 100%, but on the other, the performance of district Baran was very poor and it was less than 50%. The performance of credit plans in Jhalawar and Kota districts was moderate and more or less the same. The performance of credit plans in industrial sector in district Bundi was higher than the region; while it was lower in remaining three districts of the region.

7) The overall performance of credit plans in tertiary sector has been moderately successful and a clear rising trend has been observed in absolute amount of targets and achievements. While looking at the district-wise performance of credit plans in this sector, severe variations have been noticed. On the one hand, the overall performance of credit plans in district Bundi and Kota was excellent as it exceeded 100% mark. The performance in district Baran was modest; while it was very poor and highly dissatisfactory in district Jhalawar (only 29%). The performance of district Bundi and Kota were better than the performance of the whole region; while the performance of district Baran was more or less equal to the region, but it was far-far below in district Jhalawar.

8) In terms of sector-wise percentage share of targets in total credit plan in Hadoti region, the agriculture and allied sectors have enjoyed lion's share (71.43%), followed by tertiary sector (17.61%) and industrial sector (10.95%) respectively. This symbolises that even today, the region is pre-dominated by agriculture and allied activities and is industrially backward except the Kota city. The another important point worth mentioning here is that there has been marginal change in the percentage share of agriculture and allied sector and tertiary sector in the region; while the percentage share of industrial sector has gone down significantly over the years, which reveals this fact that inspite of lot of band-banging and pious intentions, the efforts of industrialisation didn't prove fruitful. Sector-wise percentage share of targets in total credit plans in different districts was on the pattern of the region, in terms of ranking.

9) In terms of institution-wise performance in the region, the overall percentage achievement of CBs has been extremely satisfactory as it has exceeded 100% mark; while the overall percentage achievement of RRBs has been satisfactory (around 93%). The overall percentage achievement of co-operative banks was more or less the same as that of RRBs; The overall percentage achievement of other financial institutions was satisfactory, which was marginally less than 100%.

In terms of absolute amount of overall targets and achievements, the co-operative banks in the region have remained at the top. The absolute amount of both overall targets and achievements of these banks have exceeded the combined targets and achievements of CBs and RRBs. In terms of district-wise comparative performance, the performance of CBs in the district Baran was highest and it was higher than the whole region. The performance of co-operative banks was highest in district Bundi and it was even higher than the whole region. Regarding the performance of RRBs, district Kota stood first and its performance was even higher than the whole region.

10) The percentage share of co-operative banks in total credit plan of the region was not only highest, but it was more than the half (51.49%) of the total size of credit plans. The percentage share of CBs was marginally above 1/3 (38.72%); while the share of RRBs was comparatively small (8.14%). The share of other financial institutions was negligible.

The percentage share of targets of the different financial institutions in district Baran and district Jhalawar was on the same pattern as that of the region in terms of their ranking. In Bundi and Kota districts, the percentage share of CBs was higher than the co-operative banks.

11) Comparing the percentage growth rate of total deposits of the CBs in the region during the whole period of study with the State of Rajasthan, it was slightly lower. The growth rate in total deposits of the region was 285.14% in comparison to 296.79% of the State of Rajasthan and 288.10% of the country as a whole. Thus, the overall percentage growth in deposits of CBs in the region has been more or less at par with the growth rate of deposits of these in the State of Rajasthan and India. The percentage growth rate of deposits during the whole period of study was highest in district Jhalawar, followed by districts Kota, Bundi and Baran. The percentage growth rate of district Jhalawar was higher than the whole region, but for remaining three districts, it was lower than the region.

Compound Average Annual Growth Rate (CAGR) of total deposits in the region during the whole period of study was 16.1%, which was slightly lower than the State of Rajasthan (16.5%) and much higher than all India figure (11.9%). District Jhalawar ranked first in this regard, followed by district Kota, Bundi and Baran.

12) The growth rate in total advances in the region of CBs was only 138%, which was much lower than the growth rate in the State of Rajasthan (220.52%) and of India (207.97%). Thus, a glaring difference in growth rate pattern in total advances was observed, which compels us to conclude this fact that the growth rate in total advances has not been satisfactory comparing to the State of Rajasthan and India.

The percentage growth rate in total advances of CBs was highest in district Jhalawar, followed by district Baran, Bundi and Kota respectively.

The CAGR of total advances of the CBs in the region during the whole period of the study, was 10.10%, which was slightly lower than the State of Rajasthan (13.9%) and all India (11.9%). Making district-wise comparison of CAGR, district Jhalawar stood first, followed by district Baran, Bundi and Kota respectively.

13) The overall Credit-Deposit Ratio as well as CD ratio of different years of the whole period of the study has been much higher than the State of Rajasthan. In first six years out of the total nine years of the period of study, the CD ratio of the region has been higher than the prescribed norm of the 60%, but it was slightly less than the prescribed norm in last three years of the study. The overall CD ratio was highest in district Jhalawar, followed by district Baran, Bundi and Kota respectively. The overall CD ratio in district Jhalawar, Baran and Bundi was higher than the whole region; while it was lower for district Kota.

14) The performance of CBs in financing to priority sectors in Baran, Bundi and Jhalawar districts of the region has been much higher than the prescribed norm of 40% of total advances, but it has been generally less than the prescribed norm in district Kota. District Bundi stood first in the percentage achievement of CBs in financing to priority sectors, followed by district Baran and Jhalawar. District Kota remained at bottom in the rank and its performance was also not satisfactory. The performance of CBs in priority sector financing in the region was 59.77% in 1999-2000, which was much higher than the performance in the State of Rajasthan (51.20%) and in India (43.60%). This shows clearly that the performance of CBs in priority sector financing in the region has been better in comparison to the State of Rajasthan and India.

15) The performance of CBs in direct agriculture financing in Baran, Bundi and Jhalawar districts has been excellent as it was always higher than the prescribed norm of 18% of total advances, but it was less than the prescribed norm in district Kota in all years of the study, except only for one year. The performance of CBs in financing to direct agriculture in the region in 1999-2000 was 37.38%, which was much higher than the State of Rajasthan (20.70%) and India (15.80%).

16) The performance of CBs in financing to weaker sections of society has been excellent in Baran, Bundi and Jhalawar districts of the region, as it has always been exceeded the prescribed norm of 10% of total advances, but in district Kota, it was generally less than the prescribed norm. Inter-district performance in this regard reveals that district Bundi was at the top, followed by district Baran, Jhalawar and Kota respectively in the region. The performance of CBs in financing to weaker sections of the society was 23.03% in 1999-2000, which was significantly higher that the State of Rajasthan (11.80%) and India (4.77%) respectively.

17) The performance of CBs in financing under DRI has not been satisfactory in all districts of the region as the achievement was always less than the prescribed norm of 1% of the total advances. Analsyis of inter-district comparison reveals this fact that the performance of district Baran was much better than other districts of the region. The performance of CBs in this regard in the region was 0.10% in 1999-2000; while it was only 0.05% in the State of Rajasthan. Though, the performance of CBs in the region was better than the Rajasthan, but it was not at all satisfactory.

Findings of the study are based on the sample survey of the bankers and beneficiaries both. The sample for bankers include 98 service area branches, which are 40% of the total 244 service area branches in the Hadoti region. The sample for benficiaries include 400 beneficiaries in all from the whole region selecting 100 beneficiaries from each district of the region.

The author has conducted field survey to know the response of bankers and beneficiaries of credit plans framed and implemented under the SAA. Though the detailed analysis of the response of bankers and beneficiaries has already been done in chapter VIII of the present study, but even then for sake of presenting the gist of the survey, the main findings are presented below in nutshell form :

1) 96.94% respondent bankers completed the village survey in stipulated time period. This shows that the village survey work was accorded top priority by the BMs.

2) Unfortunately, only 66.33% respondent BMs didn't updated the village profile annually. This shows updation of village profile annually is a big challenge in formulating realistic credit plans in the region.

3) The main problems faced by the bankers during the village survey as mentioned by BMs were shortage of staff (82.65%), inadequacy of

data (56.12%), illiteracy (41.84%), lack of transport facilities (36.76%), scattered lending (27.55%) and problem of language (18.37%).

4) 50% respondent BMs opined that the attitude of Govt. officials were either indifferent or non-co-operative. Thus, the problem of seeking co-operation from Govt. officials/ departments during the survey work emerged as an important problem.

5) More than 50% respondent BMs reported that they didn't receive the information/ data from Govt. departments in time. Thus, it reveals that obtaining timely information from Govt. departments is a big problem.

6) 82.65% BMs were satisfied with the accuracy and reliability of data/ information obtained from Govt. departments.

7) Exactly 50% respondent BMs mentioned that lack of proper dovetailing of DCP with DDP was a big problem for them in implementing credit plans and in making them a grand success.

8) Most of the respondent BMs reported that they have given due weightage to economic viability and technical feasibility of schemes, nature of scheme, targets of Govt. sponsored schemes, activity-wise credit requirement, attitudes of beneficiaries regarding the end use and the repayment of loans, credit worthiness of the beneficiaries, resources available with the banks and basic infra-structural facilities available in the area at the time of formulation of credit plans.

9) One of the important factor, which was affecting adversely the efficiency of bankers, was inadequate facilities at their work place.

10) As per the opinion of the majority of BMs, an ideal selection criteria of beneficiaries should have economic viability and technical feasibility of an activity, repayment capacity of borrower, need-based lending and past experience about the track record of beneficiaries as an important ingredients.

11) 66.33% respondent BMs were not found happy with the present selection criteria of beneficiaries.

12) As high as 63.26% respondent BMs mentioned this bitter truth that they didn't have any say in selecting the beneficiaries, particularly under Govt. sponsored schemes, which resulted into non-involvement of bankers and hence indifferenceness creeps in the mind of the bankers.

13) Political interference in selecting the beneficiaries was a big problem, as mentioned by the majority of bankers.

14) Lack of suitable training and training facilities were another important problems in changing the mind set-up of the bankers as most of them were orthodox in approach. As high as 62.20% respondent BMs didn't receive any training during their career, which was amazing and disgusting.

15) It was a matter of delight that more than 3/4 BMs adhered to the action calendar provided to them for completion of different stages of credit plans.

16) Lack of proper and effective system of monitoring of credit plans was a major problem, which was highlighted by around 1/3 respondent bankers.

17) There is a matter of satisfaction that around 3/4 respondent BMs were of the opinion that the level of production, productivity and income has increased due to the implementation of SAA, but note of dis-satisfaction is that this positive impact was only marginal rather substantial.

18) The another area of anxiety and concern was the profitability of the bank branches, which has adversely been affected due to the introduction of SAA. This fact has been reported by around 98% respondent BMs.

19) The most widely discussed issue and a big problem is the poor recovery of loans which has been highlighted by the majority of bankers. Around 2/3 respondent BMs have accepted that the recovery position has been adversely affected by the implementation of SAA.

20) Majority of the respondent BMs were of the opinion that the SAA in Hadoti region has been successful on the whole. Of course, there was a difference of degree in the successful functioning of SAA. 64.29% BMs expressed their opinion that the SAA was moderately successful; while 28.50% BMs were of the opinion that the functioning of SAA was successful. Only 7.14% respondents mentioned this fact that the SAA has been a failure.

21) The lack of literacy and higher education was the main hurdle in enlisting the co-operation of the beneficiaries in credit plans. The illiteracy percentage in the region was 28.50%, which was substantial. The percentage of qualified persons upto the secondary level and above was only 18.50%. This was a quite low comparatively. Thus, the lack of awareness about the different schemes of credit plans was mainly due to the problem of illiteracy and lack of good education.

22) The main problems faced by beneficiaries at the time for applying for loan as stated by them were mainly completion of loan application form (80.75%), security/ guarantee of loan (22.25%) and not getting application form (10.50%).
23) 43.25% of respondent beneficiaries made complaint that the banks took more than one month and upto two months time in sanctioning loans; while 31.50% mentioned that the time taken by banks was between 16 days to 1 month. 24% beneficiaries got their loan sanctioned in more than two months time. Thus, 67.25% beneficiaries in the region got their loan sanctioned in more than one month time. Therefore, delay in sanctioning of loan was a big problem, which diverted the beneficiaries from institutional sources of credit to non-institutional sources of credit.
24) Regarding the sufficiency of loan sanctioned by banks, 30% beneficiaries highlighted this fact that they didn't get sufficient amount of loan from banks needed for completion of their project. Obviously, such a large number of beneficiaries have to search some other non-institutional sources of loan.
25) The main problems faced by beneficiaries at the time of sanctioning of loan as reported by them, were time-lag between applying for and sanctioning of loan (42.25%), complicated procedures and unnecessary formalities (24.75%), bribe (15.25%) and recommendation (8.75%).
26) Only 62.50% beneficiaries accepted that they have used the credit for the purpose for which it was sanctioned to them. This automatically compels us to reach to this obvious conclusion that more than 1/3 beneficiaries didn't use the credit for the purpose it was sanctioned to them. Thus, post-disbursement supervision of credit emerges as a big problem.
27) The main weapons with bankers for recovery of loans were verbal reminders and written reminders, legal notices, social pressure and ultimately court cases. Only 29.75% beneficiaries reported that banks have filed cases against them for the recovery of their dues. Thus, in case of only few defaulters banks resort to the last and final weapon of filing case.
28) Majority of the beneficiaries (71%) repaid their loan out of the incremental income generated from the activity for which loan was taken. But contrary to it, the another bitter fact was that 27% beneficiaries took loan only for sake of repaying old loan. Thus, loan for sake of repaying loan was a big problem in credit management.

29) Slightly above 2/3 (69.75%) beneficiaries mentioned that they have repaid their loan in time, but 28% reported that they didn't paid their loan in time. Thus, slightly less than 1/3 beneficiaries were defaulters, which created the problem of recovery and NPAs.

30) The main reasons for non-payment of loan as reported by the beneficiaries were inadequate income generation from the activity/scheme (32.14%), possibility of loan waiver (29.46%), utilisation of loan in some other uses (23%) and no fear of legal action (16%).

31) Around 3/4 (73%) beneficiaries expressed that the level of services rendered by co-operative banks was better in comparison to CBs and RRBs. Thus, it indicates that there is much scope for improvement in the services rendered by CBs and RRBs.

32) Around 16% beneficiaries were not satisfied with the work and behaviour of the bankers. This throws light that there is a room for improvement in work and behaviour of bankers towards the beneficiaries.

33) 61% beneficiaries reported that they were dependent on institutional credit; while 32% reported that they were dependent on non-institutional credit. Inspite of serious efforts of Govt., RBI and whole banking sector, even today, a large number of people depends on non-institutional credit.

34) A vast majority of beneficiaries accepted that due to implementation of SAA, their level of income, employment, production, assets and their living standard have increased. This indicates that the launching of SAA has increased the prosperity in the region. This is a good sign and beneficient aspect of SAA.

35) Around 60% beneficiaries were of the opinion that the SAA in Hadoti region has been highly successful; while around 29% reported that the success of SAA was normal. Only 2.25% beneficiaries reported that SAA has been unsuccessful in the region. Thus, a vast majority of beneficiaries (around 90%) in Hadoti region found the SAA either highly successful or normally successful.

36) When a question regarding continuance of SAA was asked to beneficiaries, more than 86% beneficiaries expressed their opinion in favour of continuance of SAA. Thus, a vast majority of respondents were in favour of continuance of SAA in view of its overall advantages to them.

In the last, we can conclude by saying that the SAA as a rural credit delivery system and strategy for rural development should be continued keeping in view of it's overall advantages and beneficient aspects as reported by both bankers and beneficiaries despite of its several deficiencies. These deficiencies can be removed by sincere efforts of all participating agencies and by enlisting people's participation.

REFERENCES

1. Dua, H.S., Social Banking for Economic Development (Deep and Deep Publications, New Delhi), 1996.
2. Sundaram, I. Satya, Rural Development (Himalaya Publishing House, Delhi), 1997.
3. P. Arumugam, Lead Bank System and Service Area Approach in India (UDH Publishing House, Delhi), 1990.
4. Mathur, B.L., Credit Planning and Management in Indian Banking, Edited (Arihant Publishing House, Jaipur), 1995.
5. Singh, Gopal, Rural Credit Planning (RBSA Publishers, Jaipur), 2000.
6. Patel, A.R., Rural Banking : Service Area Policy Shift needed, Southern Economist, August 1, 1995.
7. Ammannaya, K.K., Service Area Approach - A New Challenge for Banks, Southern Economist, July 15, 1990.
8. Ray, Atamadip, Banks Hit Potholes on Recovery Path, FE SELECT. The Financial Express, December, 2001.
9. Capoor, Jagdish, Developmental Issues in Micro Credit, RBI Bulletin, March, 2001.
10. Thingalaya, N.K., The Rural Credit Structure : Some Imponderables, IBA Bulletin, January, 1993.
11. Vasudeva, S., Rural Banking, IBA Bulletin, Special Issue, January, 1996.
12. Sharma, S.P., Recovery of Agricultural Loans : Need for Innovative Approach, SBI Monthly Review, Sept. 1992.
13. Verma, J.R. , Bad loans write off : Accepting the Inevitable, The Hindu, July 6, 1995.
14. Singh, R., Educating Borrowers on Repayment, Financial Express, November 13, 1993.
15. Duhan, T.C., Waiving Rural Loans, Some Basic Issues, Agricultural Banker, Oct.-Dec., 1991.
16. Vasudevan, T.M.C., Recovery-Need of the Hour, The Banker, January, 1990.

□■□